INSURING THE NATION'S HEALTH

Market Competition, Catastrophic and Comprehensive Approaches

Judith Feder
Jack Hadley
John Holahan

An Urban Institute Book

 THE URBAN INSTITUTE PRESS · WASHINGTON, D.C.

Manufactured in the United States of America

LC 81-51345
ISBN 87766-298-3
UI 1049

Please refer to URI 32400 when ordering

This publication was printed by The John D. Lucas Printing Co.
from type set by Allen Wayne Ltd.

THE URBAN INSTITUTE is a nonprofit policy research and educational organization established in Washington, D.C. in 1968. Its staff investigates interrelated social and economic problems of urban communities, and government policies affecting those communities and the people who live in them. The Institute disseminates significant findings of such research through the active publications program of its Press. The Institute has two goals for work in each of its research areas: to help shape thinking about societal problems and efforts to solve them, and to improve government decisions and performance by providing better information and analytic tools.

Through work that ranges from broad conceptual studies to administrative and technical assistance, Institute researchers contribute to the stock of knowledge available to public officials and to private individuals and groups concerned with formulating and implementing more efficient and effective government policy.

Conclusions or opinions expressed are those of the authors and do not necessarily reflect the views of other staff members, officers or trustees of the Institute, or of any organizations which provide financial support to the Institute.

CONTENTS

Page

vi

TABLES

APPENDIX TABLES

FIGURES

APPENDIX FIGURE

APPENDIX CHARTS

ACKNOWLEDGMENTS

This study was funded by the Ford Foundation and by the U.S. Department of Housing and Urban Development, Office of Community Planning and Development, Legislative and Urban Policy Staff.

Special thanks are due to Robert Harris, whose support and encouragement made the monograph possible.

The authors gratefully acknowledge the following individuals for valuable comments and suggestions: Randall Bovbjerg, Richard Froh, Paul Ginsburg, Franklin James, Deborah Lewis, Harvey Pies, Andreas Schneider, Gordon Trapnell, Judith Wagner, John Wills, and Harold Wolman. We would also like to thank Priscilla Taylor for her editing and Elizabeth Straus for her assistance in preparing the manuscript.

INTRODUCTION

In the 1970s, it became almost ritual for each session of Congress to have many national health insurance (NHI) bills on its agenda. In 1979 Congress had at least ten proposals in various stages of development and consideration.[1] Although prospects for passage of a bill appear no better now than in the past, the process of introducing bills is an important mechanism for generating debate over how much and what kind of national health insurance the nation should have.

The primary purpose of this monograph is to analyze the major implications of three prominent NHI bills before Congress in 1980: the Medical Expense Protection Act introduced by Congressman James Martin as a Republican Party proposal, the National Health Plan submitted on behalf of President Carter by Congressman Charles Rangel, and the Health Care for All Americans Act introduced by Senator Edward Kennedy and Congressman Henry Waxman.[2] Although prominence is largely a function of election-year politics, it is also true that these bills represent three very different approaches to national health insurance: (1) a proposal to fill major gaps in coverage with minimal changes in health care financing (the Martin bill); (2) a proposal to fill gaps and partially reform provider payment in order to limit costs (the Carter bill); (3) a proposal to replace the current system of multiple insurance programs with a unified system of coverage and payment for the entire population (the Kennedy-Waxman bill).

The three different approaches have very different implications for Americans' access to medical care, the distribution of the burden for health financing, the share of the nation's resources devoted to health, and the role of government in the health care field. To clarify these implications we compare the Martin, Carter, and Kennedy-Waxman plans along four dimensions: adequacy of coverage and benefits, equity of financing, effects on employment, and control over expenditures and resource allocation. We also consider the administrative feasibility of each proposal throughout the analysis.[3]

Most earlier studies of NHI proposals have concentrated on each bill's provisions for benefits, coverage, sources of revenue, and the size of governments' budgets. This paper extends this evaluation in two ways. First, this study evaluates each bill's implications for cost control and resource allocation. Second, it analyzes each bill's effects on cities. Two critical issues are not fully addressed either by the bills under discussion or by this monograph: protection against the costs of long-term care and financial responsbility for delivering medical care to illegal aliens.

IMPLICATIONS OF NHI BILLS FOR COST CONTROL AND RESOURCE ALLOCATION

Cost control has become increasingly important as the NHI debate has continued. Although improving insurance protection continues to be a major goal for national health insurance, slowing the rate of increase in medical expenditures has become equally important. In terms of 1967 dollars, the United States spent almost $17 billion on public and private health care services in 1950. By 1979, national health care expenditures had exceeded $97 billion (in 1967 dollars). Constant-dollar per capita expenditures grew from $114 to $434 in the same period. Within the past quarter-century, the percentage of the gross national product committed to medical care has almost doubled, to about 9 percent in 1979.[4]

Increases in expenditures can be attributed to changes in population, prices, and the volume and intensity of services per capita. Measures are imperfect, and it is difficult to distinguish between changes in price and intensity. Price increases nevertheless seem to have been the largest single factor in medical expenditure increases (they accounted for more than 40 percent of expenditure growth since 1950), and increases in volume and intensity were a close second.[5] Before 1966, consumer prices exclusive of medical services rose at 2 percent per year, medical prices at 3.2 percent. Between 1966 when Medicare and Medicaid went into effect and 1971 when price controls were introduced, general prices increased at 5.8 percent per year and medical prices at 7.9 percent.[6] Once controls were removed in early 1974, medical price increases continued to outpace price increases for all goods and services.

Because of the government's sizable commitment to health care programs, expenditure and price inflation take their toll on the federal budget. In 1965, before Medicare and Medicaid, the federal government spent 4.8 percent of its budget, $5.2 billion, on health care. By 1969 the share of the budget allocated to health care had doubled.[7] Federal health expenditures rose to 11.4 percent of the federal budget in 1979.[8]

This experience has made costs as important as coverage in the debate on national health insurance. Recognizing that expansion of insurance to current levels has stimulated the rapid increases in medical expenditures, many NHI opponents argue that adding more coverage will make matters worse. Although some segments of the population would benefit from greater insurance protection, this argument goes, the bulk of the population would suffer from higher taxes, larger premiums, and rising costs for whatever medical bills national health insurance did not cover.

Critics have questioned even the benefits associated with expanded protection. In 1979, third parties contributed more than 90 percent of hospitals' revenues but less than two-thirds of physicians' receipts,[9] so expansion of coverage would be directed primarily at physicians' services. Critics are concerned that expanded insurance will lower consumers' medical care prices even further, and will cause them to use services for which costs exceed health benefits derived.

Fianlly, beyond pointing out these effects on the health sector, critics oppose the expansion of the federal budget that national health insurance would entail. Some object on the philosophical grounds that government should not encroach further on private sector activities. Others fear that a larger federal budget would mean greater deficit spending, to the detriment of the nation's economic health.

These considerations have been used to justify the assertion that the nation cannot afford national health insurance. This is the view of the new breed of fiscally conservative Democrats, who join with Republicans in opposing major changes in health care financing. The counter-argument, from liberal Democrats and their constituencies, is that national health insurance is essential to bring the current medical inflation under control — in other words, that the nation cannot afford *not* to have national health insurance. The challenge, as NHI proponents see it, is to design an NHI plan that can reconcile the apparently competing goals of expanding access to medical care and containing medical costs.

The bills we analyze represent three prototypical approaches toward the twin goals of expanded access and cost containment. Senator Kennedy and Congressman Waxman's bill would cover all acute health care expenses for all U.S. citizens and legal residents. At the same time, the bill would aggressively attempt to contain costs through extensive government control over provider payment and resource allocation.

President Carter's bill takes a more limited approach to coverage and payment reform. Carter viewed comprehensive coverage as too expensive in the current fiscal and political environment. His NHI plan would offer comprehensive coverage in phases, beginning with catastrophic coverage for the general population and expansion of Medicaid for the poor. The Carter bill's cost containment measures are also more limited than the Kennedy-Waxman bill's. Government would control all public and private payments to hospitals but would control only public payments to physicians and other noninstitutional providers.

Congressman Martin's bill aims to leave most of the current financing system intact but to supplement it with catastrophic protection for all citizens and legal residents. To some extent, his bill would promote cost containment by encouraging people to choose low-cost insurance that either contained significant cost sharing or relied on closed panels of physicians, as in health maintenance organizations (HMOs). But the Martin bill proposes no changes in methods of provider payment or resource allocation. Although some changes could be made without altering other features of the bill, as now written, the Martin bill favors expansion of access over cost containment as the major goal for national health insurance.

First-year cost estimates for the three plans will also be presented. These estimates, however, are not a principal criterion in evaluating the bills, for two reasons. First, comparing the current system's cost with a plan's first year costs may be a poor indicator of a plan's long-run costs. The first year may involve one-time transition costs associated with expanding benefits or upgrading provider reimbursement. Although these transition costs are important, plans' mechanisms for controlling costs over the long run are probably even more important. A plan of limited scope that fails to contain costs could ultimately cost as much as or more than a comprehensive plan that effectively controls costs. The first-year cost estimates presented below focus primarily on the effects of increased benefits and the demand for services. The estimates do not attempt to incorporate the consequences of cost control measures, primarily because their effects are so difficult to predict. Thus, these cost estimates should be treated as yardsticks for gauging differences in the bills' overall approaches, not as a major criterion for evaluating the bills.

The second reason for not emphasizing cost in this analysis is that the question of how much should be spent for medical care is a broad political issue that transcends technical analysis. The nation can clearly accommodate more health spending by reducing spending in other areas. Whether such tradeoffs are desirable, however, can only be evaluated in the much broader context of allocating the nation's resources first between public and private activities and then among competing public programs. This type of evaluation is far beyond the scope of this report.

IMPLICATIONS OF NHI BILLS FOR CITIES

Local and other governments have played a major role in health care financing as providers of last resort. Public hospitals, clinics, and other facilities serve people who cannot afford to purchase care in the private sector. Enactment of Medicare and Medicaid in 1965 reduced but did not eliminate the need for charity care, and local financing remains an essential element in supporting health care for the poor. City and county governments spent $11.7 billion for health care services in 1976, just under 10 percent of the nation's total expenditure of $120 billion.

Roughly 20 percent of local government's spending was for medical vendor (chiefly physicians) payments, 57 percent was for hospital services (including payments to private hospitals), and the remainder for general health services. The bulk of local health and hospital spending is concentrated in the more populous cities and counties; approximately half of the total expenditures (excluding medical vendor payments) was spent in cities with more than 500,000 persons and counties with more than 300,000 persons. About half of localities' health spending is supported by local revenues, raised primarily by property and sales taxes.[10]

Local governments' roles as health care providers and financiers clearly vary with federal and state health care programs and policies. In recent years, fiscal pressures have caused many states to limit Medicaid eligibility and payment levels. Low rates of payment have reduced private physicians' willingness to treat Medicaid patients. The value of Medicare coverage for physicians' services, too, has eroded over time because of medical care price inflation. As a result, the poor continue to turn to public hospitals and to other locally supported providers for medical care.

But many local governments, like state governments, face increasingly stringent budgets. Some cities have been forced to close public hospitals and to reduce other health care services. These cutbacks in turn pass on the responsibility for care for the indigent to private providers, particularly hospitals located in low-income neighborhoods. One highly visible consequence of this shift is the plea for federal support from private as well as public hospitals claiming "financial distress." A less apparent consequence may be less medical care for the poor.

This monograph assesses the way various national health insurance plans would affect these burdens on cities. To the extent that an NHI plan would expand insurance coverage, the plan would reduce the need for locally provided care. City residents, however, would have to pay for expanded coverage, either through taxes or premiums. A comparison of benefits with financing burdens will reveal whether, on balance, cities gain or lose from a particular plan. Taxes and premiums used to finance care would also affect employment levels, which in turn could affect a city's prosperity.

Cities would also be affected by NHI provisions for cost containment. In one sense, cities have benefited from rising expenditures on medical care, for more expenditures have meant more jobs and higher wages in the cities' health care sector. But these benefits must be weighed against the negative impacts of health cost increases — including the costs to a city of maintaining the public facilities (especially hospitals) to care for people who find private care beyond their means. Support for cost-containment legislation from the National League of Cities and other

xvii

urban organizations suggests that cities perceive more to gain than to lose in expenditure control. How much they would gain would depend on specific cost-containment provisions.

OVERVIEW

Our objective in analyzing and comparing the Martin, Carter and Kennedy-Waxman bills is not to conclude which is the best plan, either for the nation or for cities. That decision requires value judgments that only the political system can make: How much should government spend on medical care? How much government regulation should there be? How important are equity, income redistribution, and efficiency? Rather, our goal is to identify the differences among the plans' impacts on coverage, income distribution, employment, and resource allocation. By making these implications more explicit, we hope to contribute to the process of choosing and developing an improved national medical care system.

The main body of this monograph is divided into ten chapters. Chapter 1 outlines the major features of the Martin, Carter and Kennedy-Waxman bills. Chapter 2 considers the coverage provisions of each bill and compares them to insurance coverage under the current system.

Chapter 3 analyzes the consequences for income distribution of each bill's combination of financing and benefits. Because the details of current bills' financing provisions are not available, inferences about income distribution effects are made from analyses of earlier, similar bills.

Chapter 4 analyzes the employment effects of the Carter, Kennedy-Waxman, and the Martin bills. We consider the implications of premiums and taxes for wage and employment levels and the implications of increased health spending for employment in the health care sector.

Chapters 5 through 8 explore the bills' mechanisms for cost control, provider payment and resource allocation. In chapter 5 we focus on two major strategies for controlling costs through the market place: competition among insurance plans and consumer cost sharing. In chapter 6 we examine physician reimbursement provisions, particularly the implications of fee schedules. Chapter 7 explores hospital cost containment strategies. Since two of the three bills (Carter and Kennedy-Waxman) propose several new regulatory and administrative procedures for paying providers, chapter 8 concentrates on some of the potential problems which might arise in administering the proposed systems.

The impact of the three bills on cities is analyzed in chapter 9. This analysis focuses on changes in coverage, income distribution, employment, and resource allocation. In addition, comparisons are made between selected high-poverty and low-poverty cities.

Finally, chapter 10 summarizes our findings. Each bill's advantages and shortcomings are highlighted. We conclude with an outline of principles for an equitable and efficient national health insurance bill, drawing upon the best features of all three.

I. LEGISLATIVE PROPOSALS FOR NATIONAL HEALTH INSURANCE

As background for our analysis, this chapter outlines the major features of the Martin, Carter, and Kennedy-Waxman bills. (For summary outlines of the three proposals, see Appendix A, Charts 1, 2, and 3.) We have concentrated on provisions governing coverage, financing, and provider payment, for these relate to our main concerns set forth earlier: adequacy of benefit coverage, equity of financing, effects on employment, and control over expenditures. Other features — including quality assurance, facility regulation, utilization review — are not addressed, so these outlines are not comprehensive.

THE MARTIN MEDICAL EXPENSE PROTECTION ACT

Coverage

The Martin Medical Expense Protection Act would provide income-related, publicly financed catastrophic health insurance for all Americans in its Catastrophic Automatic Protection Plan (CAPP). The plan would pay a share of all covered medical expenses exceeding a specified level and would cover all of a family's medical bills once the family had incurred out-of-pocket medical expenses in any given year equal to a set percentage of the family's annual income as shown in the following table:

Annual Family Income	Out-of-Pocket Deductible Per Family	Coinsurance Rate (Percent Paid by Family)	Out-of-Pocket Limit Per Family
Not over $4,000	$300	10%	$500
Over $4,000 but not over $10,000	$300, plus 20% of income over $4,000	15%	$500, plus 25% of income over $4,000
Over $10,000	$1,500 plus 20% of income over $10,000	20%	$2,000, plus 20% of income over $10,000

1

Covered services would include prenatal care, well-baby care through age one, immunizations, and all services covered by Medicare (including the changes described in the paragraphs below). Payments made by private insurance plans would not count toward CAPP's cost-sharing requirements. Cost-sharing obligations would be based on family income during the preceding calendar year. Retroactive adjustments would be made when income in the current year was significantly higher or lower than in the preceding year. Once a family incurred medical expenses (not covered by insurance) that exceeded its deductible, it would pay only a portion of expenses (at the specified coinsurance rate) until its out-of-pocket limit had been reached. The Martin plan's catastrophic program would pay the remainder of expenses below the out-of-pocket limit and all expenses beyond that limit.

These provisions aim to provide catastrophic protection to people who now have little or no insurance — the working poor, the unemployed, part-time workers, and the like — and to currently insured persons whose insurance does not cover financially catastrophic medical expenses. The plan is estimated to increase total 1980 health care costs by $1 billion. Since the federal government will assume responsibility for some costs that are now privately financed, its 1980 costs would increase $5 billion.[11]

Medicare and Medicaid would remain in place, but both would change somewhat. The copayment on hospital days under Medicare Part A would be eliminated; so would the limit on hospital days. CAPP's income-related limit on out-of-pocket medical expenses would apply to Medicare beneficiaries as well as other individuals. Medicare eligibles would be allowed to count all out-of-pocket expenses incurred for certain prescription drugs as well as all Medicare deductibles and coinsurance toward the catastrophic plan's deductible. The only alteration to Medicaid would be the addition of a maintenance-of-effort provision to prohibit states from reducing the number of categories of eligible individuals or the amount of services now provided.

Individuals insured through their employers would be expected to retain private coverage. The bill proposes several changes in current tax provisions to alter that coverage, encouraging the purchase of catastrophic protection and discouraging first-dollar coverage. Current law permits employers to deduct contributions to employee health plans as a business expense without limit and excludes these amounts from employees' taxable income as well. Under the Martin plan the employer's tax exemption would be limited to $120 per employee per month, and only contributions to qualified plans would be eligible for favored tax treatment. (Qualified private plans would have to cover the same services as the bill's catastrophic plan and would have to pay all expenses once the employee or a family member had incurred $2,500 in out-of-pocket expenses.) Premium payments above the $120-per-employee limit would be taxable as employee income. (The plan could still be a qualified plan even if the employer contribution exceeded the $120 limit.)

The $2,500 limit on out-of-pocket expenses in qualified private plans would be higher for some families than their income-related limit under the federal catastrophic plan (CAPP). In such cases, qualified plans would be required to provide interim coverage for family expenses above their CAPP out-of-pocket limits; CAPP would later reimburse the private plan for such expenses. In addition, qualified plans could not impose restrictions such as waiting periods or limited coverage for pre-existing conditions, and they would be required to have open enrollment at least annually. Plans would be required to cover dependents and to continue coverage of workers and their families up to sixty days after termination of a worker's employment. In addition, plans would be required to permit employees who terminated employment to continue participating in the plan at their own expense. Premiums would be set at individual, not group, rates.

Employers would not be required to offer health insurance (qualified or otherwise). Employers would have to contribute at least half the premium for the least expensive qualified plan offered and would be required to make equal dollar contributions to employees, regardless of the plan chosen. Furthermore, if an employee enrolled in a qualified plan that cost less than the employer's fixed contribution, the employer would be required to pay a rebate equal to at least 75 percent of the difference between the employer contribution and the cost of the selected plan. (The bill would allow the employer to keep up to 25 percent of that difference to encourage employers to offer a high cost-sharing plan.) Up to $8.33 per month of the employees' rebate would not be taxable income to the employee, so long as the employer contribution was below the $120 limit. None of the rebate would be subject to Social Security, unemployment, or railroad retirement taxes.

Employees choosing not to enroll in a qualified private plan would still be eligible for catastrophic coverage under the federal plan (CAPP). They would nonetheless face a higher deductible as a penalty for not enrolling. Employees could choose to calculate the higher deductible in one of two ways: (1) the deductible would be equal to all expenses incurred in the period during which the private plan would have covered them and for 120 days thereafter, or, (2) the CAPP deductible could be increased by 50 percent of what it otherwise would have been or by $1,000, whichever is greater.

The federal catastrophic plan would be administered by the Department of Health and Human Services (DHHS), which would verify income and determine eligibility on the basis of incurred, itemized bills for services covered by the plan. Coverage would begin once bills exceeded the income-related deductible.

Financing

The federal catastrophic plan would be financed from general revenues deposited in a Social Security trust fund. The financing of Medicare, Medicaid, and other public programs would remain the same. Private insurance plan financing also would remain unchanged, subject to proposed modifications in the tax code.

Provider Payment

Participating providers would have to agree to accept the CAPP rate as payment in full for services covered by CAPP. Participating hospitals and other institutions would be paid on the basis of reasonable costs, as under Medicare. Participating physicians would be paid under CAPP on the basis of "reasonable charges," computed from physicians' own submitted bills, as in Medicare. However, unlike Medicare, CAPP would pay 100 percent of allowed reasonable charges once out-of-pocket limits are reached. The bill also would raise CAPP fees in areas where physicians are in short supply to the 75th percentile of current fees, would provide for more frequent updating of fees than is now done, and would eliminate the economic index that now restrains fee increases in Medicare. At the option of participating physicians, a physician could be reimbursed at CAPP rates for all Medicare patients, but would be required to accept that rate as payment in full.

THE CARTER NATIONAL HEALTH PLAN

Coverage

The Carter National Health Plan proposes catastrophic and maternal-infant health insurance protection for all citizens and legal residents and a federal program, replacing Medicare and most of Medicaid, to provide comprehensive health insurance for the poor, the elderly, and the disabled. Coverage would be available in three ways: (1) Employers would be required to provide their employees catastrophic and maternal-infant coverage by the "Employer Guarantee." (2) Small employers and individuals not covered through employment could obtain catastrophic and maternal-infant coverage from a federal "HealthCare" program. (3) The poor, the elderly, and the disabled (on somewhat different terms) would receive comprehensive insurance from the federal HealthCare program.

4

It is estimated that the Carter bill would raise total health care costs in 1980 by $19.5 billion, to $248.5 billion. The public sector would bear the bulk of the increase ($17.1 billion). The federal government's 1980 health care costs would increase from $62.5 billion to $80.3 billion.

Both the Employer Guarantee and the HealthCare program of the Carter plan would make catastrophic coverage available to any citizen or legal resident once family out-of-pocket medical and hospital expenses in a given year had exceeded $2,500. Under HealthCare, catastrophic benefits would be paid only after a family incurred expenses during the year of $2,500 that were not covered by a private insurance policy. In other words, HealthCare would impose a $2,500 annual deductible. In employer plans, $2,500 would be a limit on out-of-pocket expenses that employees and their dependents might incur through a variety of cost-sharing arrangements. Under both plans, expenditures on any medical or institutional services covered under the bill would count toward the $2,500 limit. Covered services would include inpatient hospital services; outpatient physical therapy; physicians' services; diagnostic tests and x-rays; medical equipment and devices; family planning services; immunizations; and prenatal, delivery, and infant care services (up to one year of age). The bill would authorize the Secretary of the Department of Health and Human Services to cover additional services for children up to age eighteen by regulation. Under both the Employer Guarantee and the HealthCare program, expenses for prenatal, delivery, and infant care services would be fully covered with no patient cost sharing.

To obtain coverage, individuals would have to enroll in either a private or public health insurance plan. The Employer Guarantee program would require employers to enroll all full-time workers and their dependents in a qualified private health insurance plan. To be qualified, a private plan would be required to offer (at a minimum) the law's catastrophic, prenatal, delivery, and infant care benefits; to meet specific financial, privacy, and reporting requirements; to charge community (not experience) rates for firms with ten to fifty employees; to continue coverage of individuals who terminated employment for ninety days after they leave the job; to allow individuals leaving employment to continue coverage subsequently at a maximum cost of 125 percent of the program's premium; to submit to review of services by government-sponsored Professional Standards Review Organizations (but not necessarily to abide by their decisions); and to adopt the government's terms of payment for prenatal, delivery, and infant care services and hospital-based physicians' services.

Employers would be required to pay at least 75 percent of the insurance premium for covered services and to offer employees a choice between a qualified, traditional insurance plan and all federally qualified health maintenance organizations (HMOs) in the area. The employer would have to contribute the same dollar amount per employee, regardless of the employee's choice of plan. If a plan's premiums were lower than that amount, the employer would have to pay the employee the difference in cash or fringe benefits. Cash rebates would be taxable on the same terms as other wages and salaries.

If an employer's premium expenses exceeded 5 percent of payroll, the government would pay the excess, provided the premiums were reasonable relative to coverage offered. The employer also would have the option to purchase coverage from the federal health insurance plan — HealthCare. For employers with ten or more employees, the HealthCare premium would be equivalent to 5 percent of payroll. For other employers, the premium would be the lower of 5 percent of payroll or the premium charged to individuals not covered through employment.

Any U.S. citizen or legal resident not covered through employment could (but would not be required to) purchase insurance for catastrophic, prenatal, delivery, and infant care expenses from the federal HealthCare program. The federal government would administer this program through fiscal agents, similar to the way Medicare is administered. Under HealthCare, catastrophic benefits would be paid after an out-of-pocket deductible of $2,500. Premiums would be charged for catastrophic benefits and would be set annually to cover the costs of benefits provided under the plan to persons who bought its protection. Premiums might vary by geographic area and family size. No premium would be required to obtain full coverage for pregnancy, delivery, and infant care expenses.

In addition to catastrophic, pregnancy, delivery, and infant care protection, HealthCare would provide full coverage of hospital and medical services for any U.S. citizen or legal resident who (1) had an income below 55 percent of the federal poverty standard; (2) was already eligible for Medicaid in any state; (3) incurred expenses (at HealthCare-allowed rates) on services covered by HealthCare (or the residual Medicaid program, which is explained in the next paragraphs) that would reduce income to 55 percent of the poverty standard; or (4) met the eligibility requirements for Medicare. Persons who meet Medicare's current eligibility requirements would be required to pay a premium equivalent to the premium now charged for Medicare Part B ($8.70 per month), raised annually to reflect increases in medical costs. There would be no premium for persons eligible for HealthCare on the basis of income.

HealthCare would improve coverage for persons now eligible for Medicare by removing limits on the covered days of hospital care, by limiting beneficiaries' out-of-pocket expenditures for health care to $1,250 per year, and by eliminating the two-year waiting period for eligibility based on disability. HealthCare would cover more people than the Medicaid program by expanding coverage beyond cash assistance eligibility categories (the aged, the blind, the disabled, and recipients of aid to families with dependent children — AFDC) to all persons meeting the income standard; by raising the income standard in several states; and by making persons in all states eligible for coverage if their medical care expenditures reduced their incomes to the eligible income standard. For children up to age eighteen, HealthCare would cover hearing services, which are not now included in Medicaid, and would cover dental and vision services that some but not all states now offer. HealthCare would not cover nursing home services that Medicaid now provides; nor would HealthCare cover other benefits, including prescription drugs. Medicaid will continue for these services, under current terms.

Financing

Benefits provided through the Employer Guarantee program would be financed through mandatory premiums, which could be considered the equivalent of a tax. HealthCare would be financed through voluntary premiums and general revenues. HealthCare would retain current Medicare financing mechanisms — premiums, payroll taxes, and general revenues — for Medicare eligibles. HealthCare would rely on federal and state general revenues to finance benefits for the poor. In the Carter plan's first two years, states would be obligated to contribute the equivalent of 90 percent of their share of an estimate of what their Medicaid costs would have been but for the enactment of the Carter plan. (This estimate is calculated as the cost of HealthCare — covered services immediately prior to enactment, projected into each of the two years after enactment by adding in each year the average annual rate of increase in state Medicaid costs for the three preceding years.) State obligations after the first two years would be calculated in the following way: Medicaid-equivalent costs (calculated as just described) would be subtracted from total HealthCare costs for low-income people. The remainder would be attributed to the NHI plan and paid by the federal government. The federal share would be inflated every year by the national rate of increase in health expenses. Each state would then pay 90 percent of its current Medicaid matching rate on the difference between actual HealthCare costs for low-income beneficiaries in the state and the federal payment calculated as just described. Thus the federal NHI share would be relatively fixed and predictable. Unusual cost increases would be a joint federal-state responsibility. The effect of this arrangement would be to make each state responsible for a share of any amount by which actual cost increases for the low-income population in the state exceeded the national rate of increase in health care costs. Alternatively, states would gain if their costs increased more slowly than national costs.

Provider Payment and Cost Containment

The Carter plan's cost control features include separately introduced hospital cost-containment legislation, limits on hospitals' capital expenditures, and limits on physician payment under HealthCare. The hospital cost-containment legislation would impose revenue ceilings on hospitals whose total expenditure increases exceeded predetermined amounts. Ceilings would apply to public and private revenues. In addition, the bill would place a per state dollar ceiling on capital expenditures that could be approved through certificate-of-need programs.

Physician payments under HealthCare would be made according to state or area fee schedules, negotiated between the federal government and physicians. The schedules would specify fees for services, regardless of who performed them, but exceptions could be made to allow fee differences that reflect specialty training. Rates for services related to pregnancy and infant care might be all-inclusive, rather than fee-for-service. Physicians could not charge HealthCare beneficiaries above the amount specified in the schedule. Except for pregnancy and infant care services, the plan would place no restrictions on physician charges under private insurance plans.

THE KENNEDY-WAXMAN HEALTH CARE FOR ALL AMERICANS ACT

Coverage

The coverage proposed by the Kennedy-Waxman bill would differ substantially from that proposed by the Martin and Carter bills. The bill does not distinguish between coverage for the poor and coverage for the general population, and it would provide all citizens and legal residents full coverage with no cost sharing. Covered services would be basically similar to those the Carter bill would provide, but the Kennedy-Waxman bill would also cover well-child care up to age eighteen, hearing aids, and drugs for treatment of chronic illness for Medicare-eligible individuals. It would not cover dental and vision care. The last two services would remain state options under a residual Medicaid program.

It is estimated that the Kennedy-Waxman plan would increase 1980 health care costs to $269.5 billion ($113.5 billion in public costs and $156

8

billion in private costs), an increase of $40 billion. The federal government's health expenditures would increase to $91 billion.

Under the Kennedy-Waxman bill, every individual would be entitled to enroll in a qualified insurance plan.[12] To be qualified, a plan would be required (1) to participate in one of five national consortia, composed of Blue Cross-Blue Shield plans, commercial insurance carriers, prepaid group practice (PGP) health maintenance organizations, individual practice associate (IPA) health maintenance organizations, and self-insurers; (2) to offer at least the specified coverage without charges above authorized premiums; (3) to conduct open enrollment periods and accept all applicants in the order in which they apply (to the limit of plan capacity); (4) to issue health insurance enrollment cards; (5) to pay providers no more than authorized amounts; (6) to make records available to agencies with responsibilities under the law; (7) to assure that any rebates or extra benefits offered to one enrollee were offered to all; and (8) to establish fair hearing procedures for dissatisfied individuals or providers.

Employed individuals would enroll themselves and their families in a plan offered by their employers. Employers would be required to offer their employees a choice of at least three qualified plans — one belonging to the Blue Cross-Blue Shield consortium; one belonging to the insurance carrier consortium; and one belonging to either of the HMO consortia. Employers could also offer a qualified self-insurance plan. Individuals who could not enroll through employment could enroll in any available qualified health plan. The government would enroll any individual who failed to enroll in a qualified plan and collect (with penalty) any premiums owed. As a result, all citizens and legal residents would be eligible for comprehensive benefits.

Financing

The Kennedy-Waxman plan would be financed through a combination of premiums and taxes, assessed in the following ways: The federal government would pay premiums sufficient to cover administrative and benefit costs for the population receiving Supplemental Security Income (SSI) payments and residents of federal institutions. State governments would pay premiums for the AFDC population and residents of state institutions. The elderly would continue to pay premiums as they now do for Medicare (supplemented by the hospital insurance payroll tax extended to apply to public as well as private employees).

The rest of the population would pay premiums directly. Because the premium would be calculated as a flat percentage of wage-related and non-wage-related income, however, the premium would really be a combination payroll and income tax. The percentage premium tax rate would be determined on a state-wide basis to cover administrative and service

9

costs in the state. The full rate would be applied to wage-related income; half of the rate would be applied to non-wage-related income. Non-wage-related income of $2,000 for individuals and $4,000 for families would be exempt from the base against which premiums were calculated. The total premium an individual would pay on wage and nonwage income could not exceed average per capita costs for operating the plan in that state.

Employers would pay at least 65 percent of wage-related premium costs for their employees. Tax credits or grants would be available to employers for a three-year period for a portion (one-half in year one, one-third in year two, and one-sixth in year three) of the amount by which newly required premiums exceeded 3 percent of payroll. For private, for-profit employers, however, this subsidy would be available only if net incomes had declined following enactment of the Kennedy-Waxman bill.

Premiums would be collected by the consortia and distributed among member insurers and HMOs on a capitation basis for enrollees in each state. Capitation payments would be adjusted to reflect cost differences in areas within the state and in individual enrollee characteristics related to actuarial risk category (for example, age, sex, and disability status). Individual insurers could attract enrollees by offering coverage beyond what the law specified or by paying dividends or cash rebates to enrollees. Cash rebates would not be taxed or treated as income for purposes of other transfer programs (such as Social Security or SSI).

In addition to having responsibility for premiums for AFDC eligible persons, states would be required to maintain their Medicaid programs for services that national health insurance did not cover. Long-term care is the major service area that would be affected. The Kennedy-Waxman bill would limit a state's total obligation for AFDC premiums and the residual Medicaid program to Medicaid expenditures before enactment of the bill, adjusted upward for increases in national health expenditures.

Provider Payment and Cost Containment

To control medical expenditures under the new plan, the Kennedy-Waxman bill would establish an annual national health budget, which would represent the total amount that could be spent on covered services in the coming year. The bill specifies that the budget could not exceed the previous year's budget by more than the average annual rate of increase in the gross national product (GNP) for the preceding three-year period. The budget would specify limits on expenditures by types of service or provider and by state. Methods for allocating the national budget among states are not specified in detail, except that (1) the percentage increase in a state's annual health budget over actual expenditures in the previous year would vary inversely with the state's per capita expenditures relative to the nation's per capita expenditures (that is, a state spending more than the national average would get a lower rate of increase); and (2) the increase could not be less than 80 percent or more than 120 percent of the rate of increase in the national health budget experienced the year before. Exceptions to the latter provision might be made for states with populations formally identified as medically underserved. Subject to budget limitations and federal government rules, boards appointed by the governor in each state would determine prospective budgets for each state's hospitals and other institutions and maximum fee schedules for physicians. Specific payment methods and levels would reflect negotiations among representatives of providers, insurers, employers, employees, and other consumers. Individual insurers and HMOs could not pay providers more than the amounts the State Health Board approved, but they could pay less than the approved amount.

II. COVERAGE CHANGES UNDER NATIONAL HEALTH INSURANCE

To assess the changes that national health insurance would make, it is necessary to clarify the current structure of private and public health insurance coverage. Together, private and public plans now provide the great majority of Americans considerable protection against the cost of illness. Yet structural characteristics of the private insurance market and of public programs exclude some people from coverage and limit the benefits available to others. The Congressional Budget Office (CBO) estimated that in 1978 as many as 18 million persons (8 percent of the population) were without coverage of any kind.[13]

This chapter describes current insurance programs, highlighting features that produce gaps in coverage. It then assesses the extent to which each NHI plan proposes to fill existing gaps. As already mentioned, our discussion, like the bills themselves, deals solely with financing acute care for citizens and legal residents.

COVERAGE UNDER CURRENT INSURANCE ARRANGEMENTS

Private Insurance Plans

Variations in purchasing power, compounded by insurers' incentives to limit their exposure to financial risk, have divided the insurance market into two segments: large employee groups and the rest of the population. Large groups obtain broad coverage at relatively low rates for a number of reasons. Favorable tax treatment of employers' contributions to insurance premiums, the reduction in risk associated with large numbers of relatively healthy persons, and the sheer volume of premium dollars have combined to make employees of large, unionized industries particularly attractive to insurers. Competition to insure these groups has held down administrative costs and has led insurers to tailor rates exclusively to costs incurred by each group's members, that is, to employ "experience rating" (as opposed to "community rating" under which members of different groups are charged the same premium). Because employed people are generally healthier than the rest of the population, experience rating means that employee groups pay lower premiums than they would if they shared the costs of the nonworking population. Better health status and lower administrative costs per capita in large employee groups make group premiums lower than premiums charged to small groups and individuals.

13

The availability of insurance through employment varies considerably with firm size. A 1977-78 Battelle survey found that only 50 percent of firms with between 2 and 9 employees offered group health insurance, as compared with 85 percent of firms with 10 to 99 employees and 100 percent of firms employing 100 or more. Fifty-six percent of workers in the smallest firms had group insurance available. The proportion rose to 89 percent in the middle-size firms and 100 percent in the largest firms.[14]

Not all employees in firms offering group insurance plans are covered by those plans. The Battelle survey reported 78 percent of employees in firms with coverage (70 percent of all private nonfarm employees in 1977-78) actually acquired coverage under their firm's plan.[15] Employees covered by group plans acquire quite extensive benefits. The Battelle survey reported that in 1977-78, 100 percent of employees with group insurance had benefits for hospital room and board and inpatient services and physicians' surgical services; more than 90 percent had benefits for physicians' office visits, outpatient lab tests and x-rays, outpatient prescription drugs, and normal maternity care. Seventy-five percent had coverage for care of sick newborns. In contrast, 49 percent had coverage for well-baby care and 65 percent for posthospital skilled nursing care. Only 25 percent had coverage for routine dental care, and 12 percent for routine vision care.[16]

A policy's coverage of a service does not assure that the policy will pay the full cost the service entails. Policies may include limits on hospital days, benefits per day, benefits for surgical services, and lifetime benefits; policies also may require deductibles and other cost-sharing features or may simply not pay full cost, leaving the balance to the insured. In addition, many policies have waiting periods before benefits go into effect. A person changing jobs can therefore be caught without insurance or with incomplete coverage.

Although limitations persist, a growing number of large group policies are aligning benefits to full service costs and raising lifetime ceilings. In 1976, 90 percent of workers in group plans in firms with twenty-five or more employees reportedly had "major medical" benefits, which pay the major part (usually 80 percent) of charges for most medical services after beneficiaries meet an initial deductible. These plans offer lifetime maximum benefits ranging from under $10,000 to $250,000 or more with a growing number of policies offering unlimited benefits. In 1976, however, less than 10 percent of workers in group plans in firms with more than twenty-five employees had unlimited benefits. Although most "major medical" plans require that beneficiaries share costs (usually 20 percent of charges after a deductible), a growing number of plans set limits on beneficiaries' out-of-pocket payments, thereby providing what

14

may be the most significant protection against catastrophic costs. Roughly 20 percent of employees in group plans in firms with more than twenty-five employees had coverage of this type in 1976.[17]

Even well-insured workers, however, face catastrophic risks in the current system. Individuals who lose their jobs because of illness tend (after a brief period) to lose their job-related insurance as well. In 1977-78, only an estimated 5 percent of employees in firms with group insurance had the opportunity to continue coverage at their own expense after terminating employment.[18] This opportunity to "convert," however, may be limited in time, and will certainly involve increased premium burdens that may be beyond the individual's financial means. No one in the current private insurance market is protected indefinitely against a debilitating illness. As this section points out, public programs are intended to compensate for this weakness in the market, but they do so imperfectly.

Although detailed information is not available on the variation in benefits by size of firm, marketing practices suggest that employees of large firms have more comprehensive coverage than employees of small firms. Insurers typically do not tailor benefit packages to small employers but offer a standard package instead. Because expenditures are more uncertain for small groups, insurers are likely to offer the more limited benefits at higher premiums. Even more important, firms smaller than a certain size are individually underwritten. This means that premiums vary with employees' health status and that coverage may not be provided for certain preexisting conditions. Insurers' marketing costs are also higher for small than for large firms, further raising premiums in relation to benefits. In these respects, small firms face the same problems as individuals in the insurance market.[19]

Part-time employees, the self-employed, and the unemployed also have limited access to group health insurance plans. Health insurance, like other fringe benefits, may not be available to part-time employees, and unemployed workers may lose their group health benefits when they terminate employment. Table 1 shows the percentages of each of these groups and of full-time workers with group health benefits in 1976. The unemployed fare better than might be expected because some group health insurance plans continue benefits during short-term layoffs. In 1974, extended benefits during layoffs were provided by plans covering 40 percent of workers with group coverage. Some plans varied the length of protection with the length of employment, and the majority of plans had protection of three months or less.[20]

People with limited access to group health insurance can buy individual health insurance policies. Individual policies, however, typically

Table 1

PERCENTAGES OF PERSONS WITH AND WITHOUT INSURANCE PROTECTION
(1976)

	Percentage of Population with Group Insurance[a]	Percentage of Population with Individual Insurance[b]	Percentage of Population with No Private Health Insurance	Percentage of Population with Neither Private Nor Public Health Coverage
Age				
Less than 19 years	65.4%	12.2%	24.4%	—
19 to 24 years	58.0	14.6	29.0	20.5%
25 to 44 years	72.3	13.7	17.7	9.3
45 to 64 years	66.6	20.8	16.5	7.6
65 years and over	18.3	38.7	38.7	1.0
Family Income				
Less than $5,000	30.8	39.3	26.9	17.4
5,000-9,999	43.5	20.4	36.7	16.6
10,000-14,999	70.1	15.8	16.6	9.2
15,000 or more	79.3	15.3	9.2	5.7
Employment Status				
Full-time wage earner	82.6	13.1	9.6	6.5
Part-time wage earner	63.2	18.5	20.0	12.1
Self-employed	33.0	41.3	24.6	14.9
Unemployed	41.5	14.9	44.9	26.8
Retired	26.2	34.4	36.0	2.0
Not in labor force	55.8	16.4	29.0	11.4
Total	61.9%	17.2%	23.0%	5.7-9.0%[c]

Source: U.S. Congress, Congressional Budget Office, *Profile of Health Care Coverage: The Haves and Have-Nots* (Washington, D.C.: U.S. Government Printing Office, 1979), tables 1 and 11. Columns do not add to 100 percent because categories overlap.

a. Includes person with group coverage only, group and individual coverage, and group and public coverage.

b. Includes persons with individual coverage only, individual and group coverage, and individual and public coverage.

c. A range is used because of conflicting estimates of private insurance coverage.

[Handwritten marginal notes:]

fewer poor are covered as income level ↓

All employed 8.2

%age only this low because category includes nonpoor who have access to temporary group health insurance benefits and can afford

16

offer fewer benefits at higher cost than group policies do. Table 2 compares the enrollment (for persons under age 65) by policy type under group and individual policies in 1978. The number of enrollees under group policies does not decline with the scope of coverage. In contrast, enrollment in individual policies declines sharply as benefits expand, which indicates that most individuals can — or do — buy only limited coverage. The small number of individual major medical policies may reflect insurers' unwillingness or inability to make this coverage available on an individual basis at an affordable premium.

Table 2

ENROLLMENT IN INSURANCE COMPANIES' HEALTH POLICIES
(1978 Data for Persons under Age 65)

Expenses Covered	Group Policies	Individual and Family Policies
Hospital Care	84,857,000	29,155,000
Surgical Services	94,109,000	15,149,000
Physicians' Expense[a] Protection	90,208,000	12,450,000
Major Medical Expense Protection	97,187,000	6,715,000

Source: Health Insurance Institute, *Source Book of Health Insurance Data, 1979-80* (Washington, D.C.: Health Insurance Institute, 1980), pp. 13-17.

a. Physicians' medical expense insurance pays physicians' fees for nonsurgical care in a hospital, home, or doctor's office. Payments are usually limited to a specified maximum amount for specific expenses.

Not only are types of coverage more limited under individual than under group policies; restrictions within types of coverage also are more widespread. Commercial insurance companies may deny individuals coverage because of poor health status, and both insurance company and nonprofit Blue Cross-Blue Shield plan policies impose exclusions or waiting periods that may preclude coverage for needed care. Blue Cross-Blue Shield plans typically offer these policies at a single rate for all individuals in the community, but this rate is likely to be higher than the employer group rate because of the relatively poorer health status of the individuals applying and the administrative costs. Insurance companies sometimes vary their premiums with an individual's health status, thereby raising costs of coverage to persons most likely to need it, if indeed such persons are not excluded altogether from coverage for some or all conditions. Finally, premiums for insurance companies' individual policies reflect extremely high administrative costs. In 1977, insurance companies spent only 54.2 percent of premium incomes under individual policies on benefits under those policies, retaining the rest to cover operating expenses and profits. This compares with a retention rate of 13.6 percent under group policies.[21]

Table 1 shows that the private insurance market as it is now structured provides more than half the population (those with group insurance) with comprehensive insurance at affordable prices; 17 percent of the population (those with individual insurance) with limited insurance at prices generally higher than for group policies; and almost a quarter of the population with no private insurance coverage at all. The table illustrates that group coverage varies with employment status, income, and age. More than 50 percent of the uninsured population have incomes less than $10,000 and almost 75 percent have incomes less than $15,000.[22] Group coverage is more limited among persons between nineteen to twenty-four years old than for any other age group except the elderly. This reflects the fact that many policies terminate coverage of dependents when they reach eighteen years of age, unless they are in school.[23]

Table 1 also shows that individual insurance does not compensate for the absence of group coverage for many people. Overall, less than half the population without group coverage purchases private health insurance, and for some groups — persons under age twenty-five, the unemployed, and persons not in the labor force — the percentage is much smaller. The people most likely to lack either group or individual private insurance policies tend to be younger than age twenty-four or older than age sixty-four, in families with incomes less than $10,000 per year, and working less than full time or not at all.

Public Insurance Plans

The gaps in private insurance coverage have long been recognized and led to enactment of Medicare and Medicaid in 1965. Medicare provides relatively comprehensive — though far from complete — insurance protection for almost all citizens age sixty-five and over.[24] A comparison of columns 3 and 4 for persons ages 65 and over in table 1 reveals the significant effect that Medicare has had on insurance protection for the elderly. In 1976, 38.7 percent of this group had no private insurance, but only 1 percent had no insurance at all. Medicare also covers medical costs for individuals who have received Social Security disability benefits for two years. This coverage ultimately protects people who are unable to work because of illness. But the two-year waiting period leaves the disabled exposed to potentially catastrophic expenditures.

Medicaid was intended to protect people who are too poor to afford private insurance and, in some states, people who become poor because of illness (the "medically needy"). Unfortunately, Medicaid's design leaves many people in both categories unprotected. Medicaid is a joint federal-state program in which eligibility standards are subject to considerable state discretion. States are required to extend Medicaid benefits to all persons eligible for cash assistance under the Aid to Families with Dependent Children (AFDC) program. States are allowed but not required to extend Medicaid benefits to other welfare recipients — that is, persons eligible for Supplemental Security Income (SSI).[25] States are also allowed to set income standards for Medicaid eligibility above cash assistance levels. With a "medically needy" program, a state can extend Medicaid eligibility to persons whose incomes less medical expenses are 133 percent or less of the AFDC payment standard. Asset tests, however, may be used to limit eligibility.

Eligibility under cash assistance programs is limited to the aged, the blind, and the disabled (under SSI) and to single-parent families. At state option, Medicaid benefits can be extended beyond these categorical eligibles to two other groups, provided they meet income eligibility standards: children under age twenty-one, regardless of whether they are members of intact families, and members of families with unemployed fathers. Coverage of unemployed fathers is of limited duration, usually six to nine months.

These Medicaid eligibility rules mean that actual eligibility for Medicaid varies considerably among states. Table 3 shows the eligibility rules that states employed in January 1979. Arizona is the only state with no Medicaid program at all. Thirty-five states and jurisdictions provided Medicaid coverage to recipients of federal SSI payments, and almost as many covered recipients of state supplements to SSI. Fifteen states did not cover all SSI recipients, employing more restrictive eligibility criteria. Thirty-three states had medically needy programs; thirty states covered unemployed fathers and their families (Michigan covered only the children of unemployed fathers); and twenty states covered all financially eligible children under age twenty-one.

Income eligibility levels also vary considerably among states and are typically below the poverty level, as defined by the Census Bureau. In 1976, the Census Bureau defined the poverty level as $5,786 for a family of four. The Medicaid program reported that:

19

Table 3

MEDICAID COVERAGE OF THE POOR, BY STATE
(January 1979)

State	AFDC	All SSI Recipients	More Restricted Standard	State Supplement Recipients: Aged	Blind	Disabled	Medically Needy	Unemployed Fathers and Their Families	Children of Unemployed Fathers	All Financially Eligible Individuals Under Age 21
Alabama	X	X		X	X	X				
Alaska	X	X		X	X	X				
Arizona[a]										
Arkansas	X	X								
California	X	X					X	X	X	X
Colorado	X	X					X	X	X	X
Connecticut	X		X	X	X	X	X	X	X	
Delaware	X	X		X	X	X	X	X	X	X
District of Columbia	X	X					X		X	
Florida	X	X		X	X	X	X	X	X	X
Georgia	X	X								
Guam	X	X		(b)						
Hawaii	X	X	X	X	X	X	X	X	X	X
Idaho	X			X	X	X	X	X	X	
Illinois	X		X	X	X	X				
Indiana	X		X	X	X	X	X	X	X	
Iowa	X	X		X	X	X	X	X	X	
Kansas	X	X		X	X	X	X	X	X	
Kentucky	X	X		X	X	X	X	X	X	
Louisiana	X	X		X			X	X		
Maine	X	X		X	X	X	X			
Maryland	X	X		X			X	X	X	X
Massachusetts	X	X		X	X	X	X	X	X	X
Michigan	X	X		X	X	X	X		X	X
Minnesota	X		X				X	X	X	X
Mississippi	X		X							
Missouri	X		X							
Montana	X	X					X	X	X	
Nebraska	X		X	X	X	X	X	X	X	

Table 3

MEDICAID COVERAGE OF THE POOR, BY STATE
(January 1979) (continued)

State	AFDC	All SSI Recipients	More Restricted Standard	State Supplement Recipients — Aged	State Supplement Recipients — Blind	State Supplement Recipients — Disabled	State Supplement Recipients — Medically Needy	Unemployed Fathers and Their Families	Children of Unemployed Fathers	All Financially Eligible Individuals Under Age 21
Nevada	X	X		X	X	X				X
New Hampshire	X			X	X	X	X	X	X	
New Jersey	X	X								
New Mexico	X	X						X	X	X
New York	X	X	X	X		X	X			
North Carolina	X		X				X		X	
North Dakota	X	X	X				X	X		
Ohio	X			X	X	X	X		X	X
Oklahoma	X			X	X	X		X	X	
Oregon	X	X		X			X	X	X	X
Pennsylvania	X	X		(b)	X	X	X	X	X	X
Puerto Rico	X	X		X	X	X	X			
Rhode Island	X	X		X	X	X	X			
South Carolina	X	X		X	X	X				
South Dakota	X	X					X			
Tennessee	X	X					X			
Texas	X	X		X			X	X	X	X
Utah	X		X	X	X	X	X	X	X	X
Vermont	X	X		(b)	X		X	X	X	X
Virgin Islands	X		X	X	X	X	X			
Virginia	X			X	X	X	X	X	X	X
Washington	X	X		X	X	X	X	X	X	
West Virginia	X	X		X	X	X	X	X	X	X
Wisconsin	X	X					X			X
Wyoming	X	X					X			

a. No Medicaid program.

b. The SSI program does not provide coverage in Guam, Puerto Rico, or the Virgin Islands. Federal-state matching programs for assistance to the aged, the blind, and the disabled remain in effect, and Medicaid is provided for these persons.

Source: U.S. Department of Health, Education, and Welfare, *Data on the Medicaid Program: Eligibility/Services/Expenditures, 1979* (Baltimore, Md., Health Care Financing Administration, 1979), pp. 26-27.

. . . as of January 1978, the majority of
states with medically needy programs had
established their medically needy standards
below the weighted average poverty
thresholds determined by the Bureau of the
Census in 1976. Only 6 of the 33 states and
jurisdictions with medically needy programs
had medically needy levels for one person in
excess of the poverty thresholds for persons
aged 65 and over. Only five states had standards in excess of the poverty threshold for
two persons, and none of the states had a
standard in excess of the poverty threshold
for a four-person family.[26]

The result of income limitations and categorical restrictions is to leave
many poor persons without Medicaid coverage. As shown in table 1, 17.4
percent of people in families with incomes of $5,000 or less and 16.6 per-
cent in families with income between $5,000 and $10,000 are without
public as well as private insurance protection.

IMPACT OF NATIONAL HEALTH
INSURANCE ON COVERAGE

National health insurance could affect coverage in two ways: (1) by expanding the proportion of the population with insurance protection and
(2) by improving benefits for the population already covered as well as
for people newly insured. This section describes the effects of the
Kennedy-Waxman, Carter, and Martin plans on each aspect of coverage.

The Kennedy-Waxman Plan

Population Coverage

Because the Kennedy-Waxman bill proposes to cover all citizens and
legal residents, its effects on population coverage would be dramatic and
straightforward — it would simply absorb all the currently uncovered
population, along with everyone else, into the NHI plan. Enrollment
would be mandatory, and any individual who failed to enroll would be
enrolled by his or her employer or the government. Coverage would be
immediate or, if necessary, deemed retroactive, so that waiting periods
for eligibility, common today even in group insurance, would no longer
exist. Under the Kennedy-Waxman plan, no citizen or legal resident
would be without coverage at any time.

Obviously, people with no insurance protection would have the most
to gain from the proposed coverage. People eligible for disability

payments through Social Security would no longer face a two-year waiting period for Medicare eligibility. Gains among the poor would be most substantial where Medicaid is now limited — in Arizona, where there is no Medicaid program, and in the southern and western states that do not cover unemployed fathers and their families or children in low-income, intact families.

Variations in population coverage would remain, however, for services not covered by national health insurance. Most important among these services are long-term nursing home care, outpatient prescription drugs for the population under age sixty-five, dental services, and eyeglasses. The Kennedy-Waxman bill would require all states to maintain Medicaid eligibility and benefits at pre-NHI levels. Poor people in states with extensive Medicaid programs would probably retain better coverage for these services than poor people in other states.

Benefits

Despite some exclusions, benefits under the Kennedy-Waxman plan would be quite comprehensive, covering all hospital and physicians' services, hearing aids, and preventive services such as basic immunizations, prenatal and postnatal maternity care, and well-child care for children up to age eighteen. With the exception of mental health, skilled nursing facility, and home health benefits, the plan would not limit days of care. What is perhaps even more significant, the plan would cover all service costs, eliminating all out-of-pocket payments for medical care. Along with persons with no insurance coverage, persons with limited insurance coverage would benefit particularly from the coverage of physicians' services and the payment of service costs. Even persons who today have relatively comprehensive coverage would acquire new benefits. Persons with major medical insurance and Medicare-eligibles would no longer face deductibles and coinsurance and would acquire coverage for many items that are often not included in current insurance policies: some skilled nursing facility care, preventive services, hearing aids, and — for Medicare beneficiaries — outpatient prescription drugs for chronic illness.

These benefits would assure everybody protection against the costs of acute illness and therefore would do much to reduce current variations in coverage by income and employment status. Employee groups that are now well insured, however, might maintain an advantage over the rest of the population. The Kennedy-Waxman bill would require that employers pay employees — in cash or benefits — any difference between premiums under national health insurance and premiums the employers paid for health benefits before enactment of national health insurance. Since health benefits would still be treated as nontaxable income to employee, this requirement might encourage employers to continue benefits — like prescription drugs or dental care — that national health insurance would not cover.

The Carter Plan

Because the Carter NHI plan would establish different types of coverage for different population groups and would not mandate coverage for the whole population, analysis of its effects on coverage is more complicated. Increases in population coverage could be expected from mandated employer coverage and from the substitution of HealthCare for Medicaid. But, as this section describes, some people are likely to remain inadequately covered.

The Employer Guarantee's Impact on Coverage

The Carter Plan's mandated employer coverage would extend health insurance to a significant proportion of the population that is not now covered, with the result that an estimated 155 million persons would be covered by employer-offered plans. Under the bill, all employers would be required to provide insurance coverage to all full-time employees and their dependents. (Full-time employees are defined as employees who have worked at least twenty-five hours per week for ten consecutive weeks; dependents include children through their twenty-second birthday or through age twenty-six if in school or disabled.) Benefits would be required to extend ninety days after termination of employment. Employers would be required to allow employees who terminate employment to purchase continued coverage at a premium rate not to exceed 125 percent of the premium for employer-covered employees.

Employer plans would be required to cover services similar to those in the Kennedy-Waxman bill. In contrast to the situation under the Kennedy-Waxman bill, however, employer plans could include cost sharing, but out-of-pocket payments on covered services could not exceed $2,500 per family per year, and no cost sharing could be charged for prenatal, delivery, or infant care services.

These requirements significantly change the benefits now available even to well-insured employees. Most of these employees now have extensive hospital and physician coverage, but many lack coverage for infant coverage during a layoff, or limits on out-of-pocket payments. In addition, most workers now lack the opportunity to retain coverage at their own expense if they quit or lose their jobs or cannot work because of extended ill health. In these areas, even well-insured workers would benefit from the Carter plan.

The plan's effects on people who now lack coverage, however, are of greater concern. The Congressional Budget Office estimated that in

1976, 6.5 percent of full-time workers — almost 20 percent of the uncovered population — had no coverage.[27] In addition, almost one-quarter of persons without coverage who were not in the labor force reportedly belonged to families whose heads had private insurance coverage.[28] By covering this population, the Carter plan would absorb another 13 percent of the population that now lacks coverage.[29] Including dependents not in school up to age twenty-two would also help cover part of the group aged nineteen to twenty-four. Finally, the Carter plan would improve coverage for more than 27 percent of the working population who now face extensive waiting periods before their employer coverage takes effect.[30] The bill establishes ten weeks as a maximum on the waiting period in any qualified plan.

Although the Carter plan would substantially expand coverage of the population, some of the benefits the population would receive might be of limited value. For services other than maternal and infant care, the plan would only require that employers offer coverage for expenses that exceeded $2,500. Employers who do not already provide health benefits would be unlikely to offer coverage exceeding this minimum. Hence employees who now lack coverage would only gain coverage for expenditures over $2,500. Because many of these employees earn relatively low incomes, an illness could cause financial catastrophe long before their new benefits went into effect. With a $2,500 deductible, workers earning $10,000 would have to spend 25 percent of their pretax incomes before they would receive any benefits under their employer-offered plans. Thus, the Carter plan would offer more apparent than real protection for currently uninsured workers.

Small employers would not be expected to obtain the newly required coverage through the private market, for that coverage has not been available at affordable premiums. To assure the availability of mandated coverage at acceptable costs, the Carter bill would encourage small employers to purchase catastrophic coverage from the government-operated HealthCare plan. The HealthCare premium would be set to equal average benefits under the plan. Because of lower marketing costs and apparent subsidies, HealthCare coverage would cost less than would similar coverage offered by private insurers.

HealthCare's Impact on Coverage

HealthCare would also be available to cover individuals who were not full-time employees — self-employed workers, part-time workers, unemployed persons, and persons not in the labor force. The coverage available would differ for the poor and nonpoor. People whose incomes exceeded HealthCare's income standard (55 percent of poverty level) could obtain maternity and infant care coverage on application, with no premium charge. For a premium, they could also obtain protection against catastrophic medical expenses, but that coverage would include a $2,500 annual deductible. The deductible would have to be met through out-of-pocket expenses, not through payments by private insurers. As already described, the value of this coverage to low-income families would be questionable, and many might choose not to buy it.

Although the Carter plan would make individuals who are not full-time employees responsible for obtaining their own coverage, it would make special provisions to protect persons for whom very low income might be a barrier to the purchase of insurance. For individuals who met specified income criteria, HealthCare would cover all service costs with no patient cost sharing. This segment of HealthCare would replace Medicaid. Its potential effects can be judged by comparing existing Medicaid eligibility criteria with those that HealthCare proposes.

Because the Carter plan would not provide for universal coverage, description of its improvements is complex. Changes differ for the aged, the disabled, and low-income families. Provisions for the aged and disabled are relatively straightforward. As indicated earlier, current Medicare beneficiaries would gain from the proposed $1,250 ceiling on out-of-pocket payments. Eligibility standards of the current Medicare program for the aged and persons suffering chronic renal failure would remain in place; but the two-year waiting period for eligibility by the disabled would be eliminated. Increases in income eligibility standards relative to current Medicaid standards would affect coverage for elderly and disabled citizens not now covered by Medicare and coverage for poor elderly and disabled persons who require more financial assistance than Medicare provides. The Carter administration estimates that the plan would cover for the first time some 500,000 persons who did not work long enough to earn Medicare entitlement but whose incomes are less than the HealthCare eligibility standard of 55 percent of poverty level.

Coverage for the disabled would also improve because HealthCare would cover all individuals who receive cash assistance through the Supplementary Security Income program. Coverage would increase in states that do not now provide Medicaid coverage for individuals whose incomes are high enough to receive only state supplements instead of federal SSI payments. Fourteen states now apply a more restrictive eligibility standard than SSI (thus excluding even some recipients of federal SSI payments): Connecticut, Hawaii, Illinois, Indiana, Minnesota, Mississippi, Missouri, Nebraska, New Hampshire, North Carolina, Ohio, Oklahoma, Utah, and Virginia. Thus the Carter plan would improve coverage for disabled individuals in those states.

The Carter plan would improve coverage for families and individuals who are not aged or disabled in three ways: (1) by setting a higher income eligibility standard than now applies in several states, (2) by mandating coverage of all families and single persons who meet the national low-income standard, and (3) by mandating a spend-down mechanism for all states. It is difficult to quantify the likely effects of these provisions on coverage of the low-income population because of the complexity of current Medicaid provisions. The Carter plan would enroll all individuals now receiving cash assistance payments, most but not all of whom are eligible for Medicaid. Current Medicaid eligibility depends on the states' standards for cash assistance eligibility. In general, states use two standards in determining eligibility for cash assistance: (1) a need standard, based on estimates of the cost of essentials such as food, clothing, and shelter; and (2) a payment standard, which may be equal to or less than the need standard. Individuals with countable income less than or equal to the payment standard are eligible for cash assistance payments and Medicaid.

Table 4 presents annualized income eligibility standards for two- and four-person families in each state. Clearly income eligibility criteria vary greatly across states. The Carter plan would attempt to lessen these inequities by covering families with incomes less than the HealthCare low-income standard — equivalent to 55 percent of the poverty level. The effect would be to increase the number of covered families in seventeen states: Alabama, Arkansas, Florida, Georgia, Kentucky, Louisiana, Maryland, Mississippi, Missouri, Nevada, New Mexico, North Carolina, Ohio, South Carolina, Tennessee, Texas, and West Virginia. In the remaining states with current payment standards higher than 55 percent of poverty level, families meeting cash assistance criteria would remain eligible for HealthCare.

Medicaid also requires individuals to meet so-called "categorical" eligibility requirements related to family status, age, or disability in addition to income requirements. The Carter plan would move away from this categorical approach by extending eligibility to all families and individuals with incomes less than 55 percent of the poverty standard. Thus, single individuals aged nineteen to sixty-four, childless couples, and all intact families would be covered if they met the low-income standard. The elimination of categorical restrictions and increase in the income eligibility standard would have its greatest impact in the South, but the effects would be felt throughout the nation. Many intact families with employed parents do not meet current Medicaid eligibility criteria but would meet the Carter Plan's low-income standard.

Table 4

ANNUAL CASH ASSISTANCE AND MEDICALLY NEEDY INCOME ELIGIBILITY STANDARDS, TWO- AND FOUR-PERSON FAMILIES

(July 1978)

	Two-Person Families			Four-Person Families		
	Cash Assistance Standard	55% of Poverty Level	Medically Needy	Cash Assistance Standard	55% of Poverty Level	Medically Needy
Alabama	$1,068	$2,400	—	$1,776	$3,664	—
Alaska	4,200	2,400		5,400	3,664	
Arizona	1,620	2,400		2,544	3,664	
Arkansas	1,596	2,400		2,256	3,664	
California	3,444	2,400	$2,200	5,076	3,664	$3,100
Colorado	2,604	2,400	3,804	3,912	3,664	5,604
Connecticut	4,092	2,400		5,904	3,664	
Delaware	2,172	2,400	4,500	3,444	3,664	6,000
District of Columbia	2,436	2,400		3,768	3,664	
Florida	1,536	2,400	3,500	2,352	3,664	3,900
Georgia	1,260	2,400		1,776	3,664	
Hawaii	4,680	2,400	4,800	6,552	3,664	6,600
Idaho	3,120	2,400		4,404	3,664	
Illinois	2,724	2,400	2,600	3,996	3,664	3,800
Indiana	2,664	2,400		3,924	3,664	
Iowa	3,300	2,400		4,740	3,664	
Kansas	3,280	2,400	4,000	4,368	3,664	4,900
Kentucky	1,620	2,400	2,200	2,820	3,664	3,800
Louisiana	1,212	2,400	1,602	2,064	3,664	2,700
Maine	2,220	2,400	3,200	3,768	3,664	5,400
Maryland	2,064	2,400	2,800	3,204	3,664	3,800
Massachusetts	3,348	2,400	4,500	4,752	3,664	5,280
Michigan	3,708	2,400	3,468	5,388	3,664	5,040
Minnesota	3,600	2,400	3,330	5,088	3,664	4,500
Mississippi	2,256	2,400		3,024	3,664	
Missouri	2,100	2,400		3,072	3,664	
Montana	2,004	2,400	3,444	3,972	3,664	4,572

Table 4

ANNUAL CASH ASSISTANCE AND MEDICALLY NEEDY INCOME ELIGIBILITY STANDARDS, TWO- AND FOUR-PERSON FAMILIES

(July 1978) (continued)

	Two-Person Families			Four-Person Families		
	Cash Assistance Standard	55% of Poverty Level	Medically Needy	Cash Assistance Standard	55% of Poverty Level	Medically Needy
Nebraska	$3,000	$2,400	$4,000	$4,440	$3,664	$5,600
Nevada	2,220	2,400		3,312	3,664	
New Hampshire	3,156	2,400	3,500	4,152	3,664	4,600
New Jersey	2,964	2,400		4,488	3,664	
New Mexico	1,848	2,400	4,400	2,748	3,664	5,000
New York	3,996	2,400	2,200	5,712	3,664	2,800
North Carolina	1,908	2,400	3,400	2,400	3,664	5,300
North Dakota	2,820	2,400		4,400	3,664	
Ohio	2,304	2,400	3,200	3,492	3,664	5,000
Oklahoma	2,376	2,400		3,768	3,664	
Oregon	3,252	2,400	4,000	4,836	3,664	4,500
Pennsylvania	3,120	2,400	4,300	4,476	3,664	6,100
Rhode Island	3,564	2,400		5,016	3,664	
South Carolina	1,728	2,400		2,748	3,664	
South Dakota	3,108	2,400		4,080	3,664	2,400
Tennessee	1,164	2,400	1,600	1,776	3,664	
Texas	1,032	2,400		1,680	3,664	
Utah	2,916	2,400	3,800	4,488	3,664	5,800
Vermont	4,140	2,400	4,224	5,724	3,664	5,724
Virginia	2,880	2,400	3,100	4,020	3,664	3,867
Washington	3,696	2,400	3,948	5,268	3,664	5,268
West Virginia	1,968	2,400	2,200	2,988	3,664	3,300
Wisconsin	3,912	2,400	5,000	5,496	3,664	6,300
Wyoming	2,940	2,400		3,660	3,664	

Source: U.S. Department of Health, Education, and Welfare, *Data on the Medicaid Program: Eligibility/Services/Expenditures*, 1979 ed., (Baltimore, Md.: Health Care Financing Administration, 1979), pp. 85-88.

Along with the new income eligibility standard, the Carter plan would retain categorical eligibility standards by making all persons now eligible for welfare automatically eligible for HealthCare. The practical effect of this provision would be to cover people in states with particularly generous welfare programs (those paying people with incomes above the amount that equaled 55 percent of poverty level).

To determine eligibility under the 55 percent of poverty-level standard, the Carter plan would establish new rules for calculating income. Actual gross income would be reduced by "disregarded" amounts, that is, 20 percent of earnings and up to $160 per month of itemized work-related expenses. Thus a four-person family with the full amount of work-related expenses could have up to $6,980 of income and still meet the plan's low-income standard. (An individual with no work-related expenses could have an income of $4,580 and still retain coverage.)

The adoption of this rule would expand eligibility in two ways. First, the rule is more generous than many states now apply in calculating income for cash assistance and, thus, Medicaid eligibility. Second, the rule would apply to individuals whether or not they had received cash assistance. In contrast, under the current system, income is "disregarded" only for people who have been poor and increased their earnings, not for people with the same earned income who have never received cash assistance. The Carter plan would treat all people with equal incomes equally, regardless of their previous welfare status. These changes would make large numbers of sporadically or part-time employed individuals with incomes above 55 percent of poverty level eligible for HealthCare. Although this feature would apply primarily to people in the South, many people in the North also would benefit. The maximum income of $6,980 would be above both the AFDC categorical and the medically needy income eligibility standards for four-person families in every state. Thus, even in states with eligibility standards above HealthCare's low-income standard, many families who now have earnings that make them ineligible for cash assistance or Medicaid would be eligible for HealthCare.

Unfortunately, these improvements in coverage would impose a significant administrative burden. Coverage would be available to persons whose incomes exceed welfare eligibility standards, but coverage would continue to depend on income. The Carter plan therefore would require the establishment of a new eligibility determination process, alongside the current process for cash assistance. This administrative duplication not only would cost money but also would confuse many of the potential recipients it aims to help.

The same conclusions apply to the Carter plan's reliance on "spend-down" provisions, similar to those now employed by Medicaid programs in thirty states. Under the current system, these states establish a medically needy income level which by federal regulation can be set at any level up to 133 percent of the highest money payment that would be made to a family of the same size under the state's AFDC program. Families with incomes less than the medically needy income level are eligible for Medicaid but not cash assistance. (The medically needy income levels in July 1978 are shown in table 4.) Individuals and families can also become eligible for Medicaid even if their incomes exceed the medically needy income levels if they "spend down" to that level in meeting their medical expenses. When income less allowable medical expenses falls below the medically needy income level (and assets have been taken into account), all subsequent medical expenses are covered by Medicaid.

The Carter plan would extend Medicaid's medically needy provision to all states. The medically needy income level in all states would be 55 percent of poverty level, with income calculated according to the plan's new rules. The mandated spend-down provision would have its greatest impact in the eighteen states, most in the South, that now do not have a spend-down provision. The new provisions, however, would also affect other states because the Carter plan would have more generous rules for income calculation than those Medicaid now employs. Medicaid's current medically needy provisions consider only total income and do not disregard any earnings or expenses.

Spend-down provisions theoretically protect anyone whose medical expenses became exorbitant relative to income. Unfortunately, Medicaid experience indicates that the spend-down mechanism has not really served this purpose in the past. Several problems have arisen in its use. First, many potentially eligible applicants are not aware of the existence of the spend-down mechanism as a means of becoming eligible for Medicaid.[31] Moreover, individuals have difficulty keeping track of expenses and incomes, and many people find it hard to understand the rules well enough to know if they should apply. To the extent that people do not understand the system, they will either go without care or they will get care through non-Medicaid resources in the community.

Second, potential "spend-downers" often cannot incur sufficient expenses to become eligible through the spend-down mechanism. Since many or most lack the cash to make payments, they may be unable to see providers unless providers will extend credit until the individual has incurred sufficient expenses to be eligible through the spend-down. Providers may never get paid for the individual's share of expenses. Hospitals may be willing to accept the risk of nonpayment because once the individual has "spent-down," the rest of the bill is paid. Physicians, however, often do not understand the spend-down process. For this and

31

other reasons, they may be unwilling to extend credit; so they may simply refuse access to those unable to pay.

HealthCare provisions would add two new problems to spend-down operations. First, the Carter plan would be less liberal than most Medicaid programs have been in calculating expenditures that count toward spend-down. Most Medicaid programs have counted any medical expenses, covered or not, in determining spend-down eligibility. In the Carter plan, only covered services at HealthCare payment rates would count toward the spend-down. For example, outpatient prescription drugs would not count, nor would that portion of a physician's fee in excess of the HealthCare fee schedule.

Second, under the Carter plan, income and medical expenses would be calculated over a twelve-month period. For a family to gain eligibility through the spend-down mechanism, the family's annual income (adjusted as already described) less annual medical expenses would have to be less than the income standard. Under Medicaid, the accounting period is six months or less. In general, the longer the accounting period, the smaller the number of families covered by spend-down provisions. A family with medical expenses that were large relative to six-months' income would receive assistance with a six-month accounting period. Over a twelve-month period, the same family's income might be high enough relative to expenses to deny the family eligibility for coverage.

Summary

The Carter plan would make major strides toward improving health care coverage for the poor and near-poor. Almost all of the steps just described would increase coverage for people who lack it and reduce inequities for those eligible for current federal financing programs. But gaps, inequities, and administrative problems remain.

The Carter plan's coverage provisions pose four major problems. First, the HealthCare program would rely on a complex eligibility determination process. To eliminate inequities and inadequacies in the current welfare system, it would impose a new, massive layer of income determinations on top of the present one. Presumably in an effort to keep costs at politically tolerable levels, eligibility would not be universal. Thus the Carter administration has indicated a willingness to incur a large administrative burden, one that is likely to be financially costly and politically unpopular.

Second, the spend-down mechanism has proved to be an ineffective income-related deductible. Its rules and provisions are difficult to understand. Even if understood, qualifying can be difficult. Many cannot afford to use it because of physicians' reluctance to provide credit or charity care during the "spend-down" period.

Third, it seems unlikely that low-income individuals who are part-time or intermittent employees would buy into HealthCare. If they were to do so, they would get protection only against expenses over $2,500 a year. Thus, whether or not they bought into HealthCare, their medical expenses might be unaffordable. They, like many low-income families now, would probably rely on public facilities for free care.

Finally, and perhaps most important, full-time employees (and their families) who earn relatively low incomes would be in a similar situation as other low-income workers. Employers who do not now provide health insurance coverage would almost certainly provide only the minimum required under the Carter mandate. For persons and families with incomes near the poverty level and even some middle-income people, the $2,500 family deductible would absorb a very high percentage of income. These people are likely either to forgo care or to seek free care from public facilities at the expense of local governments.

The Martin Plan

By providing catastrophic coverage to all Americans, the Martin plan would improve the protection of many poor and near-poor families. States would be required to maintain current levels of Medicaid coverage and benefits. Medicare beneficiaries would gain some benefits and a limit on out-of-pocket expenses. Persons who now have either no coverage or shallow coverage would receive catastrophic insurance at no direct cost. Catastrophic illness insurance of the employed population would be improved. The provisions of the plan would, however, leave substantial discrepancies in noncatastrophic coverage among individuals and families. In addition, the income-related deductibles and limits under Martin's catastrophic plan would be high in relation to income.

The Impact of Martin's Catastrophic Automatic Protection Plan (CAPP) on Coverage of the Poor

The Martin plan would leave current Medicaid eligibility criteria intact. The plan's contribution would be to provide catastrophic protection through its federal plan (CAPP) to persons not covered by Medicaid. As described earlier, Medicaid coverage of different types of individuals and families as well as Medicaid income eligibility criteria vary considerably across states. By covering the single individuals, childless couples, and intact families not now covered by many state Medicaid programs, CAPP will alleviate to some extent the inequities that exist when families at a given income level are covered in one state but not in another. Even in generous Medicaid programs, the near-poor would benefit because the CAPP deductible and limits would be lower than the Medicaid spend-down requirement. (CAPP coverage also would impose lower cost sharing than the Carter plan's spend-down provision for families with incomes of less than $12,000.)

It is important to note that while CAPP will reduce these inequities in coverage, it would not eliminate them. The plan's high deductible and limits would mean that substantial differences in the financial burdens of the same medical care expenses would remain for different types of families within any given state and among identical types of families in different states. The deductibles and limits on out-of-pocket liability of families with different income levels are shown in this table:

Family Income	Deductible	Limit	Percent of Family Income
$ 4,000	$ 300	$ 500	12.5%
6,000	700	1,000	16.7
8,000	1,000	1,500	18.7
10,000	1,500	2,000	20.0
12,000	1,900	2,500	20.8

Families with yearly incomes of $4,000 and $6,000 would have to incur medical expenses of $300 and $700 respectively before coverage would begin under the Martin plan. If medical expenses were to continue, the family would face expenditures of up to $500 and $1,000, respectively. Similar families eligible for Medicaid would have no out-of-pocket expenses.

Continuation of Medicaid in addition to CAPP would create a number of administrative problems as well. First, CAPP would require an additional set of income and medical expense determinations for persons who incurred catastrophic expenditures. While feasible, this process would be costly and cumbersome. Second, individuals would be eligible for Medicaid through that program's spend-down mechanism in some circumstances and for CAPP through the income-related deductible in other circumstances. Families would be eligible for Medicaid through the spend-down mechanism if income less medical expenses were to fall below a specified threshold. Many of the same families would be eligible for CAPP. Although CAPP would provide better protection than Medicaid as income increased, at some income levels the Medicaid spend-down requirement would be lower than the CAPP deductible.

With CAPP, the Martin bill aims to cover the unemployed, part-time employed, and self-employed who traditionally have had little or no insurance. While protection through CAPP would in most instances represent an improvement over current coverage, uncovered medical expenses would still be quite high in relation to income. For the nation as a whole, per capita health expenditures were 9.2 percent of per capita personal income in 1979,[32] as compared to the 12.5 percent minimum in CAPP (see preceding table). The medical expense income tax deduction for individuals would be eliminated and only out-of-pocket medical expenses not covered by private insurance would count toward the income-related deductible. Thus, families probably would not purchase insurance covering expenses below the CAPP deductible. If they did, such coverage would probably be quite expensive. Given CAPP's sizable deductible, low-income families may have very little increase in access to care, particularly physicians' services. Routine ambulatory care, particularly preventive care, for these people might not increase. The main effect would be coverage of large expenses, particularly inpatient hospital care. Hospitals should be less reluctant to admit members of these families because most of the incurred costs for many hospital stays would be paid. Only a few days in expensive hospitals would exhaust cost sharing and activate full CAPP payment of the hospital's "reasonable costs." CAPP would therefore provide substantial fiscal relief to hospitals that traditionally have cared for poorly insured families. Fiscal relief to institutional providers, rather than improved access to ambulatory care, could be the predominant effect of the plan.

The Impact of Changes in Tax Provisions on Coverage through Employment

It is hard to predict precisely the effects of changes in tax provisions on families with employer coverage. Because employers could only deduct contributions to qualified plans which would be required, by definition, to cover all expenses in excess of $2,500, catastrophic insurance coverage should increase. Other changes in coverage would be less certain. Because employer contributions greater than $120 per month would not be tax-free to employees, many employers would no longer contribute more than that limit. There would no longer be any advantage to providing insurance benefits rather than wages. Even if employers continued to make contributions in excess of $120 per month, employees might not purchase these more expensive policies. Thus, we could expect a reduction in coverage for those employees now receiving employer contributions in excess of $120 per month. About 25 percent of covered employees are in firms with total monthly premiums of $120 or more for family coverage.[33] Since many firms contribute less than 100 percent of premiums, even fewer employees are in firms in which employer contributions exceed $120 per month. Coverage changes would probably consist of higher deductibles or coinsurance or less coverage of relatively discretionary services.

It is particularly hard to predict the choices of employees who now receive contributions toward health insurance of less than $120 per month. The Martin plan would not change the tax treatment of employer contributions of up to $120 to a qualified plan or plans. The bill encourages employers to offer a plan covering only the minimum benefits for qualification by allowing them to retain a share of any difference between the contributions they make to premiums and actual premiums paid. As a result, employers would benefit if employees were to choose plans for which premiums were below contribution rates.

At the same time, employers are also likely to raise their contributions to the $120 monthly ceiling. The reasons are as follows: Current contributions of less than $120, when they are not taxable income to the employee, must reflect employee or employer preferences. When only one plan is offered, its terms reflect a compromise between employees who want more insurance and employees who want less. If employees are offered a choice of plans and partially taxable rebates, employees should push for higher employer contributions (in lieu of wages) because (1) those employees choosing relatively comprehensive coverage would then receive nontaxable contributions to a plan that they presumably wanted all along and (2) those employees choosing a low-cost plan would receive a rebate that would be partially free of income tax and completely free of Social Security and unemployment taxes.

If employers are indifferent to whether they provide compensation in the form of wages or fringe benefits, many firms should substitute contributions to health insurance for wages. But employers will probably not be indifferent for two reasons: (1) employers may fear that multiple plans would increase administrative costs, and (2) there is evidence that health insurance increases sick leave.[34] Thus, employers should prefer wages to increased health insurance. These factors will reduce the extent of changes in insurance offerings.

The net result of these shifts in employer-offered plans should be that coverage would increase for some families and decrease for others. The effect would vary with the attitude toward risk. It would also vary with the value of the rebate. The lower the price of the minimum qualified plan relative to the employer contribution, the greater the potential rebate. The percentage of employees choosing the minimum qualified plan is likely to vary with family income, for two reasons: (1) the pretax value of the rebate would be a higher percentage of income, the lower the family's income, and (2) since much of the rebate is subject to tax, the after-tax value of the rebate also would vary inversely with income. The rebate then should have a greater effect on decisions of low-income families, making them more likely to choose high cost-sharing plans. At the same time, the rebate should have less effect on the decisions of high-income families who would probably tend to purchase more comprehensive plans up to the $120 per month limit.

The fixed ceiling on the tax-deductible employer contribution could have important equity effects. If, as we have argued, employer contributions tend to cluster around the maximum permitted, the plan's provisions would favor low-risk groups and families in low-cost areas. The plan would permit experience rating of employer groups. Thus, insurance premiums attached to any given benefit package would vary with age, health status, and other characteristics of the covered groups as well as with medical care prices in an area. Employers would not necessarily vary their contributions with these characteristics. Thus, the plan would often result in coverage of a higher percentage of real benefits for low-risk employer-groups than of high-risk employer-groups. High-risk families with high incomes could afford to supplement employer contributions; high-risk, low-income families are less likely to be able to do so.

Similar results would follow for areas with different levels of hospital and medical care costs. Families in high-cost areas would have lower contributions to any level of real benefits than families in low-cost areas. Families in low-cost areas would be able to purchase fairly comprehensive insurance and get a substantial rebate, while identical families in high-cost areas might find that the employer contribution would not permit purchase of much coverage in excess of the minimum qualified plan. (These problems would not arise for employees in firms with national operations and uniform health benefit plans.) The effects would again vary with family income. Low-income families in high-cost areas should tend to have less coverage than high-income families in those areas and low-income families in low-cost areas.

SUMMARY

All three national health insurance plans would offer major improvements in protecting the population against the cost of illness. With its comprehensive, universal coverage, the Kennedy-Waxman plan would offer the greatest improvement, covering all those not now covered and providing all people equal coverage on equal terms.

The Carter plan, in contrast, would provide catastrophic coverage to the full population and comprehensive coverage to many poor persons not now covered under Medicaid. Its new coverage, however, would entail a costly and complex process of eligibility determination, operating alongside the current welfare system. Furthermore, under the Carter plan, people who are not full-time workers would not obtain coverage unless they paid premiums to the federal HealthCare program, and low-income persons whose incomes exceeded 55 percent of the poverty-level standard would continue to face cost-sharing obligations that would either absorb a significant proportion of their incomes or deter their use of medical care. In addition, individuals who obtain insurance through employers may face significantly lower deductibles than individuals who purchase insurance from HealthCare.

The Martin plan would make catastrophic protection automatically available to all people and would relate cost-sharing obligations to income. But the levels of cost sharing the bill would still leave low-income people with sizable out-of-pocket obligations. The Martin bill would also leave people who are categorically eligible for Medicaid with more comprehensive coverage than other equally poor people, would allow differences in coverage between employees whose employers offer coverage and other individuals, and would foster inequities between covered employees in high- and low-risk occupations and high- and low-cost areas (hospital and medical care). At the same time, however, the Martin plan's proposed ceiling on out-of-pocket expenditures would improve protection against the costs of illness for many people.

III. FINANCING AND INCOME REDISTRIBUTION

The method of financing national health insurance can have substantial effects on income distribution. Funds to pay for medical care can be raised by any combination of premiums, payroll taxes, income taxes, other taxes, and out-of-pocket payments. Each approach has very different implications for the share of total costs that families and individuals in different income classes bear.

The primary objectives of this chapter are to describe in general terms the different methods of financing health care and to discuss their implications for income distribution. The first section describes the aggregate flow of funds under the existing health system. Then comes a discussion of the redistribution implications of premiums and out-of-pocket payments, payroll taxes, and income taxes as methods of financing medical care expenditures. Each plays a prominent role in the NHI bills being considered.

The net burden of a financing plan, however, also depends on benefits received, which include payments by the insurance plan for services received, the use of free medical care, and subsidies returned to households by other provisions of the tax system. The third section assesses each bill's financing method in terms of its implications for income redistribution by family income.

THE FLOW OF FUNDS IN THE HEALTH SYSTEM

People pay for medical care by direct payments to providers of medical services and by indirect payments through various financial intermediaries. Direct payments include payments for uninsured services as well as coinsurance and deductibles paid as part of insurance plans. Indirect payments include insurance premiums, earmarked payroll taxes, and all other forms of taxation used to raise general revenue. The last is important because of the government's role as a direct provider or financer under various programs such as Medicaid, maternal and child health, the Veterans Administration, the Indian Health Service, and the armed services. In addition, local governments are frequently providers of last resort for the medically indigent.

39

To some extent various subsidies provided by the federal tax code off-set individuals' payments for medical care. The three major subsidies operate through the exclusion from taxable income of employers' payments for health insurance premiums, the deductibility of much of personal payments for health insurance premiums, and the deductibility of uninsured medical expenses in excess of 3 percent of income. The values of these subsidies to a taxpayer depend on the taxpayer's employment status and marginal tax rate, and on the itemization of deductions.

Figure 1 illustrates these flows and table 5 reports their dollar magnitudes in 1975. (Figures may not be consistent among sectors because of differences in sources.) Throughout this discussion we treat government as simply another financial intermediary. This reflects our assumption that the *size* of the federal or total public budgets for medical care is not crucial for the issues being discussed here. The extent of public involvement is, of course, critical from philosophical, regulatory, and aggregate economic perspectives, but these issues are not considered here. Similarly, the issue of how much *should* be spent in the aggregate on medical care exceeds the scope of this paper.

In 1975, the nation spent almost $115 billion for personal health care services. Thirty-one percent was paid out-of-pocket, 30 percent by public and private insurance premiums, 8.7 percent through payroll taxes, and the remainder, 30.3 percent, by other taxes (primarily income taxes). Tax subsidies for private health insurance premiums and deductible medical expenses amounted to 5.5 percent of total spending, while free medical care services (medical care received at no cost to the patient because of entitlement rather than prepayment) accounted for approximately 23 percent of total expenditures. Of the $32.8 billion spent for private health insurance premiums, almost 60 percent was paid by employers.[35]

Table 6 reports some of the same data by family income. Both out-of-pocket and health insurance premium expense rise gradually with income; families in the highest income class spend about 55 percent more on these two categories than do families in the lowest income bracket. In spite of this, however, expenditures as a percentage of family income decline as family income rises. In 1970, families below the near-poverty line spent 8.9 percent of their incomes on medical care while all other families had average medical care expenses that were 4 percent of family income.[36] When families' tax payments for medical care and the receipt of free services are taken into account, the current financing system becomes less regressive. However, families in the lowest income category still spend the largest share of their income on medical care, about 10 percent, while families with incomes of $15,000 or more spend about 3 percent of their incomes on medical care.

Figure 1

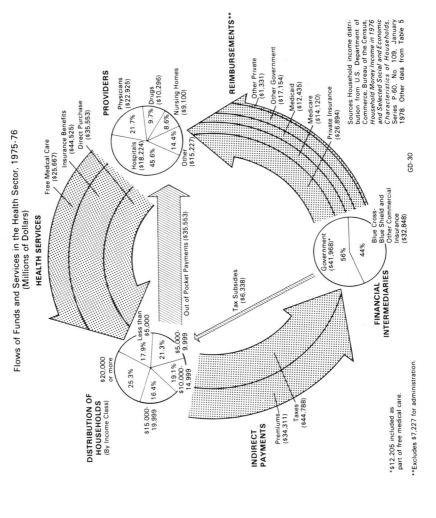

Flows of Funds and Services in the Health Sector, 1975-76
(Millions of Dollars)

HEALTH SERVICES

Free Medical Care
($25,667)

Insurance Benefits
($44,525)

Direct Purchase
($35,553)

PROVIDERS

Physicians
($22,925)

Hospitals 21.7%
($18,224)
45.6%

Drugs 9.7%
($10,296)

8.6%
Nursing Homes
14.4% ($9,100)

Other
($15,227)

REIMBURSEMENTS**

Other Private
($1,331)

Other Government
($17,154)

Medicaid
($12,435)

Medicare
($14,120)

Private Insurance
($26,894)

GD-30

**DISTRIBUTION OF
HOUSEHOLDS**
(By Income Class)

$20,000
or more

25.3%

$15,000-
19,999
16.4%

19.1%
$10,000-
14,999

21.3%
$5,000-
9,999

17.9% Less than
$5,000

Out of Pocket Payments ($35,553)

Tax Subsidies
($6,338)

**FINANCIAL
INTERMEDIARIES**

Government
($41,968)*
56%

44%

Blue Cross-
Blue Shield and
Other Commercial
Insurance
($32,848)

**INDIRECT
PAYMENTS**

Premiums
($34,311)

Taxes
($44,788)

*$12,205 included as
part of free medical care.

**Excludes $7,227 for administration.

Sources: Household income distri-
bution from U.S. Department of
Commerce, Bureau of the Census,
*Household Money Income in 1976
and Selected Social and Economic
Characteristics of Households,*
Series P-60, No. 109, January
1978. Other data from Table 5

41

Table 5

AGGREGATE FLOWS OF FUNDS IN THE HEALTH SECTOR
(in $ millions)
(1975)

Payments by Households

Direct Payments for Health Services	$ 35,553
Private Insurance Premiums[a]	32,848
Medicare Premiums	1,463
Payroll Taxes[b]	9,992
All Other Taxes[c]	34,796
Total Payments[d]	114,652

Tax Subsidies

Employer Paid Health Insurance Premiums	5,518
Deductions for Health Insurance Premiums and Excess Medical Expenses—Personal Income Tax[e]	820
Total Tax Subsidies	6,338[f]

Payments by Intermediaries

Private Health Insurance	26,894
Medicare	14,120
Medicaid (federal, state, and local)	12,435
Other Government[g]	17,154
Philanthropy and Industry	1,331
Expenses for Administration (Public and Private)	7,227

Health Services Received

Hospital Care	48,824
Physicians' Services	22,925
Drugs and Drug Sundries	10,269
Other Professional Services	10,000
Nursing Home Care	9,100
Other Health Services	5,227
Total Care Received	105,745

Free Medical Care

Medicaid	12,435
Veterans Administration	3,280
General Hospital and Medical Care[h]	3,203
Department of Defense	3,063
Other[i]	3,716
Total Free Medical Care	25,667

Table 5

AGGREGATE FLOWS OF FUNDS IN THE HEALTH SECTOR
(in $ millions)
(1975) (continued)

a. Computed as the sum of payments by private insurance plus expenses of administration.

b. Medicare payroll taxes only.

c. Federal income taxes plus all other federal, state, and local taxes (calculated as a residual).

d. Excludes expenditures for research and medical facilities construction ($7.6 billion).

e. 1970 estimates from Mitchell and Vogel extrapolated to 1975 by multiplying by Consumer Price Index.

f. S. Long and M. Cooke, "Financing National Health Insurance," unpublished discussion paper, NHI Financing Team, DHEW, January 6, 1978, estimate this total to be $7.8 billion.

g. Includes temporary disability (medical benefits), workers' compensation (medical benefits), maternal and child health, general hospital and medical care, Department of Defense, Veterans' Administration, government public health activities, and medical vocational rehabilitation.

h. Assumed to be one half of total general hospital and medical care expenditures.

i. Includes maternal and child health, government public health, and medical vocational rehabilitation.

Sources: Robert M. Gibson and Marjorie Smith Mueller, "National Health Expenditures, Fiscal Year 1967," *Social Security Bulletin* 40 (April 1977): 3-22 (Sections I, III-V); Bridger Mitchell and Charles Phelps, "National Health Insurance: Some Costs and Effects of Mandated Employee Coverage," *Journal of Political Economy* 84 (June 1976): 566 (Section II.2); Bridger Mitchell and Ronald Vogel, *Health and Taxes: An Assessment of the Medical Deduction* (Santa Monica, Calif.: The Rand Corporation, 1973), p. 11.

Table 6

HEALTH CARE EXPENDITURES PER FAMILY,
BY INCOME CLASS
(1975)

Family Income	Out-of-Pocket Expenses	Health Insurance Premium[a]	Average Tax Burden[b]	Value of Free Care[c]
Less than $5,000	$448	$121	$ 106	$203
5,000-9,999	518	171	314	117
10,000-14,999	572	204	586	21
15,000-19,999			855	
20,000-24,999			1,191	
25,000-34,999	651	228	1,616	35
35,000+			3,889	

a. Excludes employers' contributions.

b. Includes all federal, state, and local taxes used to pay for medical care.

c. Data for 1970 extrapolated to 1975 by multiplying by Consumer Price Index.

Sources: U.S. Department of Health, Education, and Welfare (DHEW), National Center for Health Statistics, *Family Out-of-Pocket Health Expenses, United States, 1975,* DHEW Publication No. (PHS) 79-1555, (Hyattsville, Md.: National Center for Health Statistics, 1979), p. 11 (columns 1 and 2); S. Long and M. Cooke, "Financing National Health Insurance," unpublished discussion paper, NHI Financing Team, DHEW, January 6, 1978, p. 20 (column 3); Ronald Andersen et al., *Expenditures for Personal Health Services,* DHEW Publication No. (HRA) 74-3105 (Rockville, Md.: Health Resources Administration, 1973), p. 6 (column 4).

METHODS OF RAISING REVENUES[37]

The four basic sources of revenue for financing the health care system are insurance premiums, out-of-pocket payments, payroll taxes, and income taxes. (In addition, a small portion of total revenues is raised by state and local governments through poverty and excise taxes.) This discussion focuses on the relationship between family income and the amount paid under each method.

Premiums and Out-of-Pocket Payments

Premiums are fixed payments, generally independent of income, made to insurance intermediaries (either public or private). Use of premium financing is common in NHI plans that rely on private sector financing. Most group insurance plans offer two premiums, one for individual subscribers and the other for families. (The former are not to be confused with purchasers of nongroup, "individual," policies for themselves or their families.) If everybody's policies had identical benefit levels, the annual premium would be roughly equivalent to the cost of medical services covered by the policy plus insurer-retained funds which include the costs of selling and advertising, claims processing, customer relations, taxes, general overhead, risk premium, reinsurance, and profit (or dividends, in the case of mutual companies).

This form of financing is highly regressive because premiums are not related to family income. As a result, the ratio of premiums to family income falls steadily as income increases. Furthermore, as shown in table 7, family premiums do not increase proportionately with family size. As a result, small families' premiums effectively subsidize those of larger families. Since many two-person families consist of either elderly or young couples who generally have lower incomes than larger families, this structure further increases the regressivity of premium financing.

The effects of out-of-pocket payments on income distribution are similar to those of premiums. Although the poor have greater access to free medical care, they also have much less private insurance coverage. (See tables 1 and 6.) As a result, average per family out-of-pocket expenditures increase only slightly with income. Higher out-of-pocket expenditures by high-income families reflect both the greater use of preventive health services, which are frequently not covered by insurance, and higher-priced medical care, particularly physicians' services. Nevertheless, the share of family income devoted to out-of-pocket expenses for medical care falls sharply with income (see table 6).

Payroll Taxes

A payroll tax is generally a fixed percentage tax rate applied to earned income (wages, salaries, and sometimes self-employed income). The current Social Security/Medicare payroll tax system sets a limit on the amount of income subject to taxation. As a result, the payroll tax is a proportional tax (neither progressive nor regressive) up to the taxable income limit, after which it becomes a flat payment much like a premium. Thus, the ratio of payments to income is constant up to the maximum income level, and thereafter declines. As a result, a payroll tax is regressive overall. Nevertheless, the use of payroll taxes rather than premiums to raise a given amount of revenue results in a subsidy of lower-income families by higher-income families — that is, the maximum tax under a payroll tax plan exceeds the average premium assessed on all insurance plan subscribers. Finally, the distributional consequences of a payroll tax are also affected by the fact that nonlabor income (dividends, interest, rents, capital gains) is not subject to the tax. This increases the tax's regressivity, because higher-income families generally receive a larger

Table 7

HEALTH INSURANCE PREMIUMS, BY FAMILY SIZE AND INCOME
(1975)

Family Size and Income	Premium Expenses	Premium Expenses per Person
All Incomes		
Individuals	$ 91.00	$ 91.00
2-person families	210.00	105.00
3-person families	196.00	65.33
4-person families	187.00	46.75
5 + -person families	180.00	—
Less than $5,000		
Individuals	80.00	80.00
2-person families	157.00	78.50
3-person families	69.00	23.00
4-person families	77.00	19.25
5 + -person families	69.00	—
$5,000-$9,999		
Individuals	97.00	97.00
2-person families	219.00	109.50
3-person families	146.00	48.67
4-person families	121.00	30.25
5 + -person families	98.00	—
$10,000-$14,999		
Individuals	110.00	110.00
2-person families	217.00	108.00
3-person families	216.00	72.00
4-person families	176.00	44.00
5 + -person families	195.00	—
$15,000 or more		
Individuals	108.00	108.00
2-person families	222.00	111.00
3-person families	235.00	78.33
4-person families	234.00	58.50
5 + -person families	222.00	—

Source: U.S. Department of Health, Education, and Welfare, National Center for Health Statistics, *Family Out-of-Pocket Health Expenses, United States, 1975,* DHEW Publication No. (PHS) 79-1555 (Hyattsville, Md.: National Center for Health Statistics, 1979), p. 11.

share of their income from unearned sources. A study of the payroll tax using data from the Old Age, Survivor, Disability, and Health Insurance (OASDHI) tax in 1969 illustrates the tax's overall regressivity.[38] The effective rate was a flat 9.41 percent of income up to $7,800; the rate fell to 3.17 percent for earnings income over $15,000 (see appendix B, table 1).

Income Tax

The third major source of funds is government's general revenues, which are raised predominantly by personal and corporate income taxes. (State and local governments rely more on property, sales, and excise taxes, but these are only a small share of the total and will not be discussed separately.) In general, the personal income tax structure appears highly progressive because marginal tax rates increase steeply as income rises. Various deductions, exclusions, credits, and other modifications to the basic structure, however, make the effective tax rate far lower than the marginal rate, particularly at the higher income levels. As a result, the income tax is only a slightly progressive tax with no limit on taxable income. In other words, the ratio of tax payments to family income increases gradually with income up to the middle income level, and then remains roughly constant at higher income levels. Table 8 illustrates the combined effects of federal payroll and income taxes for a four-person family with one wage earner at five-year intervals between 1963 and 1973. (Note that the effective payroll tax rate drops from 11.7 percent at $10,000 to 5 percent at $25,000.)

Combined Financing and Net Effects

The effects of the three financing methods other than out-of-pocket spending on families' budgets are clearly illustrated by table 9. (This example assumes equal cost sharing for each method.) These data are based on a hypothetical NHI plan requiring total revenue of $50 billion and 1975 data on tax rates, tax structure, and the distribution of families by income. If it is assumed that the average premium is equal to average expected benefits, then the difference between the premium payment and the income or payroll tax payment represents the net per family benefit (or loss) resulting from each financing plan at each level of income. Thus, there would be no income redistribution under a system financed solely by insurance premiums of the type just described. Under the payroll tax in table 9, all families with incomes less than about $13,000 would receive positive net benefits. (That is, the monetary value of the medical care services consumed by a family is greater than their direct and indirect expenditures for medical care.) Finally, the income tax-financed plan would result in positive net benefits for families with incomes less than approximately $18,000.

Table 8

FEDERAL INDIVIDUAL INCOME AND PAYROLL TAXES FOR A FOUR-PERSON FAMILY WITH ONE EARNER, SELECTED EARNINGS
(1963, 1968, and 1973)

Earnings and Tax Items	1963	1968[a]	1973
$5,000 Earnings			
Income tax	$ 420	$ 308	$ 98
Payroll tax[b]	348	440	585
Total tax	768	748	683
Effective income tax rate	8.4%	6.2%	2.0%
Effective payroll tax rate[b]	7.0	8.8	11.7
Total effective tax rate	15.4	15.0	13.7
$10,000 Earnings			
Income tax	$1,372	$1,198	$ 905
Payroll tax[b]	348	686	1,170
Total tax	1,720	1,884	2,075
Effective income tax rate	13.7%	12.0%	9.0%
Effective payroll tax rate[b]	3.5	6.9	11.7
Total effective tax rate	17.2	18.8	20.8
$25,000 Earnings			
Income tax	$4,889	$4,362	$3,890
Payroll tax[b]	348	686	1,264
Total tax	5,237	5,048	5,154
Effective income tax rate	19.6%	17.4%	15.6%
Effective payroll tax rate[b]	1.4	2.7	5.0
Total effective tax rate	20.9	20.2	20.6

a. Includes income tax surcharge.
b. Includes both employee and employer taxes.

Source: Edward R. Fried, Alice M. Rivlin, and Nancy H. Teeters, *Setting National Priorities: The 1974 Budget* (Washington, D.C.: The Brookings Institution, 1973), table 3-4. Reproduced from Rita M. Keintz, *National Health Insurance and Income Distribution* (Lexington, Mass.: Lexington Books, 1976), p. 138.

Table 9

DISTRIBUTION OF FINANCING COSTS, BY FAMILY INCOME

| | Pure Financing Methods | | | Combined Financing Methods | |
| | If Plan is Financed by: | | | If Plan is Financed by a Combination of: | |
Family Income	Premium	Payroll Tax	Income Tax	Premiums and Income Tax	Payroll Tax and Income Tax
$ 3,000	$850	$210	0	$ 570	$ 140
6,000	850	400	$ 100	600	300
9,000	850	610	260	650	490
12,000	850	780	400	700	650
15,000	850	970	560	760	840
20,000	850	1,060	930	880	1,020
30,000	850	1,060	1,910	1,200	1,340
40,000	850	1,060	3,080	1,590	1,730
50,000	850	1,060	4,330	2,010	2,150

Source: Bridger M. Mitchell, "Basic Elements of Financing National Health Insurance," Rand paper P-5610 (Santa Monica, Calif.: The Rand Corporation, 1976), pp. 5, 10.

Clearly, however, the distributional implications of these pure financing forms can be modified by combining two or more approaches within a single NHI plan. This, in fact, is what most NHI schemes propose. The result of joint financing is generally more progressive than under premium-only financing, and less progressive than under pure income tax financing. These effects are shown in the righthand portion of table 9 for hypothetical $50 billion plans which are financed by a combination of income tax (one-third) and payroll-tax or premium (two-thirds). Under these schemes, more families would receive some positive net benefit under the premium-income tax combination, but the size of the per family subsidy would be generally larger under the payroll-income tax mix. (See appendix B, figure 1, for graphs of these tables.)

Progressivity can also be affected by building income-related tax credits or subsidies into the financing plan. For example, premiums or out-of-pocket payments can be eliminated or tied to income for families below some income threshold. Medicaid constitutes this type of subsidy, although it is based on categorical eligibility as well as on family income. Other subsidies are provided by the existing tax code's treatment of insurance premiums and uninsured medical expenses in excess of 3 percent of income. This latter class of factors tends to increase the regressivity of the health financing system, since the size of the subsidy depends on a person's marginal tax rate, employment status, and the likelihood of itemizing deductions. As a result, higher-income families generally receive higher per family subsidies.

Finally, the net effect of an NHI plan's financing scheme on a family's fiscal status also depends on medical care subsidies it receives. These now take two main forms: receipt of free medical care and reductions in personal income taxes for health insurance premium and large medical expenses. As shown in table 6, the quantity of free medical care received declines with rising income. According to the Congressional Budget Office, the exclusion from taxable income of employers' contributions to employee health insurance plans in 1977 reduced tax payments by $26 for taxpayers earning between $5,000 and $10,000; the savings for taxpayers in the $50,000-to-$100,000 bracket was $386 (see appendix B, table 2).[39] Similarly, tax reductions associated with personal income tax deductions for health insurance premium and medical expenses also increases with income: $103 per taxpayer for the $5,000-to-$10,000 bracket compared to $310 for the $50,000-to-$100,000 bracket[40] (see appendix B, table 3). The overall effect, then is to reduce the direct cost of medical care at all income levels. The next section of this chapter examines more closely the consequences for income redistribution of specific NHI bills.

IMPLICATIONS FOR INCOME REDISTRIBUTION

Financing Structures of Alternative Bills

The net effects of an NHI plan's financing scheme on income redistribution depend on interactions among several complex factors: the combination of methods used to raise revenues; the use of offsetting direct subsidies, tax credits, and tax deductions; the amount of free care provided; the definition of the insured unit (persons, households, families, families by size); and the distributions of different types of income by family characteristics. Unfortunately, many of the data needed are not available in sufficient detail to compute the net effects of current plans. Nor are the financing approaches outlined in the Martin, Carter, and Kennedy-Waxman bills sufficiently specific to allow their implications for income redistribution to be quantified in detail. Therefore, this section relies on estimates of net benefits by income class based on the financing plans of earlier NHI proposals. In particular, we focus on the Comprehensive Health Insurance Plan (CHIP) proposed by the Nixon administration in 1973 and the Health Security Act (HSA) developed under the sponsorship of Senator Edward Kennedy and Representative James Corman. These plans proposed financing methods similar to those advocated by the Carter and Kennedy-Waxman bills, respectively. CHIP will serve as the model for intermediate NHI plans, such as the Carter proposal, which build upon and extend the current system, while HSA will represent plans that call for comprehensive reform of the current system. Inferences about the redistributive effects of minimal change plans, such as the Martin bill, which would modify the existing financing system the least, will be based on an analysis of income redistribution under the current system.

As noted in chapter 1, the Carter bill would rely primarily on premium financing to raise revenues. People enrolling only in the catastrophic portion of the plan would pay premiums based on expenditures for catastrophic illnesses; those enrolling in private insurance plans would also pay premiums, with employers contributing at least 75 percent of the cost. Cost sharing would probably continue to be a major feature of plans covering expenses below the catastrophic threshold; and low-income households would be eligible for an expanded Medicaid program (included in HealthCare) funded by federal and state general revenues.

The earlier intermediate plan (CHIP) also relied exclusively on premiums and out-of-pocket spending (cost sharing) to finance care for families which were not poor. At the same time, however, any family's maximum liability was limited to $1,500 (in 1973), which is similar to the Carter plan's catastrophic provision. Poor families' premiums and cost-sharing liabilities were to be subsidized from general revenues. The Carter proposal's plan to expand Medicaid coverage appears more generous. Thus, net benefits — the difference between a family's total costs and the value of the insurance package/protection it receives — would probably be somewhat smaller at low-income levels under the intermediate plan than under the Carter plan and somewhat larger at high family incomes.

The comprehensive plan (HSA) is almost identical to the current Kennedy-Waxman plan in terms of cost sharing, coverage, benefits, and eligibility. Private insurance would play a much larger role in the Kennedy-Waxman plan than in the Health Security Act, although this feature does not affect the calculations reported here. The two bills' financing approaches appear quite different but in reality are fairly similar. Health Security was to obtain half of its funds from a payroll tax and the other half from general revenues. The Kennedy-Waxman bill, conversely, appears to emphasize premiums. In reality, however, premiums for the SSI population, AFDC recipients, and residents of state and federal institutions would be paid from federal and state general revenues. Although the remainder of the population would pay premiums, the actual payment would depend on the application of a constant premium rate to earned income. The premium rate, estimated to be between 7 and 8 percent, would be applied to all payrolls.[41] In addition, one-half the rate would be applied to unearned income above specified amounts ($2,000 for individuals and $4,000 for families). Employers would be required to pay at least 65 percent of the premium on earned income. As a result, the premium would really be an expanded payroll tax, that is, a fixed percentage tax rate with a maximum personal payment set at the average per capita (or per family) health expenditure in the person's state.[42] (Note, however, that employer contributions would not count toward the maximum personal payment.) Without a more detailed analysis, which would require information on actual tax rates and maximum premiums by state, it is hard to assess the exact divergence between the Health Security Act's and the Kennedy-Waxman proposal's financing methods. On average, though, it appears that Kennedy-Waxman would raise a larger share of revenues through the quasi-payroll tax method. Therefore, the simulations reported here, which are based on the Health Security Act, may overstate the amount of income redistribution implicit in Kennedy-Waxman.

Finally, the Martin bill would leave intact the existing financing systems for private insurance, Medicare, Medicaid, and other government health programs. Revenues to pay for the catastrophic portion of the Martin plan would be raised from federal general revenues. At the same time, however, the Martin bill would reduce the drain on the federal treasury by lowering tax expenditures associated with tax deductions for health insurance premiums and excess medical expenses. The Congressional Budget Office estimated that in 1980 tax expenditures arising from exclusion of health insurance premiums and the deductibility of excess medical expenses amounted to $12.97 billion for the former and $3.59 billion for the latter.[43] The Martin bill would reduce these expenditures by not permitting individuals to exclude monthly employer premium contributions in excess of $120 from their personal income taxes, and by repealing the medical expense deduction. (The $120 limit would be increased over time to adjust for inflation.) Some additional revenues would also be raised by including as taxable income a portion of employer rebates to employees who chose private insurance plans less costly than the employer's fixed contribution. Estimating the exact impact of these changes from available secondary data is impossible. However, given the magnitudes of the existing tax expenditures, a plausible estimate of the amount of revenue that the Martin bill would raise is $4.5 billion.

The Martin plan's catastrophic feature would be activated when a family's out-of-pocket expenses for medical care (i.e., those *not covered* by any other private or public insurance) exceeded specified income-related thresholds. As noted in chapter 1, these thresholds range from 12.5 percent for a gross family income of $4,000, to 20 percent at $10,000, and to 24.4 percent at $100,000. Although the limits for upper-income families seem quite high, the great majority of these families are likely to have private insurance that provides protection against regular medical expenses. (In addition, those people covered by an employer plan would have a $2,500 maximum liability, which is less than the computed liability for incomes above $15,000.) Data on the magnitude of covered expenses in excess of these percentages are not readily available. Using 1970 income tax returns, Mitchell and Vogel estimated that $1.68 billion of medical expenses (2.25 percent of total health spending) exceeded 15 percent of income that year.[44] Applying a 2.25 percentage to an estimate of 1980 health spending produces a projected expenditures under CAPP of approximately $5 billion.

Extrapolating 1970 conditions to 1980 is likely to underestimate CAPP expenditures for several reasons. First, the 1970 estimate excludes catastrophic expenses incurred by families and individuals who did not file itemized tax returns. Presumably, local governments, private philanthropy, and implicit subsidies from private insurers now absorb these expenditures. Second, some proportion of persons with individual private insurance policies would probably drop their coverage in favor of CAPP. Thus, some expenses that private insurance now covers would be shifted to CAPP. Third, medical care costs have risen more rapidly than family incomes in the last ten years. Finally, open-ended insurance coverage for catastrophic expenses is likely to shift the pattern of care toward longer hospital stays, the use of more expensive procedures, and the application of "heroic" measures if there is any possibility, no matter how small, of a successful outcome. Again, it is impossible to estimate the exact magnitude of CAPP expenditures, but a plausible guess is about $9 billion to $10 billion in 1980.

Overall, then, it appears that the Martin bill would have only a minimal effect on the existing financing system, since only about $1 billion in new revenues would be required. (We assume that $5 billion in new CAPP expenditures would be offset by $4 billion in new revenues. In addition, $4 billion of existing catastrophic expenditures would be shifted to federal general revenues from other sources.) The small increase in total spending, however, understates the amount of income redistribution implicit in the plan's financing. In general, the regressivity of the existing financing system would be reduced. As was indicated earlier, subsidies provided by tax expenditures benefit high-income families more than low-income families. These would be reduced. Second, the use of the federal income tax to generate new revenues would mean that high-income families would pay more per family than low-income families. Third, fewer low-income families would be paying premiums for individual insurance policies. Finally, CAPP benefits should be skewed toward low-income families, since they are most likely to be unprotected by existing private or public insurance.[45]

Table 10 summarizes the financing approaches of the three bills being analyzed. It also describes the analogs that will be used to evaluate the bills' distributive implications. Intermediate and comprehensive plans, such as the Carter and Kennedy-Waxman proposals, will be represented by CHIP and HSA. The effects of a minimal-change plan like the Martin bill will be based on estimates of income redistribution under the existing financing system. It should be noted that these estimates account for increases in the demand for care induced by each plan, but do not adjust for the effects of cost-containment provisions. Thus, the relative costliness of the three plans could change over time depending on how effectively costs were controlled.

The estimates of each bill's total costs and distribution of costs among channels of payment clearly illustrate the differences in approaches among the three plans. The Martin bill would have the smallest aggregate impact and only a slight increase in the size of the public sector, from about 39 to 41 percent of total costs. The Carter plan would be more expansionary than the Martin plan, with most of the additional coverage being financed by the federal government. The Kennedy-Waxman plan, on the other hand, embodies the most comprehensive approach to coverage, benefits, and system reform.[46] Out-of-pocket payments (for uncovered services, primarily dental and long-term care) are only 14.1 percent of total spending, compared with 24.7 percent under Carter and 27.9 percent under the present system. Finally, in terms of overall costs, the Carter bill would add about 8.5 percent to total spending under the current system, while the Kennedy-Waxman bill would add 17.7 percent ($21 billion more than the Carter plan).

Net Benefits under Alternative Plans

For any particular family or household, the net income gain or loss resulting from the medical care system is the difference between the family's total expenditures for medical care (out-of-pocket payments, taxes, and health insurance premiums) and the monetary value of the medical care actually used. Although the share of a family's income to purchase medical care both directly and indirectly declines as family income rises, the current system still redistributes income from high- to low-income families. Table 11 illustrates the extent of redistribution using crude estimates of average family benefits and costs by family income intervals in 1975. Benefits are assumed to be equal to the value of free and purchased medical care consumed by a family. (Free care includes services provided by Medicaid, care provided by tax-supported institutions to people for whose care there was no other payment, services provided to the armed forces, and care provided at no cost by other public programs.) As is readily apparent, the average quantity of free

Table 10

FINANCING PROVISIONS AND COSTS OF ALTERNATIVE NHI PLANS (1980)

The Current System and a Minimal Change Plan

Current	Minimal Change (Martin)

Financing Structure

Private Insurance

Premiums paid by individuals or employee-employer groups. Individual premium payments over $150 are deductible from taxable income. All employer premium payments are deductible from taxable income.

Medicare

Payroll tax supplemented by federal general revenues.

Medicaid

Federal, state, and local general revenues.

Direct Payments

Out-of-pocket payments from consumers to providers. Payments in excess of 3% of adjusted gross income are deductible from taxable income.

Catastrophic Automatic Protection Plan (CAPP)

Federal general revenues.

Private Insurance

Same as current with following changes: (1) employer share required to be at least 50%; (2) employer contributions over $120 per month would be taxable as employee income; (3) up to $100 per year of insurance premium rebate would be tax-free; (4) 50% of individual premium payments up to maximum of $250 would be tax deductible.

Medicare

No change.

Medicaid

No change.

Direct Payments

Medical expense deduction would be eliminated.

Channels of Payment, 1980

	Amount (in $ billions)	Percent	Amount (in $ billions)	Percent
Out-of-pocket	$ 64.0	27.9%	$ 63.0	27.4%
Private Insurance	71.0	31.0	70.0	30.4
Other Private	4.0	1.7	3.0	1.3
Federal Government	62.5	27.3	67.5	29.3
Govt. Insur. Premiums	4.0	1.7	4.0	1.7
State & Local Govts.	23.5	10.2	22.5	9.8

Costs by Sector, 1980

Private	$139.0	60.7%	$136.0	59.1%
Public[a]	90.0	39.3	94.0	40.9

Total Cost, 1980

Total Cost, 1980	$229.0	100.0%	$230.0[b]	100.0%

Table 10

FINANCING PROVISIONS AND COSTS OF ALTERNATIVE NHI PLANS (1980) (continued)

Intermediate Bills

Comprehensive Health Insurance Plan of 1973 — CHIP	The Carter Bill

Financing Structure

Employer Plan

Employer-employee premium payments, with employer paying 75% of premiums (65% for first 3 years). Temporary federal subsidies for employers with unusually high increases in payroll costs. Special provisions to assure coverage for small employers.

Assisted Plan

Premium payments from enrollees according to family income (none for lower income groups). Balance of costs from federal and state general revenues; state share would vary with state per capita income.

Plan for the Aged

Continuation of present Medicare payroll taxes and premium payments by aged (but no premiums for low-income aged). Federal and state general revenues used to finance reduced cost sharing and premiums for low-income aged.

Private Insurance

Employer-employee premiums with 75% paid by employer up to 5% of payroll; no mandated change in cost sharing below catastrophic threshold.

HealthCare (catastrophic only)

Premiums based on expenses for catastrophic care.

HealthCare (elderly)

Same as current Medicare.

HealthCare (low-income)

State and federal general revenues.

Channels of Payment, 1980

	Amount (in $ billions)	Percent	Amount (in $ billions)	Percent
Out-of-pocket	$ 59.5	23.7%	$ 61.3	24.7%
Private Insurance	76.5	30.4	76.6	30.8
Other Private	3.5	1.4	3.5	1.4
Federal Government	77.0	30.6	80.3	32.3
Govt. Insur. Premiums	11.5	4.6	4.5	1.8
State & Local Govts.	23.5	9.4	22.3	9.0

Costs by Sector, 1980

Private	$139.5	55.5%	$141.3	56.9%
Public[a]	112.0	44.5	107.1	43.1
Total Cost, 1980	$251.5	100.0%	$248.5[b]	100.0%

56

Table 10

FINANCING PROVISIONS AND COSTS
OF ALTERNATIVE NHI PLANS
(1980) (continued)

Comprehensive Bills

Health Security Act of 1973 — HSA	The Kennedy-Waxman Bill

Financing Structure

National Plan

50% from federal general revenues; 50% from special taxes raised as follows: on payroll (1.0% for employees and 2.5% for employers), self-employment income (2.4%) and unearned income (2.5%). Income subject to tax: amount equal to 150% of earning base under Social Security (i.e., $22,950 in 1976). Employment subject to tax: workers under Social Security and federal, state, and local government employment. Federal general revenues: equal to amount received from special taxes.

SSI, AFDC, and Public Institutions

Premiums paid by state and federal general revenues.

Elderly

Same as Medicare.

Remaining Population

Premiums based on per capita health expenses in state; premium *rate* applied in full to wage income above $2,000 for individuals and $4,000 for families; employers pay 65% of wage-related premiums up to 3% of payroll with partial subsidy after 3% for first three years of plan; maximum personal payment cannot exceed average per capita health expenses in state.

Channels of Payment, 1980

	Amount (in $ billions)	Percent	Amount (in $ billions)	Percent
Out-of-pocket	$ 30.0	10.8%	$ 38.0	14.1%
Private Insurance	9.0	3.2	115.5	42.9
Other Private	2.5	0.9	2.5	0.9
Federal Government	222.5	80.3	91.0	33.8
Govt. Insur. Premiums	1.5	0.5	1.5	0.5
State & Local Govts.	11.5	4.2	21.0	7.8

Costs by Sector, 1980

	Amount (in $ billions)	Percent	Amount (in $ billions)	Percent
Private	$ 41.5	15.05%	$156.0	59.7%
Public[a]	235.5	85.0	113.5	42.1
Total Cost, 1980	**$277.0**	**100.0%**	**$269.5**	**100.0%**

Note: Spending for services not covered under the various NHI bills has been included in all cost estimates. Adjustments have been made for increases in demand induced by the bills. No adjustments have been made for the effects of cost-containment provisions.

a. Excludes impact of changes in public revenues due to NHI bills, except for Martin plan.

b. The Martin plan is assumed to cost $10 billion, half of which would be new expenditures and half, existing catastrophic. The $5 billion in new expenditures would be partially offset by $4 billion of new revenues. Also, $4 billion of existing revenues would be transferred from nonfederal to federal revenue ($1 billion each from out-of-pocket, from private insurance, from other private sources, and from state and local governments).

Sources: All cost estimates except those for the Martin bill were provided by Gordon Trapnell of the Actuarial Research Corporation, personal communication, June 9, 1980.

Table 11

INCOME REDISTRIBUTION UNDER THE CURRENT FINANCING SYSTEM, BY FAMILY INCOME (1975)

	Benefits[a]			Expenditures				Net Benefits
	(1)	(2)	(3)	(4)	(5)	(6)	(7)	Col. (3)–Col. (7)
Income Class	Purchased Care	Free Care	Total	Out-of-Pocket	Premiums	Taxes	Total	
Less than $5,000	$ 571	$203	$ 774	$448	$121	$ 106	$ 675	$ 99
5,000-9,999	849	117	966	518	171	314	1,003	– 37
10,000-14,999	978	21	999	572	204	586	1,362	–363
15,000+	1,373	35	1,408	651	228	1,405[b]	2,284	–876

a. Weighted averages of data for smaller income categories, extrapolated to 1975.

b. Weighted average of tax burdens of families in four income classes. See table 6, column 3.

Sources: U.S. Department of Health, Education, and Welfare, National Center for Health Statistics, *Family Out-of-Pocket Health Expenses, United States, 1975*, DHEW Publication No. (PHS) 79-1555, (Hyattsville, Md.: National Center for Health Statistics, 1979), p. 11 (columns 4 and 5); S. Long and M. Cooke, "Financing National Health Insurance," unpublished discussion paper, NHI Financing Team, DHEW, January 6, 1978, p. 20 (column 6); Ronald Andersen et al., *Expenditures for Personal Health Services*, DHEW Publication No. (HRA) 74-3105 (Rockville, Md.: Health Resources Administration, 1973), p. 6 (columns 1 and 2).

care per family declines sharply as income rises. At the same time, tax payments increase progressively with income levels. The result is that low-income families receive medical care worth about $100 more than they actually pay for, while high-income families make payments more than $800 in excess of the value of the medical care they actually consume.[47]

In order to illustrate the impact of the Martin bill, we assume that the federal government would have to raise $5 billion in new revenues through the income tax. This amount corresponds to new medical care benefits that would be distributed to families whose out-of-pocket medical care bills (based on incurred expenses) exceed the plan's maximum out-of-pocket liability. Although this liability would vary with income, we shall assume for simplicity that the limit would be a flat 15 percent of income.[48] This assumption permits us to allocate the new benefit among income classes in the same proportions as the distribution among income classes of uninsured medical expenses in 1970. Using Mitchell and Vogel's estimates, 39.9 percent would be allocated to families with incomes less than $5,000, 32.1 percent to families with incomes between $5,000 and $10,000, 11 percent to families with incomes between $10,000 and $15,000 and 17 percent of the total to families in the highest income class.[49] It is also assumed that families and unrelated individuals would each receive 50 percent of the new benefit.[50] Estimates of the additional tax burden are based on simulations made by Long and Cooke for DHEW.[51] In order to allocate these costs, we assume that families would contribute 80 percent of the total revenue raised.

Table 12 indicates the changes in costs and benefits that might be induced by the Martin plan. Net benefits under the current system are reproduced from table 11 for comparison. In all, the plan appears likely to have a fairly dramatic impact. Benefits would be heavily skewed toward low-income families, while costs would be borne primarily by high-income families. As a result, low-income families would receive more than twice the amount of income redistributed by the current system, and lower-middle-income families would switch from net payers to net beneficiaries.

These estimates focus only on new expenditures induced by the Martin plan. If data were available, the estimates of net benefits in table 12 would have to be adjusted for changes in the financing of existing catastrophic expenses. In other words, the plan would also shift some catastrophic financing from out-of-pocket, health insurance premium, and state and local sources to federal general revenues. Since there might be offsetting effects among these shifts, no attempt has been made to identify the incremental redistribution that might occur.

Table 12

AVERAGE ESTIMATED NET BENEFITS UNDER THE
MARTIN PLAN, BY FAMILY INCOME
(1975)

Income Class	Average Additional Benefits	Average Additional Costs	Average Net Benefits— Martin Plan[a]	Average Net Benefits Current System
Less than $5,000	$137	$ 2	$234	$ 99
5,000-9,999	63	14	12	- 37
10,000-14,999	20	34	-377	-363
15,000 +	20	131	-987	-876

a. Net benefits under the current system plus the change in net benefits caused by the Martin plan.

b. From table 11.

Mitchell and Schwartz have calculated net benefits at various income levels based on the structures of intermediate (CHIP) and comprehensive (HSA) NHI proposals.[52] (As we noted earlier, we are using these two bills as analogs for the Carter and Kennedy-Waxman bills to assess the latter pair's redistributive effects.) The plans' estimates are calibrated to a family of four with one full-time worker at specific income levels, and therefore are not strictly comparable to the estimates in table 12, which are based on all families in various income intervals. Figure 2, taken from the Mitchell and Schwartz study, illustrates the distribution of net benefits under the two bills. Note that under the intermediate plan low-income families would have higher benefits because they would face smaller cost-sharing obligations than middle- and upper-income families. As a result, the low-income families would use more services (receive more benefits) but have lower total burdens than other families. Under the comprehensive plan, benefits would be higher than under the intermediate plan and uniform for all families, since no family would have any cost sharing for covered services.

The cross-hatched areas in figure 2 show the range of net income gain (where benefits exceed costs) and the lined areas show the range of net income loss. Under the comprehensive plan, both benefits and costs are higher, and the breakeven point (total benefit equals total burden) occurs at a much higher level of income, about $14,000, compared with approximately $5,500 under CHIP. Table 13 reports Mitchell and Schwartz's estimates of net benefits per family at selected family incomes. (These numbers correspond to the net gains and losses illustrated in figure 2.)

Figure 2

INCOME REDISTRIBUTION UNDER AN INTERMEDIATE (CHIP) AND A COMPREHENSIVE (HSA) BILL, 1975

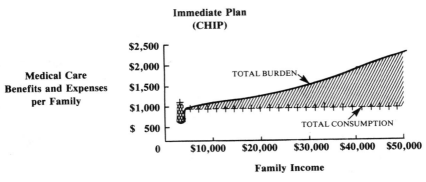

The cross-hatched area below the "total consumption" line represents net gains of income and the shaded area above the consumption line represents net losses. The average total consumption of services has been assumed constant, except for low-income groups. The higher values shown for the total consumption of low-income families are accounted for by reduced requirements for out-of-pocket payments by such families.

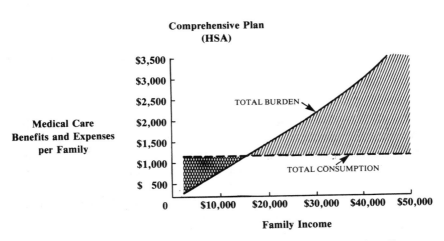

The cross-hatched area below the "total consumption" line represents net gains of income and the shaded area above the consumption line represents net losses. Because the bill has no cost-sharing provisions, the average total consumption of services has been assumed constant for all income groups.

Source: Bridger M. Mitchell and William B. Schwartz, *The Financing of National Health Insurance,* Rand Publication No. R-1711-DHEW (Santa Monica, Calif.: Rand Corporation, 1976), p. 11.

61

Table 13

INCOME REDISTRIBUTION UNDER
INTERMEDIATE (CHIP) AND COMPREHENSIVE (HSA) BILLS
(Family of Four with One Full-Time Worker)

	Redistribution[a]	
Family Income	Intermediate (CHIP)	Comprehensive (HSA)
$ 3,000	$ +400	$ +960
6,000	-40	+740
9,000	-90	+480
12,000	-140	+250
15,000	-190	-10
20,000	-300	-450
30,000	-580	-1,170
40,000	-910	-2,020
50,000	-1,270	-2,930

a. Redistribution (net gain or net loss) is equal to total consumption less total burden under each bill.

Source: Bridger M. Mitchell and William B. Schwartz, *The Financing of National Health Insurance,* Rand Publication No. R-1711-DHEW (Santa Monica, Calif.: The Rand Corporation, 1976), p. 12.

Finally, table 14 provides another perspective of these two bills' implications for income redistribution. As was indicated in table 6, the current financing system is moderately regressive, that is, the share of a family's income spent for medical care (through taxes, premiums, and out-of-pocket payments) declines as family income rises. The intermediate plan's financing scheme, because it would place so much emphasis on premiums, would sharply increase the degree of regressivity. A family of four with an income of $3,000 would be estimated to spend 26.6 percent of disposable income on medical care. Yet, at the highest income level, a family with a gross income of $50,000 would devote only 6.2 percent of its disposable income to medical care. The comprehensive plan, however, would create a mildly progressive financing system. The share of disposable income spent for medical care would steadily rise from 7.9 percent for families with gross incomes of $3,000 to 11.3 percent for families at the highest income level.

Table 14

TOTAL BURDEN (TAX + OUT-OF-POCKET PAYMENTS + OTHER COSTS) AS A PERCENTAGE OF INCOME UNDER INTERMEDIATE AND COMPREHENSIVE NHI PLANS, BY INCOME LEVEL
(Family of Four with One Full-Time Worker)
(1975)

Family Income	Disposable Family Income[a]	Intermediate (CHIP)		Comprehensive (HSA)	
		Total Burden	(Percent of Disposable Income)	Total Burden	(Percent of Disposable Income)
$ 3,000	$ 2,410	$ 640	(26.6%)	$ 190	(7.9%)
6,000	4,700	990	(21.1)	410	(8.7)
9,000	6,960	1,040	(14.9)	670	(9.6)
12,000	9,260	1,090	(11.8)	900	(9.7)
15,000	11,550	1,140	(9.9)	1,170	(10.1)
20,000	15,280	1,240	(8.1)	1,610	(10.5)
30,000	22,380	1,520	(6.8)	2,320	(10.4)
40,000	29,440	1,860	(6.3)	3,180	(10.8)
50,000	36,050	2,220	(6.2)	4,080	(11.3)

Note: The income tax component of the tax burden includes the indirect burden of the corporate profits tax, as well as the direct burden of the personal income tax.
a. Calculated from total effective tax rates in 1966 for federal, state, and local taxes. These rates include the individual income tax, corporate income tax, property tax, sales and excise tax, payroll taxes, and personal property and motor vehicle taxes.
Source: Bridger M. Mitchell and William B. Schwartz, *The Financing of National Health Insurance*, Rand Publication No. R-1711-HEW (Santa Monica, Calif.: The Rand Corporation, 1976), p. 10.

SUMMARY

The current health care system is financed by a combination of premiums, taxes, and out-of-pocket payments. Taxes (federal income and payroll, and state and local) are the source of about 40 percent of total health care expenditures ($105 billion in 1975). Each of the other two payment sources contributes about 30 percent of expenditures. Households also receive subsidies associated with the use of medical care. These include reduced tax payments and the receipt of free medical care through Medicaid, the Veterans Administration, and state and local care for the indigent. In 1975, subsidies to households exceeded $30 billion.

One effect of this complex financing scheme has been to redistribute income from the rich to the poor. Because the poor have lower tax liabilities and use more free medical care than the rich, low-income persons receive positive net financial benefits from the consumption of medical care. Nevertheless, the poor still have substantial out-of-pocket payments. As a result, the share of family income devoted to medical care declines as family income rises.

The Martin plan would make few changes to the current financing structure and would have a negligible impact on total spending (at least in the short run). Nevertheless, it would still redistribute income by eliminating subsidies to higher-income persons, by shifting revenues from regressive sources (out-of-pocket, insurance premiums) to a progressive source (federal general revenues), and by allocating a disproportionate share of new benefits to lower-income persons.

The Carter plan's financing scheme is very similar to the current system. It would rely on a mix of mandated premiums (which are equivalent to a tax), existing taxes, and out-of-pocket payments to pay for care. The HealthCare program would effectively eliminate cost sharing for low-income families who qualified and thus would redistribute additional income to the very poor. Many of the near-poor, however, might still have difficulty paying for medical care.

The Kennedy-Waxman financing approach differs from both the current system and the Carter and Martin plans in two important ways. First, it would eliminate all out-of-pocket payments for covered services. Second, it would raise the bulk of the revenues needed to pay for care through a combination of income taxes and an expanded payroll tax. (The latter would be called a premium, but in effect it would be a proportional tax applied to all wages and nonwage income that exceeded specified amounts. The maximum personal payment under this tax would be an actuarially determined premium determined separately in each state.)

Each of the three plans analyzed would redistribute income by subsidizing medical care consumption for various low-income persons and families. However, available data do not permit exact calculations of the extent of income redistribution or the degree of progressivity of the three plans' financing mechanisms. It does seem clear, however, that the Kennedy-Waxman plan would be progressively financed overall, and would redistribute more income and be more progressively financed, than the other two plans. The very poor, those below 55 percent of the poverty line, who are not now eligible for Medicaid, would fare about as well under the Kennedy-Waxman and Carter plans, and would be much better off than under the Martin bill (or the current system), since they would incur no cost sharing for covered services. However, poverty households above the 55 percent threshold and lower-middle-income persons should receive larger net benefits under the Kennedy-Waxman plan than under either alternative.

64

IV. EMPLOYMENT EFFECTS

NHI plans that emphasize increases in payroll taxes, mandated employer paid health insurance premiums, or both to raise revenues would cause employers' labor costs to increase in the short run. Because it is relatively hard to reduce *current* money wages, employers would bear the additional expenses for health insurance at first. Research on the incidence of employee-related taxes and payments made by employers shows that over time the employees bear the full cost of such levies.[53] Employers eventually pass the higher costs to workers by increasing wages less rapidly than would have been the case without the new taxes or premiums. In the short run, however, firms might respond by reducing employment.[54]

Another effect of national health insurance bills would be to increase health sector employment. In 1976, more than 6.6 million employees — 6.4 percent of the employed labor force — had some work experience in the health and medical industries.[55] In the ten years after enactment of Medicare and Medicaid, health sector employment grew by 67 percent; this figure contrasts with the 18 percent increase in aggregate employment during that time.[56] Because all NHI plans are likely to spur aggregate demand for health services, employment in the health industry could receive another substantial boost.

Both the Kennedy-Waxman and Carter proposals emphasize employer contributions to employee health insurance plans as a major element of their financing schemes. Under the former, the per person premium would be paid by applying a fixed percentage premium-tax rate to wage-related income. Family premiums would be determined by multiplying the per person rate by the number of family members up to four. Total personal payments could not exceed a predetermined annual premium. Employees would be required to pay at least 65 percent of premium costs with no limit on their contribution. If the *increase* in premiums exceeded 3 percent of payroll and if the employer's net income fell, then federal tax credits, financed by general revenue, would be available for a portion of the higher premium costs. (Public and private nonprofit employers would receive federal grants for a portion of premium increases that exceeded 3 percent of payroll.)

Under the Carter plan, employers would be required to pay 75 percent of premium costs. Premiums would vary with individual insurance policies' structures and benefits. Employers' premium expenses could not exceed 5 percent of payroll. If expenses did exceed this limit and if the firm's insurance plan did not contain overly generous benefits, then the federal government would pay the excess over 5 percent.

The Martin plan, on the other hand, should have little direct impact on employment. All new revenues would be raised through the federal income tax. Employers would not be required to offer insurance plans; nor would the minimum premium and employer-share guidelines be very different from existing conditions. Finally, the bill would have only a small impact on total medical care spending, so health sector employment would also be largely unaffected. As a result, it is unnecessary to discuss the Martin plan further in this chapter.

Many employers now pay the major share of employees' premiums for generous health insurance plans. For these firms, the NHI bills' financing methods would affect existing arrangements very little. This would not be the case, however, for firms which do not now contribute to employees' health insurance plans or which do not offer policies that would meet NHI requirements. Thus, both the Carter and Kennedy-Waxman plans would force many employers to incur higher labor costs in the short run.

This chapter examines the employment implications of these two proposals. The first section focuses on potential increases in aggregate unemployment induced by the financing schemes. The second section explores growth in health employment. Particular emphasis is placed on the consequences for employment of minority and low-income persons.

CHANGES IN AGGREGATE EMPLOYMENT

The magnitude of short-term employment effects and the amount of time it takes for these effffects to work themselves out depend on several factors: the rates of increases of labor productivity and product prices, the proportion of workers at the minimum wages, the treatment of part-time workers, the proportion of currently uninsured workers, the difference between current and mandated premiums/payroll taxes, and the existence of premium subsidies. The first two factors govern the rate at which the firm can absorb the incrased labor costs. The faster labor productivity (output per worker), product prices, or both grow, the more quickly employers can pass their higher costs back to employees by not increasing money wages as rapidly as the growth in the value of output per worker. This assumes that as long as workers receive some increase in money wages, they are willing to accept an increase that is less than the rate of inflation in exchange for expanded health insurance coverage. This adjustment process will take longer for employees receiving the minimum wage since its rate of increase is governed by law. As a result, employers will have greater difficulty in reducing the rate of growth of money wages for these employees. Thus, the adjustment period would be longer for industries with high concentrations of workers receiving the minimum wage.

The impact on part-time workers would depend on whether the premiums were a fixed amount per employee or a graduated payment (e.g., a payroll tax), and if part-time employees were exempt from mandated coverage. Fixing the premium amount per employee would cause labor costs to rise more for part-time workers than for full-time workers. Thus employers would be expected to replace part-time employees by extending overtime work or simply by reducing production. Making employers' contributions a percentage of workers' payrolls up to a ceiling also would create a bias against part-time workers; extending work hours for an employee who had already paid the maximum tax would eliminate an employer's requirement to pay the tax or premium for an additional part-time worker. Conversely, exempting part-time workers from mandated coverage would make them relatively cheaper than full-time employees (although this raises the question of how adequate the part-timers' insurance coverage would be). Establishing percentage contributions without a ceiling on taxable payroll would create the fewest distortions among different types of labor. Clearly, though, a subsidy, usually in the form of tax credits or deductions, that offsets higher premium costs could mitigate these adverse effects. The amount of the subsidy would depend on the level of payments required to trigger the subsidy and the amount of the excess premium or payroll tax that is subsidized.

Gauging the differential impact of the two NHI bills on employment requires information on the extent of existing insurance coverage, average premiums, and average employer contributions. In addition, information on the composition of the work force and the distribution of minimum wage employees by industry would indicate which sectors might be hardest hit by increased unemployment.

The most current data are provided from a survey conducted at the end of 1978 of a national sample of private, nonfarm U.S. establishments.[57] In 1977-78, 70 percent (47.6 million workers) of all private, nonfarm employees were covered by employer-offered group health policies, 20 percent chose not to enroll in the plan(s) offered by their employer, and 10 percent worked in firms which did not offer plans. (The 20 percent figure includes workers who voluntarily declined to enroll and workers who were excluded from participation, primarily because of seasonal or part-time employment. These data do not distinguish between these two groups of employees.)

Table 15 reports these data by major industry groups. Coverage was lowest in the construction, retail trade, and service industries. The primary reason for noncoverage in the first two industries was employment in a firm that did not offer health insurance. The last column of the table, which was based on a 1976 household survey, shows total coverage by private insurance by industry. Since total coverage is significantly higher than employer-offered group coverage, it follows that many workers who were not covered by their employers were covered by someone else's (typically a spouse's) policy, or purchased private insurance individually, through a voluntary association, or otherwise.[58] Nevertheless, workers in the construction, retail trade, and service sectors still had the least private insurance.

Data on the proportions of nonsupervisory employees at or near the minimum wage by industry are available for 1970. These workers and the firms that employed them would have the greatest difficulty absorbing higher health insurance costs (see appendix B, table 4). The overwhelming majority of employees earn more than the minimum wage except in the service and retail trade industries, where 15.8 and 19.2 percent of employees earned less than the then-minimum wage of $1.60. Furthermore, an increase in wages of five cents, which is just over 3 percent and approximates the possible effects of an increased payroll tax or health insurance premium, would have raised the proportions of employees at the minimum wage to 20.8 and 27.6 percent in these two industries.

As might be expected, workers at low income levels also have less coverage than other workers. Twenty-three percent of employees earning $6,000 or less were in firms that did not offer health insurance, compared with 10 percent of employees earning between $6,000 and $10,000, and only 4 percent of employees with earnings over $10,000.[59] Again, the construction, retail trade, and service industries had the lowest coverage rates at each earnings level. In addition, 25 percent of part-time employees were not covered by employer plans, compared to only 10 percent of full-time workers.[60] Part-time workers were also most heavily concentrated in the retail trade and service sectors.

Expanded coverage of workers is only one source of cost increase employers will face. The others are the costs of expanded benefits and higher employer contributions. Using data from the 1978 survey of establishments, estimates were made of average premiums, employer shares, and the ratio of employer contributions per worker to average payroll per worker by industry.[61] These estimates are reported in table 16. Assuming average premiums to roughly measure the comprehensiveness of the benefits offered, the average for all industries is $1,002 worth of benefits. The transportation and utilities industry is the most generous at $1,287, while the retail trade industry is the least generous at

Table 15

DISTRIBUTION OF EMPLOYEES BY COVERAGE THROUGH EMPLOYER-OFFERED HEALTH INSURANCE, BY INDUSTRY
(thousands of employees)
(1977-78 and 1976)

Industry	Workers Not Covered by Employer Plan, 1978						Workers Covered by Employer Plan 1978		Percentage of Workers Covered by Private Insurance, 1976
	Establishment Offers Insurance		Establishment Does Not Offer Insurance		Total Without Employer Coverage				
	(No.)	(%)	(No.)	(%)	(No.)	(%)	(No.)	(%)	(%)
Construction	588	18.4	1,092	34.2	1,680	52.6	1,512	47.4	80.0
Manufacturing	3,970	16.2	444	1.8	4,414	18.0	20,149	82.0	93.5
Transportation and Other Utilities	430	15.2	245	8.6	675	23.8	2,162	76.2	92.0
Wholesale Trade	910	16.9	490	9.2	1,400	26.1	3,970	73.9	92.0
Retail Trade	2,429	22.9	3,044	28.7	5,473	51.6	5,131	48.4	83.0
Finance, Insurance, and Real Estate	803	15.6	340	6.6	1,143	22.2	3,995	77.8	87.0
Services	4,316	27.2	1,612	10.1	5,928	37.3	9,961	62.7	82.7
Private, Nonfarm Sector	13,448	19.9	7,267	10.7	20,715	30.6	46,879	69.4	87.0

Sources: 1977-78 data from Malhotra et al., "Employment Related Health Benefits: A Survey of Establishments in the Private Nonfarm Sector," Final Report, vol. 2 (Seattle, Wash.: Battelle Human Affairs Research Center, 1980), pp. 26, 35; 1976 data from U.S. Congress, Congressional Budget Office, *Profile of Health Care Coverage: The Haves and Have-Nots* (Washington, D.C.: U.S. Government Printing Office, 1979), p. 53.

Table 16

ESTIMATES OF COVERAGE, AVERAGE PREMIUMS, EMPLOYER SHARES, AND EMPLOYER BURDENS, BY INDUSTRY

(1980)

Industry	Employees Covered (1977-78)[a]		Average Premium[b, c]	Average Employer Share[c]	Employer Share as Percentage of Average Payroll per Worker[d]
	All Firms (%)	Firms with Plans (%)	($)	(%)	(Firms with Plans) (%)
	(1)	(2)	(3)	(4)	
Construction	47%	72%	$1,088	65.6%	3.27%
Transportation and Other Utilities	76	83	1,287	84.2	5.07
Wholesale Trade	74	81	934	75.4	3.46
Retail Trade	48	68	835	66.6	4.60
Manufacturing	82	84	969	83.4	4.20
Services	63	70	1,048	67.0	4.49
Total All Industries	70%	78%	$1,002	76.0%	4.47%

a. From Malhotra et al., "Employment Related Health Benefits: A Survey of Establishments in the Private Nonfarm Sector," p. 26.

b. Inflated to 1980 by multiplying 1977 average premium by change in medical care component of Consumer Price Index.

c. Average premium and average employer share computed from data in appendix B, table 5, under assumption that 80 percent of covered workers have family policies.

d. Employers' costs were computed by multiplying columns (2), (3), and (4), and then dividing by average payroll per worker inflated to 1980.

$835. Average employer shares vary by about the same extent, from just over 66 percent in the retail trade and services sectors to almost 85 percent in transportation and utilities. The average employer share over all industries is 76 percent.

The average burden on employers who offer plans is measured by the ratio of the employer's premium cost to average payroll per worker. This ratio is lowest in the construction industry and highest for transportation and utilities. (Although average coverage levels, premiums, and employer shares are lowest in retail trade, relatively low average earnings and payrolls nevertheless make health insurance a relatively expensive fringe benefit in this sector also.) The average burden over all establishments with plans is 4.47 percent of payroll (3.13 percent if establishments without plan are included).

The key factors in gauging an NHI plan's impact on employment are the additional premium costs mandated by the plan and its provisions for subsidizing additional premium expenditures. Table 17 presents crude estimates of additional costs by industry for three types of workers: employees now covered by group health plans, uncovered employees in firms that offer plans, and uncovered employees in firms without plans. (Table 15 showed industry distributions of the employees.) Estimates of the additional costs imposed by the Kennedy-Waxman plan are based on the following assumptions: the premium rate applied to employers' payrolls is 7.5 percent; employers without plans pay 65 percent of the premium (4.88 percent of payroll); and employers currently offering plans pay either 65 percent or their current share, whichever is higher. For the Carter plan estimates, it is assumed that all full-time employees would buy coverage through their employers (i.e., those now holding individual policies would switch to employer-offered plans) and that uninsured part-time workers would not be affected; that 63 percent of part-time workers in firms with plans have group insurance;[62] that currently insured employees would maintain existing coverage; that employers would contribute 75 percent or their current share, whichever is higher; and that employers would enroll their uncovered employees in HealthCare, the government-sponsored plan. The last assumption probably understates premium costs for some employers, since employers who now offer plans might simply choose to add uncovered employees to the existing plan. Thus, the estimates based on HealthCare premium costs are lower bounds of the potential cost increases.

Examination of the effects of the Kennedy-Waxman plan reveals several interesting facts. Since the premium would be income related, the average contribution per worker would vary by more than a factor of two, from $379 in the low-earnings retail trade sector to $817 in the transportation and utilities industry. For firms now without plans, these

71

Table 17

AVERAGE ADDITIONAL COST OF HEALTH INSURANCE PREMIUMS PER WORKER, BY INDUSTRY
(1980)

Kennedy-Waxman Plan

| | Firms with No Insurance | | Firms with Insurance Plans | | | | Industry Average[a] | |
| | | | Uncovered Workers | | Covered Workers | | | |
	($)	(% of Payroll)	($)	(% of Payroll)	($)	(% of Payroll)	($)	(% of Payroll)
Construction	$725	4.88%	$749	1.41%	$229	1.11%	$495	3.33%
Transportation and Utilities	817	4.88	948	0.96	58	0.29	217	1.29
Wholesale Trade	760	4.88	835	1.01	148	0.77	320	2.05
Retail Trade	379	4.88	379	1.56	-157	-1.37	120	1.54
Manufacturing	745	4.88	938	0.98	147	0.81	286	1.87
Services	504	4.88	504	1.46	-96	-0.65	128	1.24
All Industries	$612	4.88%	$655	1.15%	$ -8	-0.05%	$189	1.51%

a . Weighted average using distribution of employees by coverage category (from table 15) as weights.

Table 17

AVERAGE ADDITIONAL COST OF HEALTH INSURANCE PREMIUMS PER WORKER, BY INDUSTRY
(1980) (continued)

Carter Plan[a]

| | Firms with No Insurance[b] | | Firms with Insurance Plans | | | | Industry Average[c] | |
| | | | Uncovered Workers[b] | | Covered Workers | | | |
	($)	(% of Payroll)	($)	(% of Payroll)	($)	(% of Payroll)	($)	(% of Payroll)
Construction	$410	2.47%	$410	0.69%	$ 77	0.37%	$230	1.05%
Transportation and Utilities	410	1.86	412	0.37	0	0.00	90	0.19
Wholesale Trade	410	1.84	410	0.45	35	0.18	97	0.24
Retail Trade	410	3.43	410	1.21	132	1.15	207	1.39
Manufacturing	410	2.10	447	0.44	0	0.00	74	0.09
Services	410	2.67	410	0.97	132	0.89	216	1.00
All Industries	$410	2.32%	$410	0.61%	$ 51	0.32%	$134	0.50%

a. Data on part-time employees in firms with and without plans are from Malhotra et al., "Employment Related Health Benefits: A Survey of Establishments in the Private Nonfarm Sector," p. 27.

b. The cost of insuring currently uninsured workers is slightly underestimated, because the Carter plan would require firms with 10 or more employees to pay a flat 5 percent of payroll as the premium charge. Firms which could enroll their currently uninsured workers in existing plans at a lower cost would obviously do so. However, only 11 percent of workers in firms which offer insurance would be affected. Malhotra et al., p. 25.

c. Weighted average using distribution of employees by coverage category (from table 15) as weights; uncovered part-time workers excluded from Carter plan weights.

premiums would represent a flat 4.88 percent of each one's payroll. Since most workers in firms that offer policies are already covered, the cost of adding uncovered workers would range between about 1 and 1.5 percent of payroll; it would be highest in the sectors that have the highest proportions of uncovered employees: construction, retail trade, and services. Additional costs for currently covered workers would be the smallest share. In fact, in two sectors, retail trade and services, firms would pay less for currently covered employees because the NHI income-related premium would be less than the existing capitation premium. Overall, the plan would increase employers' costs by 1.51 percent of payroll, with the greatest impact in construction, which has low existing coverage and relatively high payrolls.

The Carter plan would have a smaller impact on employers' costs, primarily because HealthCare would be a much less expensive (and less comprehensive) insurance plan. The mandated premium for workers enrolled in HealthCare by their firms is estimated to be a flat $547 per employee.[63] In addition, part-time employees, who make up almost 30 percent of workers in firms without plans, are assumed to remain outside of employer-offered group plans. The requirement that employers would have to pay at least 75 percent of the premium would raise the cost of improving benefits for already covered workers only slightly because the average is now 70 percent. (If employers reduced coverage for currently insured workers, however, NHI-imposed costs would go up less.) The overall impact of the Carter plan on costs would be much smaller than that of the Kennedy-Waxman proposal; costs would rise by an average of only 0.5 percent of payroll in all firms. The burden of the additional costs, however, would be greatest for the sectors with the lowest average payrolls and existing coverage rates: construction, retail trade, and services.

Both plans would attempt to offset possible increases in unemployment by offering subsidies to firms that meet certain criteria. Under the Kennedy-Waxman plan, firms whose premium costs *increase* by 3 percent or more of payroll and whose profits decline would be eligible for tax credits (grants for public and nonprofit employers) equal to one-half the increased premium costs in the year the plan is implemented, and to one-third and one-sixth of additional premium costs in the next two years. As a result, all firms not now offering plans and meeting the reduced-profit criterion would receive subsidies from the Kennedy-Waxman plan, since their cost increases would amount to 4.88 percent of payroll. The subsidy would cut costs by half in the first year, making the average impact of the premiums over all firms very close to the premium imposed by the Carter plan — 2.44 percent of payroll versus 2.32 percent. Among firms that now offer group insurance, most establishments would not qualify for subsidies under the Kennedy-Waxman proposal, primarily because the income-related premium reduces costs for low-wage employees. Only firms in the construction industry, which has high wages and low coverage, would probably become eligible.

The Carter plan would require the government to pay all premium costs in excess of 5 percent of payroll. Since the Carter bill has a higher subsidy trigger than the Kennedy-Waxman bill, firms now without plans which enroll their employees in HealthCare would probably not qualify and would receive no subsidies. Firms in the retail trade and service sectors that now pay premiums greater than 4 percent of payroll and would have increased premium costs of 1 percent or more would receive subsidies. Under the Carter plan, these subsidies would continue indefinitely, but the cost ceiling, 5 percent, would be slightly higher than the 4.88 percent that unsubsidized firms would pay under the Kennedy-Waxman plan.

Neither the Kennedy-Waxman nor Carter plans indicate how their tax subsidy systems would be administered. Both would face serious administrative problems: the definition of a "firm," treatment of firms that are in business for less than a full year, verification of premium costs in the previous year, and evaluation of profit declines (under Kennedy-Waxman) and the reasonableness of insurance policies' benefits (under Carter). One clear advantage of the Kennedy-Waxman approach, however, is its recognition of the short-term nature of the induced unemployment and the subsequent gradual phasing-out of the subsidy system over three years. The Carter plan's subsidy scheme, on the other hand, would be permanent and might create incentives for firms near the proposed 5 percent ceiling to expand their insurance policies past this point, since the costs of additional benefits would be free, subject to a regulatory evaluation of their reasonableness.

What impact would these increased costs have on unemployment? Mitchell and Phelps estimated the effects of hypothetical NHI bills on employment by industry in 1970.[64] Although the plans they analyzed are not identical to the Carter and Kennedy-Waxman proposals, it is probably safe to associate their intermediate plan with the Carter bill and the high-level plan with the Kennedy-Waxman bill. Both hypothetical plans would mandate employer shares of at least 75 percent. The intermediate plan would impose premiums of $200 for individual coverage and $600 for family coverage. The corresponding premiums for the high-level plan would be $320 and $1,000. Their analysis estimated cost increases of 1.2 percent and 2.9 percent of payroll for the intermediate and high plans, respectively.[65] These are roughly double the estimates for 1979 reported in table 17.[66]

Several factors explain these differences in estimates of cost increases. First, as Phelps has recently pointed out, group insurance coverage grew much more rapidly between 1970 and 1975 than they had estimated.[67] Thus, mandated NHI coverage would exceed current coverage by less than Mitchell and Phelps estimated. This factor would tend to reduce the cost implications of an NHI plan partially financed by mandated employer premium contributions. Second, the Carter bill's mandated plan is less expensive (in constant dollars) than the Mitchell-Phelps intermediate plan. In addition, the Carter plan would exempt part-time employees from mandated coverage. Finally, the Kennedy-Waxman plan would use an income-related premium with a fixed premium rate rather than a capitation premium with a fixed dollar cost. As a result, firms in low-wage industries would pay much less under the Kennedy-Waxman plan than they would under the Mitchell-Phelps high-cost plan.

The estimates Mitchell and Phelps made of the impact of higher costs on unemployment assumed that firms respond by increasing hours for full-time workers and reducing employment for part-time workers, because the mandated premium is independent of employment status. They also analyzed the effects of subsidies similar to those proposed in the Carter and Kennedy-Waxman bills. They found increases in short-term unemployment of 0.6 percent and 1.1 percent induced by the intermediate and high-cost plans, respectively. For the reasons cited above, however, these estimates are probably too high, perhaps by at least a factor of two.[68] Thus, we would predict that the Carter plan would increase short-term unemployment by between 0.20 and 0.30 of a percentage point and the Kennedy-Waxman plan by between 0.45 and 0.55 of a percentage point.

Finally, as noted at the beginning of this chapter, the duration of the induced unemployment would depend in part on the rate of inflation, which affects how rapidly the higher premium costs can be passed back from employers to employees. If prices were increasing at a rate of between 8 and 10 percent, as they have been in recent years, then the higher premium costs could be shifted back to labor relatively quickly, probably within six months.[69] Thus, the adverse employment effects should dissipate fairly quickly.

HEALTH SECTOR EMPLOYMENT EFFECTS

The health industry is one of the largest and most rapidly growing employers in the national economy. As such, it has been an important source of income growth and labor stability. These characteristics are particularly important because of the demographic composition of the health labor force. Except for physicians, who make up about 8 percent of health workers, the health labor force is predominantly female (about 75 percent), primarily employed in institutions, and disproportionately black.[70] (Blacks constitute 13.6 percent of health workers compared with 9.6 percent of all other workers.) The occupational mix of the health labor force also differs significantly from that of U.S. industries as a whole. In 1970, 37.7 percent of health workers were in professional, technical and related occupations, and 38.4 percent in service occupations.[71] By comparison, only 14.1 percent of all employed persons held jobs in professional, technical, and related occupations, while 10.3 percent of all employed persons held jobs in service occupations.[72] As a result of these differences in occupational composition, average earnings for nonprofessional workers (persons with less than eighteen years of schooling in the health sector) tend to be lower than earnings for nonprofessionals in other industries. In 1969, these health workers averaged annual earnings of $4,492, compared with $6,294 for nonhealth workers (hourly earnings were $2.75 and $3.56, respectively).[73] Thus, expansion of health sector employment could have significant distributional effects.

Both of the NHI bills being considered here would expand the demand for medical care. Clearly, however, the Kennedy-Waxman bill would have a greater effect on aggregate demand because of universal eligibility and the absence of cost sharing. How this increased demand would be distributed cannot be precisely estimated without better data and more detailed analysis. However, based on studies of the use of medical care in Montreal, Canada, following adoption of a universal insurance plan with no cost sharing, it is probable that the poor and near-poor would increase their medical care consumption more than other people.[74] This should occur despite the current distribution of Medicaid benefits, because Medicaid does not cover many poor families with two parents or a working head. Furthermore, much of the increased demand would be for outpatient and ambulatory medical care. The poor now obtain most such care from hospital outpatient clinics and emergency rooms, and freestanding ambulatory care clincs.

To gauge the impact on employment of the Carter and Kennedy-Waxman proposals, we analyzed the pattern of health sector employment and aggregate expenditures between 1967 and 1978. Table 18 reports these data. Health employment refers to all active, office-based, patient-care physicians, employees of all short and long-term hospitals; and employees of physicians' offices.[75] Simple regression analysis of these data strongly suggests that employment and expenditures increase at the same rate.[76]

Table 18

HEALTH SECTOR EMPLOYMENT AND
TOTAL HEALTH EXPENDITURES
(1967-78)

	Health Employment[a]	Health Expenditures (in billions of dollars)
1967	3,201,400	$ 52.7
1968	3,411,600	58.9
1969	3,666,500	66.2
1970	3,901,400	74.7
1971	4,116,800	82.8
1972	4,315,900	92.7
1973	4,574,900	102.3
1974	4,858,900	115.6
1975	5,149,100	131.5
1976	5,377,100	148.9
1977	5,639,600	170.0
1978	5,851,300	192.4

a. Total health employment was computed as the sum of total full-time equivalent personnel in federal, state, and local government hospitals; total employment in the private, nonfarm health service sector; and total non-federal, office-based physicians.

Sources: Center for Health Services Research and Development, *Distribution of Physicians in the U.S.,* 1967-1978 eds. (Chicago, Ill.: American Medical Association, 1967-78), table 6; American Hospital Association, *Hospital Statistics,* 1979 ed. (Chicago, Ill.: American Hospital Association, 1979), table 1; U.S. Department of Labor, Bureau of Labor Statistics, *Employment and Earnings, United States, 1909-78,* Bulletin 1312-11 (Washington, D.C.: U.S. Government Printing Office, 1979), p. 810; Robert M. Gibson, "National Health Expenditures 1978," *Health Care Financing Review* 1 (Summer 1979), table 1.

Cost estimates reported in table 10 in the previous chapter indicated that the Carter bill would increase total expenditures by about 8.5 percent and the Kennedy-Waxman bll by about 17.5 percent. Applying these figures to an estimated health sector employment of 5.5 million people implies that the bills would add 467,000 and 963,000 new jobs, respectively. Many of these new health workers would, of course, be drawn from other industries. Thus, these employment gains, which amount to between 0.5 and 1.0 percentage point of aggregate national employment would not necessarily offset the short-run unemployment increases discussed in the previous section. An analysis on interindustry worker migration is, however, beyond the scope of this study.

SUMMARY

NHI plans that relied on mandated employer premiums might have adverse effects on short-term employment levels. Since current money wages generally are inflexible downwards, employers would bear the higher premium costs at first. As a result, there might be pressures to reduce employment levels until the higher costs could be shifted back to employees.

Both the Kennedy-Waxman and Carter plans would rely on mandated employer-paid premiums to finance large shares of their NHI plans' expenses. (As already noted, the Martin plan should have little direct impact on employment.) The bills differ, though, in the way they would use the employer premium to raise revenues. Foremost is the difference in the type of premium. The Kennedy-Waxman plan would apply a fixed premium rate to an employer's entire wage bill, while the Carter plan would impose a flat dollar premium per worker. In effect, the former is an income-related premium and the latter is a capitation premium. Second, the bills propose different mechanisms for subsidizing firms hit hard by the tax-like premiums. Third, the Kennedy-Waxman bill would apply the same premium rate to all employees in a state, while the Carter bill would exempt part-time workers from the mandated premium and require only that employers offer a plan that met minimum requirements and therefore would have different effects on different firms.

As a result of these differences, the Kennedy-Waxman plan would impose increased labor costs of about 1.5 percent of payroll — roughly three times the increased costs imposed by the Carter plan. The Kennedy-Waxman bill would distribute this burden fairly evenly across industries, essentially because the premium would be income related. The Carter plan would focus a disproportionate share of the total increase on the retail trade and service industries. Under both plans, however, most of the higher costs would be incurred by providing insurance for workers not now covered by employer plans. Finally, the Kennedy-Waxman bill would partially subsidize all firms that do not now offer plans, while the Carter bill, which has a higher trigger, would target most of its subsidies at firms in the retail trade and service sectors.

The net effect of these factors on unemployment is estimated to be relatively small increases of between 0.20 and 0.30 of a percentage point under the Carter bill, and roughly twice this amount, 0.45 to 0.55 of a percentage point, under the Kennedy-Waxman bill. If general price inflation should continue at relatively high rates, between 8 and 10 percent per year, then the higher unemployment should dissipate fairly quickly, possibly within six months.

Another effect of national health insurance bills would be permanent gains in health sector employment. In the past, health sector employment appears to have grown at essentially the same rate as total, constant-dollar health expenditures. Using estimates of each bill's impact on total health care expenditures, we estimate that the Carter plan would add about 467,000 jobs and the Kennedy-Waxman plan about 963,000 jobs to the approximately 5.5 million jobs already in the health sector. In each case, the number of new jobs would be twice the size of the increase in aggregate unemployment induced by mandated, employer-premium financing. Finally, expansion of health sector employment would redistribute earnings toward women, minorities, and service workers.

V. COST CONTAINMENT THROUGH
THE MARKETPLACE

Opponents of regulation have questioned payment restrictions and other forms of regulation as a means to limit and allocate health care expenditures. Control over spending, they argue, requires reductions in current pressures to spend. Specifically, they call for restructuring the insurance market to increase consumer sensitivity to the price of insurance and to prices for medical services. At present, an estimated three-fourths of the privately insured population do not face the full price of health insurance. They obtain insurance through employment, and employers' contributions to premiums (like other fringe benefits of employment) are treated as nontaxable income.[77] Many critics have argued that this tax exemption encourages employers to offer comprehensive insurance coverage, which in turn stimulates expenditures on medical care. In addition, employers do not encourage employees to compare or evaluate the benefits of insurance plans in relation to their premium levels. Employers rarely offer employees a choice among insurance plans and, if they do, they typically vary contributions to employee premiums with premium levels. As a result, employees are neither penalized for choosing higher-cost plans, nor rewarded for choosing lower-cost plans.

In recent years, several legislators have proposed to alter the employer-based insurance market.[78] An increasingly popular proposal is to encourage or require employers to offer employees a choice among different types of insurance plans, to set limits on the amount of the employer contribution to health insurance that is excluded from taxable income, and to reward employees for choosing a lower-cost plan. Favored plans are of two types: (1) health maintenance organizations or other closed-panel arrangements, in which fixed prepayment encourages providers to limit rather than maximize the service they provide, and (2) traditional insurance plans with significant patient cost-sharing requirements. (Plans with cost sharing may include limits on out-of-pocket expenditures in order to assure all employees catastrophic protection.)

These two types of plans represent two different schools of thought on the nature and role of competition in the medical market.[79] Proponents of patient cost sharing argue that making consumers sensitive to prices at the time of service is the best way to assure efficient service delivery. Advocates of HMOs and other closed panels disagree. They argue that individual consumers — particularly when they are sick—have neither the information nor the will to weigh the costs of medical services relative to their benefits. Instead, they believe consumers should be encouraged to weigh the costs and benefits of alternative insurance plans. Consumer sensitivity to the price of insurance, they argue, would stimulate insurers and providers to develop more efficient delivery mechanisms. The primary feature of such mechanisms (typified by but not limited to the HMO) would be the replacement of fee-for-service and cost reimbursement with a payment structure that would reward providers for limiting rather than increasing the use of resources.

Both cost sharing and competing insurance plans have strengths and weaknesses as strategies for cost containment. This chapter examines this evidence and evaluates each bill's provisions for controlling costs and improving resource allocation through mechanisms which enhance competitive forces.

COMPETITION AMONG INSURANCE PLANS

All three bills have provisions to encourage the development of HMOs and to increase competition among insurance plans. The belief that insurer competition will contain costs rests on several unanswered questions. If tax provisions were to change, would consumers face a choice among different types and prices of insurance plans? If they did, would differences among plans represent true differences in the costs of providing medical care rather than differences in the health status characteristics of their enrolled populations? Would consumers choose among these plans on the basis of price? If some people chose on the basis of price and new types of plans develop, would the existence of these plans generate sufficient pressure on remaining fee-for-service providers to constrain overall increases in medical expenditures? Affirmative answers to these questions require a variety of behavioral changes. The obstacles and uncertainties surrounding these changes can be outlined briefly.

First, changing the tax treatment of insurance premiums and mandating certain types of choices would not guarantee that employees would actually face a choice between fee-for-service and closed-panel insurance plans. Along with limited market opportunities, closed panels — typically HMOs — have had to face opposition from the medical profession, problems in recruiting able managers, and difficulties in accumulating start-up capital, all of which limit their availability.[80] In addition, HMOs require a certain population density to operate successfully and are unlikely to develop in sparsely populated areas. The opportunity for choice may also be limited by employer reluctance to expand the number of insurance plans they offer employees. Anecdotal evidence suggests that employers are reluctant to alter the insurance practices to which they are accustomed. Although there is no evidence of increased administrative costs associated with expanded offerings, fears of such costs may inhibit change.[81]

Employers have also been reluctant to support actions such as utilization controls that employees might perceive as a reduction in benefits. This is particularly true where employers and their employees represent only a small share of an area's medical market. Providers have, in fact, been known to discriminate against insured individuals whose insurance companies have been aggressive in cost containment. Furthermore, in industries dominated by a few firms, most if not all employers are more concerned with employee satisfaction than with saving money, because higher product prices that result from rising insurance premiums do not appear to damage the employer's competitive position in the market.[82] With the exception of some employers whose employees represent a significant share of an area's population,[83] employer concern with rising premium costs has produced more rhetoric than action.

Changes in the economy, however, could alter employers' attitudes. In times of recession, employers facing declining profits are more likely to take a hard look at practices that can reduce labor costs. Closed-panel arrangements may look particularly appealing since they may offer an opportunity to save money while maintaining comprehensive benefits for employees.

Advocates of competing insurance plans recognize that entrenched attitudes and procedures make it difficult to get closed panels off the ground. Although enrollment in HMOs is increasing by 18 percent per year,[84] in 1977-78, only 7 percent of employees in the private nonfarm sector whose employers offered group insurance had an opportunity to join an HMO,[85] and only 3 percent of the population was enrolled in HMOs.[86] Although changes in tax structure and other legislation (inside or outside of an NHI plan) could stimulate the development of HMOs and other closed panels, it is likely to be some time before closed panels are available to, let alone used by, a major segment of the population. Closed-panel advocates hope that as more and more plans overcome existing barriers, the barriers themselves will disappear.

If this assumption is correct and consumers face a choice among closed-panel and fee-for-service plans, a second question arises: Will this choice reflect real differences in the costs of medical care? The competing insurer strategy for cost containment rests on the assumption that closed panels' provider payment mechanisms will induce more efficient resource use than occurs in the fee-for-service system. In a review of research to date, Luft reports that the evidence on HMO performance is ambiguous on this question.[87] Luft found that "the total cost of medical care (premium plus out-of-pocket costs) for HMO enrollees is lower than for apparently comparable people with conventional insurance coverage."[88] For group practice HMOs, costs were 10 to 40 percent lower, primarily because of lower hospital admission rates. A careful look at the people who chose between HMOs and conventional plans, however, suggested that HMOs' low hospital admission rates might reflect self-selection into HMOs by people who are already low users of hospital care. If self-selection rather than efficiency explains HMOs' lower costs, the expansion of HMOs will lead to segmentation of the insurance market, not lower total costs. Furthermore, it is not clear that new HMOs will be as successful as existing ones in controlling resource use. Although evidence on HMO performance is limited, Luft advises caution in assuming dramatic savings from the expansion of closed-panel plans.

Even if we assume there are efficiencies in closed panels, they can only be fully realized if consumers are willing to join closed-panel plans. If consumers face a broad array of plans that vary in minor as well as major ways, they may find it difficult to compare costs and benefits and choose accordingly. Hence, even if closed panels offer better value for premium dollars, consumers may not perceive their advantages. If consumers can make rational comparisons, they are likely to consider the style as well as the cost of medical care associated with a particular plan. Many people may not like the restrictions of a closed panel of physicians, even if the closed panel costs less. Reinforced by physicians' preferences for open fee-for-service practice, these people may continue to purchase traditional insurance protection rather than join a closed panel. The preference for traditional insurance seems particularly likely if joining a closed panel entails choosing a new physician.

Evidence from the Federal Employees Health Benefit Plan suggests a strong consumer commitment to traditional insurance and fee-for-service medicine. Unlike most employers in the current market, the federal government does offer employees a choice of plans and contributes a fixed percentage (up to a maximum) of premiums, regardless of the plan chosen.[89] Meyer observes, however, that "most federal workers who have the option of choosing prepaid plans do not take this option."[90]

Conflicting evidence, however, comes from studies of University of California employees and employees in the Minneapolis-St. Paul area.[91] At the University of California, employees apparently responded to rising Blue Cross premiums by opting increasingly for the Kaiser HMO. While the number of Blue Cross enrollees remained stable over a ten-year period, employee enrollment in the Kaiser plan more than doubled. A recent study in Minneapolis-St. Paul also reported major shifts in enrollment from traditional plans to HMOs, even where HMO premiums exceeded traditional insurance premiums. (HMO benefits were also more extensive than those offered by the traditional plan.) At Honeywell, apparently one of the few companies in which HMOs had lower premiums as well as broader benefits than traditional plans, 33 percent of employees reportedly switched from Blue Cross-Blue Shield to HMO membership in the first year. A year later, the proportion had risen to 45 percent. Despite rapid growth (27 percent per year between 1971 and 1978) in enrollment in HMOs in Minneapolis, however, only 12.4 percent of the area's population had enrolled in HMOs by 1978.[92]

It is not necessary for all consumers to choose closed panels in order to create competitive pressure on the fee-for-service system. If traditional fee-for-service insurers lose some of their market to closed panels, both the insurers and their participating providers might alter their behavior in order to maintain competitive premium levels. As Luft reports in a recent review, experience in California, Hawaii, Rochester, and Minneapolis suggests that the growth of HMOs may induce Blue Cross-Blue Shield plans to control their subscribers' use of hospital care and may stimulate physicians to create individual practice HMOs in which they can monitor one another's service delivery.[93] As noted above, however, the creation of closed panels does not guarantee more efficient resource use. In Minneapolis, for example, it is interesting to note that more than half the Honeywell employees who joined an HMO enrolled in the HMO with the highest premium — an individual practice HMO. The study's authors attribute this to "the accessibility of (the plan's) 1,200 participating physicians and the likelihood that an employee can enroll without changing physicians . . . ."[94] Although the individual practice associations (IPAs) in question reported lower hospital use, in general, individual practice associations have not demonstrated savings comparable to group practice HMOs.[95] Because IPAs allow individuals to retain their current physicians while gaining the apparent out-of-pocket payment advantages of the HMOs, they may reduce the attractiveness of group practice HMOs and limit their impact on the overall market.[96]

Even more important, enrollment shifts in favor of closed panels may represent segmentation of the market between high and low users, rather than actual changes in resource use. In Minneapolis, for example, Luft reports that the growth in closed-panel enrollment produced no change in overall rates of hospitalization in Minneapolis, despite the creation of IPAs and reported lower rates of hospital use by their members.[97] Luft also finds evidence of market segmentation in the University of California experience.[98] The rate of increase in Blue Cross premiums was practically twice the increase in Kaiser premiums over the decade studied.

Luft finds it unlikely that cost differences alone could create such a sizable differential and concludes that Blue Cross was probably attracting an increasing proportion of high users of hospital care. If market segmentation rather than greater efficiency proved to be the major consequence of expanded choice, the costs of medical care would be shifted (from low to high users), not contained.

This analysis suggests caution in relying on the competing insurance plan strategy to achieve cost containment. The impact of insurer competition on medical costs is uncertain and difficult to predict. Even advocates of the competing plan strategy recognize that the massive changes it requires would take place gradually.[99] Although enhanced competition may indeed be desirable, in the short run, other mechanisms — especially changes in provider payment methods — would be necessary to contain costs.

All three national health insurance plans have adopted some elements of a market strategy. The Martin bill proposes the most extensive changes in current tax provisions in order to stimulate competition through increased cost sharing and HMOs. The bill proposes no changes in provider payment, making competition its only strategy for containing costs. The Carter plan makes fewer changes in tax treatment of insurance plan and encourages HMOs more than expanded cost sharing. In this plan, competition accompanies changes in provider payment as efforts to curtail costs. Of the three bills, the Kennedy-Waxman plan relies least on competition, eliminating cost sharing and establishing an extensive budgeting process to contain costs. Even the bill, however, includes incentives to individuals to seek lower cost insurance plans. The remainder of this section outlines the positions of the Carter, Martin, and Kennedy-Waxman bills with respect to competition among insurance plans and analyzes the likely effects of each plan's provisions on insurance coverage and service use.

The Martin Plan

Unlike the Carter and Kennedy bills, the Medical Expense Protection Act would not require employers to offer, or employees to purchase, insurance. The plan would provide strong incentives in this direction by maintaining the existing exclusion from taxable income of employer contributions up to $120 per month to qualified plans. If a firm chose to offer a qualified plan, the employer would be required to pay at least half the costs of its lowest-cost plan. The employer would not be required to offer employees a choice of insurance plans, but if more than one plan were offered the employer would be required to make equal contributions for employees regardless of the plan chosen. The employer would be required to provide rebates up to 75 percent of the difference between the fixed contribution and the cost of the selected plan. Rebates would not be subject to Social Security taxes and would be partially exempt from income taxes (i.e., rebates up to $100 per year would be exempt from income tax). To encourage employers to offer a choice of plans, including a low-cost, high cost-sharing option, the bill would allow employers to keep up to 25 percent of the difference between their premium contributions and actual premiums paid.

The plan contains several features intended to affect the market for insurance. Specifically, the plan would provide incentives for enrollment in plans with high cost sharing and in HMOs. To determine the effect of these incentives on costs of medical care, we have to assess how choices of insurance coverage would change in the aggregate.

Individuals whose employers now contribute more than $120 per month would probably choose lower-cost plans, because the contributions above $120 per month would be taxable as income under the plan. People who have a strong preference for comprehensive care might choose HMOs. The likelihood of HMO growth under these arrangements was discussed earlier. There is evidence that HMOs provide comprehensive care at lower cost than the traditional plan. If these results from past experience reflect efficiency and not careful risk selection, HMOs should be able to compete successfully by offering more benefits for a given premium. As already noted, there is limited evidence that HMOs have done well under choice arrangements with fixed, equal contributions. The main obstacle to substantial HMO growth would seem to be consumer resistance to changing physicians and to accepting the HMO style of care delivery. Families who prefer comprehensive care might find IPAs attractive in this regard, but IPAs might have more difficulty limiting the cost of premiums. Other types of closed panels are in experimental stages, and it is difficult to predict their likely availability or impact.

Individuals whose employers now contribute less than $120 per month would also have greater incentives to choose either HMOs or plans with high cost sharing. Many people, however, might end up with more comprehensive coverage than they now have. As was suggested earlier, employer contributions in many cases are likely to increase to the $120 level. Current contribution levels reflect a compromise in negotiations (implicit or explicit) over employee compensation, between employees who prefer less insurance and higher wages and others who prefer the opposite. The opportunity to choose levels of coverage would allow some employees to purchase more comprehensive insurance and others to purchase less and receive the difference as partially tax-exempt wages. Individuals and families wishing to avoid or to minimize risks could purchase more comprehensive coverage. Other employees could purchase plans with high cost sharing and receive a cash rebate. All employees would benefit from an increase in employer contributions to $120 per month.

The choice that families or individuals would make in large part would depend on the attractiveness of the rebate. The intention of the plan appears to be that a rebate would provide a monetary incentive to choose plans with higher cost sharing, thereby encouraging consumers to weigh costs against benefits as they use health care services. Given the intention, it is not clear why the incentives in the bill are not stronger. Employers could have been required to rebate all of the difference between the fixed contribution and the cost of the plan, though this might have discouraged employers from actively marketing multiple plans. The rebate could also be completely exempt from taxation. Failure to adopt these requirements encourages the choice of plans that cost $120 per month.

The apparent rationale for taxing the rebate is the fear of losing federal tax revenues. The result is less incentive to purchase policies with high cost sharing which the bill seeks to encourage. Moreover, low-income families, with low marginal tax rates, would benefit more from the rebate than would high-income families. Low-income families therefore would be more likely to choose plans with higher cost sharing than they now have. Higher-income families, which should be the ones encouraged to purchase plans with high cost sharing, would be less likely to alter their cost-sharing terms.

The plan intends that consumers should become more sensitive to the price of insurance: individuals choosing comprehensive coverage should pay for it; individuals choosing less comprehensive coverage should benefit financially. However, with experience rating, not only would the prices of insurance affect consumer choices, but also the prices of insurance would be affected by consumer choices. If relatively young and healthy families chose plans with high cost sharing, costs of those plans would be lower than if individuals and families representing a mix of risks chose such plans. Plans with high cost sharing would be available to high-risk groups, but at higher prices than are available to low- or mixed-risk groups. Similarly, if relatively unhealthy groups chose more comprehensive care, prices of plans for these groups would be higher than if groups with different risks selected comprehensive plans.

The fixed ceiling on tax-exempt employer contributions also means that low-risk groups would receive greater percentage contributions to their health insurance costs than would high-risk groups. The latter, to receive a comparable degree of coverage, would have to make greater supplementary payments. Alternatively, low-risk groups would receive greater rebates when choosing plans with high cost sharing. The effect of risk (health status) on choice of coverage would probably depend on income. Because employer contributions up to $120 per month would not be taxable while rebates remain less valuable the higher one's income, one would expect high-income individuals in any risk group to be more likely to choose comprehensive coverage. The likelihood of choosing comprehensive coverage should decline with income.

Somewhat similar problems exist for individuals and families living in different geographic areas. The fixed ceiling on tax-exempt employer contributions would permit different insurance packages in different areas. The maximum nontaxable contribution of $120 per month would permit purchase of more comprehensive coverage in areas with low hospital and medical care costs than in areas where costs are high. In high-cost areas, individuals and families would have to supplement employer payments to have the same degree of coverage, or they would choose less coverage (more cost sharing). In low-cost areas, families and individuals should be able to purchase quite comprehensive coverage for $120 per month. At the same time, the premium differential between plans with high and low cost sharing among areas should not differ among areas, so rebates would be larger in low-cost areas.

The effects on choice of coverage again should depend on relative incomes. Since families and individuals in low-cost areas have, on average, lower incomes and lower marginal tax rates than individuals in high-cost areas, their rebates would be larger, increasing their incentive to choose plans with high cost sharing. Despite the higher premium costs, the bias in the tax provisions should lead to more comprehensive coverage in high-cost areas, because these areas have higher per capita incomes. However, while high-income areas should have more comprehensive coverage than low-income areas, such coverage may be less comprehensive than it now is because of the limit of $120 per month on the exclusion of employer contributions from taxation.

The net result of the Medical Expense Protection Act would probably be fewer comprehensive insurance plans costing more than $120 per month. Persons whose employers now contribute less than $120 could change coverage in either direction. Some would probably increase coverage as employer contributions increase while others would probably reduce coverage to receive the rebate. On balance, the change in current tax provisions would probably be too little to greatly change the degree of coverage. Nonetheless, assuming equivalent levels of risk aversion, low-income families would be more likely than high-income families to have high cost sharing. Similarly, high-income localities would generally have more comprehensive insurance coverage than low-income areas.

This discussion has addressed ways in which the demand for insurance would respond to the tax provisions of the Martin bill and has neglected supplier or insurer behavior. With experience rating, insurers can adjust premiums to the expected costs of different groups. Although insurers might still avoid insuring certain high-risk groups, that type of competition would be less likely to occur under experience rating than with community rating. Competition among insurers would probably be centered upon search for the most attractive combination of benefit coverage, cost sharing, and premiums. The plan also would provide incentives for insurance firms to compete by controlling unnecessary utilization, or by restructuring provider payment systems to encourage physicians and hospitals to deliver services efficiently.

The Carter Bill

In both its Employer Guarantee and HealthCare plan, the Carter national health insurance bill would encourage consumer choice. The Employer Guarantee would require employers to permit employees to enroll in any federally qualified HMO in the area or to accept the firm's traditional insurance offering. The bill would require employers to pay an equal dollar amount toward all the insurance plans the firm offers. That amount would be set equal to the employer's share (at least 75 percent) of the premiums for the plan the firm identified as its "primary plan." If other plans cost less than the primary plan, the employer would be required to compensate the employee, in salary or fringe benefits, for the difference. The compensatory salary payment — or rebate — would be subject to personal income and payroll taxes.

The major ways the Carter bill would change current practice would be in expanding employees' choices of insurance plans and in rewarding employees for choosing a low-cost plan. Most employers do not now make equal contributions across all offered plans. As a result, employees do not bear the financial consequences of choosing a more costly plan or gain from choosing a less expensive plan. Equal contributions would give employees a greater incentive to consider costs in relation to benefits.

It is hard to predict what effect this incentive would have on the choice of plan. The bill's provisions encourage HMOs more than plans that require significant cost sharing. The Carter NHI bill would not require employers to offer plans with significant cost sharing. Indeed, it would support comprehensive coverage by allowing employers to supplement the mandatory maximum $2,500 deductible and by retaining open-ended tax exemptions for premiums. Although the bill would offer employees money or other fringe benefits if they chose a lower-cost, high-deductible plan, employers (and unions) might be reluctant to offer insurance that they perceive as an undesirable reduction in benefits. In addition, evidence from the Federal Employees Health Benefits Plan (though not perfectly analogous), indicates that employees may have a strong preference for comprehensive coverage. Only 16 percent of federal employees chose the low-option plan in 1977.[100] Employees might find a plan with more cost sharing attractive if rebates associated with the plan's lower premium exceeded the expected out-of-pocket medical expenses under the plan. The taxable status of rebates, however, reduces this possibility.

The Carter bill would require employers to offer employees an opportunity to enroll in HMOs as well as traditional insurance plans. Since the Carter plan would continue to exempt from taxation whatever amounts employers contributed to health insurance, employees who now offer comprehensive traditional insurance would probably choose that insurance plan as their "primary plan," setting contributions accordingly. Employees would find HMOs more attractive than the traditional plan if HMOs offered broader benefits at an equal or lower premium, or equal benefits at a lower premium. The primary advantages of HMOs over comprehensive traditional insurance have been the absence of cost-sharing requirements, the superior coverage of ambulatory care, and the provision of maternity and some preventive care. Under the Carter bill's mandatory benefit requirements, traditional plans would have to expand maternity and preventive benefits and would have ceilings on their cost-sharing requirements. Although this change would reduce HMOs' relative advantages, HMOs would nevertheless continue to offer the prospect of lower out-of-pocket payments (especially on ambulatory care) and presumably lower total costs than do traditional plans. Against this advantage, employees who already had physicians would have to weigh the cost of changing physicians, a significant cost that appears to have impeded HMO enrollment.[101]

Obviously, these benefits must be considered in relation to premium levels. If premiums in HMOs were higher than premiums in traditional plans, employees might choose to maintain their current insurance arrangement, preferring higher cost sharing to higher premiums. Employees who expected to use a lot of ambulatory care might opt for HMOs. If premiums in HMOs were lower than premiums in traditional plans, more employees could be expected to turn to HMOs. Relative premium levels differ somewhat by firm and area, making it difficult to assess likely results. The Congressional Budget Office reported that in 1978, average prepaid group practice (PGP) HMOs had family premiums of $95 per month, as compared with $107 per month for the Federal Employees high-option traditional plan.[102] The Carter plan's requirements for expanded benefits in traditional coverage would further increase the likelihood that HMO premiums would be less than those for traditional plans.

Overall, it is hard to predict what effect the Carter plan would have on enrollment in HMOs. Mandatory offerings and the opportunity for rebates should enhance HMOs' attractiveness. However, the bill would limit competition by maintaining open-ended tax exemptions for higher-cost plans and by taxing rebates. Perpetuation of these tax policies makes it unlikely that the Carter bill would induce major changes in the employer-based insurance market.

Like the Employer Guarantee plan, the Carter bill's HealthCare plan seeks to encourage individual choice, but HealthCare would not encourage a choice among insurance plans. The program would be the only insurer. Beneficiaries would choose among providers, one type of which is the health maintenance organization. HealthCare, like similar proposals for Medicare, aims to promote the use of HMOs on the assumption that they would cost the program less and provide beneficiaries more service than fee-for-service providers.

Two factors would influence the use of HMOs under the HealthCare plan: (1) the financial and benefit advantages of HMOs relative to fee-for-service would determine whether HealthCare beneficiaries would seek HMO enrollment; and (2) the way HealthCare would pay HMOs would determine whether HMOs would serve HealthCare beneficiaries. On the first point, HMOs would probably be most attractive to Medicare-equivalent beneficiaries (the elderly and disabled) who would continue to face cost-sharing obligations that HMOs might reduce. HealthCare beneficiaries below 55 percent of the poverty line might choose an HMO if it offered benefits superior to those from fee-for-service providers.

The willingness of HMOs to serve beneficiaries will depend on the way they are paid. In contrast to the Employer Guarantee plan, which would permit HMOs to charge what they please, HMOs could charge HealthCare beneficiaries only the actuarially determined equivalent to the cost-sharing obligations these people would face outside the HMO. Additional charges could be made for non-covered services but these too would be limited. The premiums that HealthCare pays would be a critical determinant of HMO participation.

HealthCare's approach to setting premiums (like Medicare's situation today) would differ from that of employers who are offering HMOs. Under the Carter bill, employers would pay a given amount toward health insurance. If HMO premiums exceeded that amount, individuals would pay the difference. Alternatively, if HMO premiums were below that amount, individuals would gain. Under HealthCare, individuals could not supplement government payments. If payments were low relative to HealthCare costs, HMOs (1) might not serve any HealthCare beneficiaries, (2) might limit service or reduce quality of care for HealthCare beneficiaries, or (3) might try to limit enrollment to low-risk beneficiaries. If government payments were high relative to HMO costs, the government would encourage HMO growth but might pay more for HMOs than the government would have had to pay for care in the fee-for-service system.

The Medicare program has long tried to find a payment method that would encourage HMO participation, assure adequate care, and keep costs below fee-for-service levels. Current proposals for Medicare payment are similar to the Carter bill's proposals for HMO payment under HealthCare. The Carter bill proposes to set payment rates to HMOs for HealthCare beneficiaries equal to 95 percent of the "adjusted average per capita cost" (AAPCC) of service to similar individuals in the area who are treated outside the HMO. Interim payments would be made to HMOs on a monthly basis but could be adjusted according to retroactive calculation of the AAPCC. If the payments made to the HMO exceeded an estimate of the premium it would have charged the beneficiary under a community rating system, the HMO would not be entitled to keep the difference as profit or to use at its discretion. Instead, the bill would require the HMO to add benefits equal in value to the difference.[103]

Like previous Medicare policies, this proposal reflects the government's ambivalence in dealing with health maintenance organizations. At the same time that the bill proposes to offer HMOs financial incentives to enroll HealthCare beneficiaries, it proposes to avoid the accumulation of what might be seen as excessive profits that would occur if HMOs engaged in cream skimming (enrollment of low-risk individuals). To limit the size of the HMO payments, the bill would tie HMO payments to fee-for-service costs for an allegedly comparable population. Because comparable populations are hard to find, the plan would impose constraints on HMOs' use of savings. The current Medicare approach, which limits the amount of savings HMOs can keep but does not restrict the use of savings, may therefore be preferable. The Carter plan approach would probably limit the growth of HMOs and discourage them from serving HealthCare beneficiaries.

The Kennedy-Waxman Bill

Like the Carter Employer Guarantee plan, the Kennedy-Waxman bill would offer individuals a choice among insurance plans. Unlike the Carter bill, the Kennedy-Waxman bill would offer all individuals the same type of choice. Options, however, would not include variations in cost-sharing requirements, for the bill would eliminate all cost sharing.

Plans could compete for enrollees by offering benefits not covered by the NHI plan and dividends or cash rebates to enrollees. Dividends and rebates would be exempted from income tax. Plans would pay for these benefits from the difference between their actual costs and the payments they received from their consortium. Consortium payments to insurers would be set to reflect average per capita costs for enrollees in the state (as reflected in the state budget), adjusted for area costs (as budgeted) and enrollees' actuarial risk (assessed according to age, sex, institutional status, disability status, etc.). New HMOs (less than five years old) might receive supplements to these payments if they submitted prospective budgets for state board approval. Supplements would pay for approved expenditures that exceeded premium revenues.

Under these rules, insurers and HMOs could incur costs below premium income if their administrative costs, payment rates, or total volume of services used were below the average rates for their area. New HMOs could also afford to pay rebates if their costs were below approved budgets.

With cost sharing precluded and provider payment levels constrained by government negotiations, competition among insurers and HMOs would probably focus on service use and administrative costs. In principle, service use could be limited by selecting favorable risks or by putting controls on service delivery.

The bill proposes actuarial adjustments in payments to insurers and HMOs to steer them away from the current competition to enroll low risks. Although the bill's provisions aim to align insurer revenues with the probable costs of their insured population, the proposed actuarial adjustments may not be sufficient to control for both obvious and subtle differences in factors affecting the use of health services. Other variables that probably would be highly correlated with beneficiaries' use of health services include presence and kind of chronic illness, income, education, marital status, and living arrangements. Control for all these variables would require extensive data and careful analysis. Failure to control for the most important of them, however, would result in crude estimates of appropriate premium income. If the consortium were to distribute premium income according to these crude estimates, an insurer with a low-risk population would profit, and the incentive to selectively insure low-risk populations would therefore remain. Capacity limits, discrimination in service, and location of providers are some of the mechanisms that insurers or HMOs could use to avoid high-risk enrollees, despite the bill's requirements that enrollment proceed on a first-come, first-served basis.

The likelihood of cream skimming, however, would be reduced by the Kennedy-Waxman bill's ceiling on total premium income and requirement that insurers divide that income among themselves. Because insurers would be competing against each other for a fixed amount, they probably would police each other's enrollment and service patterns carefully. If cream skimming were nevertheless to occur, it could affect the distribution of premium costs, perhaps reducing the net premium (income-related premium minus a rebate) for the healthy and increasing it for the sick. But unlike the Carter bill, the Kennedy-Waxman bill would limit individual premiums to the community average. Hence high risk individuals would be protected from the costs of significant market segmentation, if it occurred.

The control of health care expenditures through budget allocations to states and then to providers would leave limited room for insurers and HMOs to compete by controlling the price or quantity of services delivered. If hospital budgets were restricted, hospitals would control all utilization, not simply that of the most efficient insurer or HMO. By controlling fees as well as use of physicians' services, the plan in effect would create for all physicians an environment almost identical to that of an individual practice association HMO. As will be discussed in chapter 6, which analyzes physician reimbursement, all physicians would be penalized if utilization exceeded specified targets. Since all physicians participating in the NHI plan would be affected, specific insurers or HMOs would probably find it hard to control their costs by cutting utilization. Past HMO success has come from reducing utilization below that found in an unconstrained outside environment. By constraining that environment, the Kennedy-Waxman bill might make it hard even for HMOs to do better. Favorable risk selection could therefore become the most attractive route to profit making.

As the Kennedy-Waxman bill intends, insurers and HMOs also seem likely to compete on administrative efficiency. Under the current system, competition to enroll large employer groups appears to have constrained administrative costs. Under the Kennedy-Waxman bill, competition for enrollees will continue, encouraging administrative efficiency.

COST SHARING AND COST CONTAINMENT

The second major element of market-oriented strategies for controlling expenditures is patient cost sharing. Both the Carter and Martin bills would rely on cost sharing to increase consumers' cost consciousness in seeking and using medical care. The Kennedy-Waxman plan, in contrast, would specifically prohibit the use of prices for medical services as a cost-containment mechanism. This section reviews some of the evidence and arguments regarding the effects of cost sharing and analyzes the likely effects on service use of provisions of the three bills.

The architects of the Kennedy-Waxman bill reject cost sharing on the grounds that it is both an inequitable way to restrain medical care use and an ineffective mechanism for reducing inflation. With regard to equity, they fear that deductibles, coinsurance, or both impose relatively greater burdens on low-income families than on high-income families. As a result, it is argued, use of medical services varies not solely with illness but also with income. Karen Davis has provided evidence that Medicare's equal cost-sharing terms have supported continuing discrimination against (and reduced access to medical care for) the low-income elderly.[104] Enterline and associates have argued that the absence of cost sharing in Canadian national health insurance has eliminated this problem and in fact has redistributed physician services toward the poor.[105]

With regard to efficiency, critics of cost sharing argue that patients have insufficient knowledge to make rational calculations of benefits and costs of their medical choices and that physicians and other providers who presumably possess adequate information are only indirectly affected by the prices facing consumers. Cost sharing, it is argued, might deter people, especially the poor, from seeking necessary care early, thereby adversely affecting health and leading to greater use of services in the long run. The Kennedy-Waxman bill would substitute budgeting, reimbursement reform, and regulation for cost sharing to contain costs.

Eliminating cost sharing completely, however, would expand demand for services and thus increase pressure on the budgeting process. Newhouse, Phelps, and Schwartz have used evidence from available research on the demand for hospital and ambulatory care to estimate the effects of different NHI cost-sharing arrangements.[106] They estimate that an NHI plan offering full coverage could increase demand for inpatient services from 5 percent to 15 percent. Given current hospital occupancy rates, the authors argue that the capacity of the system would not be seriously strained. Thus, barring successful control through other mechanisms, increases in demand for inpatient services would probably be reflected in utilization. Because hospital inpatient services (including inpatient physician services) already account for approximately 55 percent of medical care expenditures, however, even these relatively small percentage increases would be quite important.

Because insurance now covers ambulatory services less comprehensively than it covers hospital care, the change in demand for ambulatory service that national health insurance would generate would be comprehensively greater than the change in demand for inpatient services. Increases in demand for ambulatory services, however, would probably not be translated into increases in utilization because of existing supply constraints. Newhouse and associates concluded that without cost sharing, the demand for ambulatory care would dramatically increase, and that other rationing devices, with their own cost implications, would have to be imposed. This rationing, they argued, could take the form of delays in obtaining appointments, increased waiting time, and reductions in the amount of time physicians spend with each patient.

Government control over budgets would not eliminate such rationing. If the public became dissatisfied with these rationing devices, they would probably press politically for expansion of services. Dissatisfaction could be expressed at the national level with requests for supplementary appropriations by Congress or locally with demands for supplementation by state or local governments. National supplementation would defeat the cost control objectives of the program; local supplementation would also affect equity of access across states or localities.

As argued previously, the Carter bill would probably do little to increase cost sharing among individuals insured through employment. For groups who are now uncovered or poorly covered by insurance, and for Medicare beneficiaries, cost-sharing obligations would decrease, not increase, under HealthCare. Most persons with little or no coverage would, at a minimum, have full coverage (i.e., no further cost sharing) once their expenses exceeded $2,500. Medicare beneficiaries will have no cost sharing beyond $1,250 of expenses. In sum, the prime effect of the Carter Employer Guarantee plan would probably be to retain (rather than to extend) existing cost-sharing requirements. The prime effect of the Carter HealthCare plan would be to cut the amount of cost sharing moderately. These changes in cost-sharing obligations appear unlikely to affect medical costs significantly.

Similarly, for reasons already given, the Martin plan would probably not result in dramatic increases in cost sharing. Some families and individuals would face more cost sharing, but others would face less. The absence of cost sharing for Medicaid beneficiaries would continue. The plan would eliminate cost sharing under Medicare's Part A and would remove Medicare's limitation on covered days. People who now have poor or inadequate insurance coverage would come under the Martin plan's catastrophic plan (CAPP). Although CAPP has fairly high income-related deductibles and coinsurance rates, its presence would expand coverage beyond what now exists. These families and individuals would still face substantial financial barriers to care before meeting their deductibles. But most of these people already face high cost sharing, so the net effect should be a reduction in cost sharing.

As the previous section noted, we would expect some increase in cost sharing from the changes in current tax provisions. The changes in the tax treatment of employer contributions, however, would not appear to be sufficient to cause major reductions in first-dollar coverage. Some families would choose less coverage; others would choose to increase coverage. The net effect should be to increase cost sharing, but by how much is uncertain.

The types of families changing coverage could reduce the apparent impact on service use. If policies with high cost sharing were chosen by families whose utilization rates tend to be low and comprehensive policies were chosen by families whose utilization rates tend to be high, the Martin plan might affect service demand much less than changes in coverage would lead one to predict. Similarly, for reasons already suggested, we believe that families in low-income areas would probably have, on average, less comprehensive policies (e.g., higher deductibles) than families in high-income areas. High income areas typically have more medical resources; thus the capacity to provide services would be abundant in the same geographic areas where money costs (at time of use) are low. Similarly, money costs should remain high in the areas where resources are more limited. So, utilization rates would probably be high in areas where they are now high and low where they are now low.

If a national health insurance bill were to go beyond the Martin bill's tax reforms — reducing the tax-exempt premium level and requiring a full, nontaxable rebate of differences between actual premium and employer contributions.[107] High-income as well as low-income families might find policies with high cost sharing attractive. Then service utilization rates might decline in areas where they are now high. Until consumers reached their deductibles, they might well be conservative in their use of medical care.

Although cost sharing would moderate the demand for some services, the effect of cost sharing on total expenditures is likely to be limited by the availability of protection against catastrophic costs in both the Carter and Martin plans (and most other bills promoting competition among insurance plans). To the extent that competing insurance plans emphasize high deductibles, cost sharing would affect only the demand for lower-cost services, particularly consumer-initiated primary care. Cost sharing would not constrain the resources devoted to the more expensive services (surgical and hospital care) for which costs exceed out-of-pocket ceilings. As long as a major share of provider revenue came from services beyond the ceiling, cost sharing would have a limited effect on total resource use. The Congressional Budget Office reported that, in 1978, hospitals earned more than 60 percent of their revenues from admissions in which expenditures exceeded $2,500 and that catastrophic expenditures are rising more rapidly than other medical expenditures.[108] This finding suggests that deductibles alone would have little impact on hospitals' delivery of services. To the extent that plans emphasize coinsurance (e.g., 20 percent paid by consumer), cost sharing would have a weaker effect on a larger share of provider resources. Cost sharing nevertheless can help other cost-containment mechanisms work, by keeping consumers aware of the need for insurer or government cost-containment measures.

SUMMARY

Critics of the private health insurance market have identified three problems in current arrangements: (1) the limited choice of plans that employers offer employees; (2) the unequal employer contributions across plans; and (3) the tax-exempt status of employer contributions to premiums. All three features of the current market reduce employees' sensitivity to the price of insurance and encourage the purchase of comprehensive coverage — thereby insulating consumers from the price of medical care. Each of the three NHI bills under examination addresses these concerns in a different way. Of the three, the Martin bill appears most likely to influence consumers to change their insurance coverage in ways that would alter their use of medical services.

The Martin bill proposes four major reforms: a limit on the monthly employer-paid premium that is exempt from taxes; an incentive to employers seeking such exemptions to offer employees a choice of insurance plans, including a plan with significant cost sharing; a requirement that these employers make equal contributions to employees' premiums regardless of the plan chosen; and a partial tax deduction for rebates that employees receive if they choose a lower-cost plan. These reforms would increase the attractiveness of insurance plans with high cost sharing and, to individuals who prefer comprehensive coverage, would increase the attractiveness of HMOs as relatively low-cost comprehensive plans.

The Carter bill proposes fewer reforms and therefore would have a more limited effect on insurance offerings. Because it would place no ceilings on tax-exempt employer contributions and would require only that employers offer HMOs in addition to their traditional plan, the bill would promote comprehensive plans more than plans with high cost sharing. The primary effect of the bill's mandatory offerings and taxable rebates would be to increase the attractiveness of HMOs relative to traditional insurance plans.

The Kennedy-Waxman plan would totally eliminate cost sharing and its relevance to the choice of an insurance plan. The bill's tax-deductible rebates, however, would nevertheless reward employees for choosing comparatively more efficient traditional plans or closed panels.

The impact of any of the bills' reforms on the use and price of medical care is hard to predict. Measures that would stimulate the development of HMOs and other closed panels offer the potential for more efficient service delivery. But realizing this potential would depend on massive behavioral changes that are too uncertain to predict. The effects of changes in cost sharing are somewhat more predictable. The Kennedy-Waxman bill's elimination of cost sharing would significantly expand the demand for services, putting considerable pressure on the budgeting and regulatory mechanisms the bill would establish to contain costs. The Carter bill would have little impact on current cost-sharing levels. The Martin bill might increase cost sharing among employed individuals who are already insured, but it would reduce cost sharing for the newly insured. If the bill were to strengthen its incentives for the selection of high cost-sharing plans, the net effect could be to reduce the demand for medical services, producing lower prices and lower total expenditures. Given limits on out-of-pocket expenditures, however, no change in cost sharing is likely to have a major impact on the use and total cost of high-priced services, especially hospital care.

Competition among insurance plans (with or without cost sharing), however, could affect the distribution of the cost of insurance. To minimize their premiums, relatively healthy individuals could choose lower-cost plans and insurers could compete for low-risk insureds. The result of this behavior would be that relatively healthy people will pay lower premiums than the relatively sick, reducing the risk spreading that insurance traditionally provides. The higher the reward to the individual for seeking a lower cost plan, the more likely such behavior becomes. The potential for fragmenting the market would be reduced but not eliminated through all the bills' requirements for open enrollment. The Kennedy-Waxman bill also would reduce the possibility that insurers would avoid high-risk individuals by relating insurer revenues to the health status of their insured population and encouraging insurers to police one another's behavior.

VI. PHYSICIAN REIMBURSEMENT

The method chosen to pay for physician's services has important implications for both cost control and access to care.[109] Both the Carter and the Kennedy-Waxman plans call for fee schedules. In the former plan, fee schedules would apply to HealthCare beneficiaries; in the latter, the fee schedule would apply to services received by everyone covered by the plan. The Carter plan would adjust the fee schedule annually, but it makes no provision for controlling or monitoring expenditures on physicians' services. The Kennedy-Waxman plan would directly control the rate of increase in physician expenditures through the budget-setting process. Beyond this, the plans are not very specific. The proposed use of fee schedules in both plans reflects widespread dissatisfaction with the "customary, prevailing, and reasonable" (CPR) charge systems employed by Medicare, many Medicaid programs and Blue Shield plans, and several commercial insurers. The Martin bill would not alter existing methods of paying physicians.

CPR systems typically limit reimbursements to the lowest (the reasonable) of the following: a physician's actual charge, the physician's median charge in a recent prior period (the customary charge), or the seventy-fifth (or other) percentile of charges in that same period by physicians in the same specialty and geographic area (the prevailing charge*). The principal advantages of CPR reimbursement have been its general acceptability to physicians and its flexibility. It has usually provided physicians generous reimbursement and it guarantees that fees will increase at rates largely within their control. The system is flexible in permitting rate differences among physicians on the basis of quality, location of practice, or scope of service. The system also permits relatively rapid adjustments to procedural and technological changes.

CPR systems have three main problems: they are administratively complex, they have inevitable inflationary consequences, and they reinforce what may be inappropriate price differentials. The administrative complexity of CPR systems is often underestimated. Determination of customary charges requires arraying all physicians' charges for each

---

*The Medicare program has termed *usual* charges as *customary* and *customary* charges as *prevailing*. Medicaid and most Blue Shield programs use the terms *usual* and *customary*.

procedure performed in a computation period. All excessively high or low charges are eliminated; the median charge for each procedure is identified and called the customary charge. All customary charges are then arrayed, and the 75th (or other) percentile is identified and called the prevailing. In practice, the system has proven quite difficult to implement and administer because of the complexity of the definition of "customary" charges and the substantial data manipulation required to calculate them.

The system has also permitted rapid escalation of fees. The customary and prevailing charge screens are updated annually through examination of the previous calendar year's billing behavior of physicians. Assuming that the system is enforced and that rates are annually updated, physicians always have a clear incentive to bill at a high rate. Submitting high actual charges will increase the individual physician's customary charge for the coming year. If replicated in the behavior of other physicians, this practice will increase the prevailing charge level used to set a ceiling on payment rates. Hence physicians have an incentive to bill not only at the maximum allowable charge (the plan's current reasonable fee), but actually at higher rates.[110]

Customary and prevailing charge systems also tend to sustain historical differences in charges and incomes among and within specialties and geographic areas — differences that may become inappropriate over time. The profile of customary charges will be determined by a physician's own pricing behavior. The profile of prevailing charges will depend on pricing patterns of all physicians in the group. Differences in fees among physicians may tend to change slowly and reflect historical considerations, including the length of practice and the insurance coverage of a physician's clientele when the customary and prevailing charge system began.

Fee schedules have certain clear advantages over customary and prevailing systems. First, the fee schedule approach has much greater potential to control costs because the payer at least would gain some control over unit prices.[111] Fee schedules in either the Carter or the Kennedy-Waxman plan would ultimately be based on a relative value schedule negotiated between physicians and either the federal government (Carter) or state governments (Kennedy-Waxman). This schedule would establish the value of all procedures relative to some chosen standard procedure. Once the system of relative values was established, the government would then determine the price or conversion factor for the standard procedure and consequently determine all prices. The government could control the rate of increase in the schedule or reduce some charges when a surplus of services exists while increasing or holding others constant. Because the rates of increase of conversion factors in a fee schedule would be administratively determined, with the availability of government funds being one criterion for setting rates, the mechanism for controlling rates would be inherent in the payment method.

Fee schedules also could help achieve purposes other than cost control. Unlike CPR profiles, which reinforce what may be undesirable relative prices established over time, fee schedules would permit the program to move toward certain redistributive objectives. In particular, fee schedules could be used to change the relative values given different procedures and to redistribute income among specialties and among physicians in geographic areas.

The main difficulty with fee schedules is that they do not permit variation in absolute or relative fees among individual physicians in a group. It would be hard to incorporate adjustments to the fee schedule for higher-quality service because there are no tangible measures of quality. Higher absolute levels of fees could be permitted for board-certified relative to non-board-certified specialists. But this practice would not capture many aspects of quality that a market, and perhaps a CPR, system might reward. It was noted above that CPR systems recognize differences in fees among physicians; some of these differences are justified on grounds of quality. To the extent they are not, however, CPR systems can be inequitable. By eliminating all differences in fees among physicians, fee schedules could also impose inequities.

One of the most difficult aspects of implementing a fee schedule would be the transition from current fee levels. At present, physicians' charges vary widely even within areas and within specialties. Uniform fee schedules might imply extreme changes, both up and down, for many physicians. The implications of this will become clearer by examining provisions of the Carter and Kennedy-Waxman bills separately.

THE CARTER PLAN

The Carter plan proposes fee schedules to pay physicians who treat patients covered under HealthCare. These physicians would be required to accept the HealthCare fee as payment in full for services rendered. Private plans would be encouraged but not required to use the HealthCare fee schedule. Insurance plans would also be required to provide enrollees with lists of physicians in the state who agree to accept the insurance plan's reimbursement as payment in full.

The Carter plan would set the HealthCare fee schedules initially at "average Medicare physician payment levels." This language is somewhat loose and it is not clear whether the plan envisages paying at the mean of Medicare customary charges, at the 50th percentile of customary charges, or whether area or specialty designations would be employed. The plan would probably adopt the current Medicare payment screens. Since 1976, Medicare has employed an "economic index" to control the rate of increase in prevailing charges (the maximums allowed physicians of a given specialty). Over time, Medicare's prevailing charges have fallen below the 75th percentile of customary charges. How far below varies with area and specialty. "Indexed prevailings" have been used in Medicare reimbursement since 1976, are readily available, and approach average customary charges. Thus, even though these are not average payments it is likely they would be adopted. This is the assumption made in the remainder of this section.

The Carter plan's provisions for physician reimbursement would affect the fees paid on behalf of different individuals in different ways. The differences result from variations in the current structure of fees and variations built into the Carter plan. Individuals who are now uncovered or poorly covered by insurance are generally unable to pay physicians' private charges; they therefore have access to relatively few physicians and, as a result, tend to obtain ambulatory services from hospital outpatient departments or emergency rooms.[112] Under the Carter plan, these individuals would be covered under HealthCare or the Employer Guarantee program. For people fully covered under HealthCare, payment at the fee schedule should dramatically increase access to private physicians, at least initially. For people covered under the Employee Guarantee program, payment levels would depend on the nature of the plan purchased by the employer. If the plan met only the minimum standards, the high deductible would limit their ability to pay physicians' charges. Many of these individuals would continue to use public hospitals for ambulatory care. Once the deductible was met, reimbursement would, of course, be at levels established by the plan.

Medicaid programs now pay physicians on the basis of customary and prevailing charges or fee schedules. Most of the larger states (e.g., California, New York, Massachusetts, Pennsylvania, New Jersey) use fee schedules. The HealthCare fee schedule would increase fees in virtually every state now using a fee schedule. Increasing the fees would increase physicians' willingness to serve these patients,[113] and reduce pressure on public sector outpatient departments and emergency rooms. Even in states with CPR systems, HealthCare fees would probably be higher than current payment levels. While there is variation among physicians in reimbursement rates in CPR states, current regulations do not permit Medicaid fees to exceed Medicare's. HealthCare would remove this restriction, improving access for Medicaid beneficiaries.

The effect on current Medicare recipients would be more complicated because of physicians' current freedom to choose to accept or to reject "assignment" on each individual procedure financed by Medicare. If "assignment" is accepted, the physician must accept as payment in full the allowable Medicare ("reasonable") charge for that procedure regardless of the actual charge billed. Under this arrangement, the patient pays the 20 percent cost-sharing amount on the Medicare reasonable charge (following payment of the deductible).

A physician who bills on a nonassignment basis is responsible for billing the patient, who then is reimbursed by Medicare. Under the nonassignment alternative, Medicare still reimburses only 80 percent of the reasonable charge (following payment of the deductible), but the physician can bill the patient for more than 20 percent of the reasonable charge. The patient's outlay is equal to 20 percent of the reasonable charge plus the full amount by which the actual exceeds the reasonable charge.

Physicians who do not accept assignment generally charge Medicare patients the same fees they charge other patients. Under the Carter plan, physicians would be required to accept HealthCare fee schedules as payment in full. For many physicians, the HealthCare fee schedule would be far below their normal private charges. Consequently, some of these physicians will refuse to participate in HealthCare. Current Medicare patients would as a result find their choice of physicians more limited under the new program. Some higher-income Medicare beneficiaries would choose to insure themselves privately and pay physicians' private charges. Others would have to find new physicians willing to accept the HealthCare fee. Out-of-pocket costs for these patients would be reduced because patients would no longer have to pay the difference between the physicians' actual and reasonable charges.

Physicians who accepted assignment prior to enactment of national health insurance would not have their fees significantly changed. We have assumed that HealthCare would use current indexed prevailing fees (which act as ceilings on current Medicare payment) as the fee schedule. By definition, this means that national health insurance would pay equal or higher amounts in all cases. Many physicians whose pre-NHI Medicare customary charges were below the fee schedule would have their fees increased. These physicians could increase the proportion of Medicare patients in their practice and absorb some of the effect of the reduced participation mentioned above.

Individuals insured privately before enactment of national health insurance should not experience much change in the fees paid on their behalf. Insurers would be asked to use the HealthCare fee schedule as a guide and to provide information to beneficiaries on physicians who accept the fee schedule, but there is no evidence that this would be effective in moderating fee inflation since patients would have little incentive to economize. Private fees should increase because of the increased insurance coverage.

Although the mandated plans contain high deductibles, no one would have worse insurance than at present, many would have improved coverage, and all would have full coverage after the deductible was met. Offsetting this to some degree would be the reduced demand from the Medicare nonassigned population, but this would be a small group relative to the entire population. Private fees thus should continue to vary among physicians even within areas and within specialties. Privately insured individuals and families will provide an attractive alternative to the HealthCare fee schedules for many physicians. For others, the HealthCare fee schedule would probably become their minimum charge.

This upward pressure on fees is likely to cause problems for the Carter plan administrators. If private fees increase over time because of improved insurance and general inflation, the plan would have to increase the HealthCare fee schedules to assure access for HealthCare beneficiaries. Failure to raise fees would create a two-class system, with a smaller and smaller number of physicians willing to accept HealthCare patients. The large number of individuals covered by the Employer Guarantee program plus the potential for increased utilization among a well-insured population would probably permit many physicians to practice outside HealthCare. Without increases in HealthCare fees, many HealthCare patients would either go without care or rely on hospital outpatient facilities — both of which courses could increase costs over time and lead to inefficient resource use.[114] On the other hand, continuously increasing public fees to stay close to private fees adds to medical care inflation. To simultaneously control fee inflation and maintain access for HealthCare beneficiaries, the plan would eventually have to control both public and private fees.[115]

THE KENNEDY-WAXMAN PLAN

The Kennedy-Waxman bill would employ fee schedules initially based on the maximum reimbursement rates under Medicare, presumably Medicare's indexed prevailing charges. The bill would allow these reimbursement rates to be adjusted in three ways: First, relative value scales could be used to adjust relative fees if Medicare rates were judged not to reflect the time required, the level of skill involved, the cost of providing services, or the cost-effectiveness of the services. Second, Medicare fees would be adjusted among areas to reflect the relative costs of practice, relative earnings of nonphysicians, rates of change in fees, and need to encourage provision of services in underserved areas. Finally, when individuals in two or more health personnel categories are qualified to perform a service, the maximum fee for the service would be that for the lowest-paid category.

Each of these discretionary adjustments would move the structure of fees under national health insurance away from their current distribution under Medicare. They call for many complex judgments; how they would be made is difficult to predict. However, the likely implications of the general provisions of the Kennedy-Waxman plan can be discussed. First, as with the Carter plan, use of a fee schedule would eliminate most of the inter-physician differences in fees within areas and specialties. Second, because the same fee schedule would apply to all individuals and families, physicians would have no incentive to treat rich and poor differently — a major change from the differential incentives of the present payment system or the Carter plan.

Individuals who are now uncovered or poorly covered would have full coverage under Kennedy-Waxman. Payment at Medicare fee levels would mean a large increase in collectible fees for physicians who serve these individuals. The same reasoning applies to individuals now covered by Medicaid because rates paid under the Kennedy-Waxman plan would be higher than those now paid under Medicaid. In general, private physicians should respond to the opportunity for higher income by treating more of these people, which would reduce the use of care at hospital outpatient departments and emergency rooms.

Physicians who now accept assignment under Medicare would experience no overall change in fee levels in serving the elderly under national health insurance, but their fees would be adjusted by the guidelines mentioned above. Physicians who do not now accept assignment would receive lower fees from the Kennedy-Waxman plan than they do now for serving the elderly and all others, in some cases much lower. But these physicians would have less reason to discriminate among patients in their practice. Although they could practice outside the NHI plan if they chose, inside the plan they would receive the same fees from all patients. This should reduce any preferential treatment of high-income elderly.

The Kennedy-Waxman plan would have somewhat the same effect on privately insured individuals. Because a large number of physicians' private fees are higher than Medicare prevailing fees, the Kennedy-Waxman plan would mean a reduction in fees for many physicians, and probably some loss of income for those with well-insured clients. There would be less reason for physicians to favor privately insured individuals over previous Medicare, Medicaid, or uncovered patients. Thus, private high-income patients' access to care relative to the access of the elderly and the poor should decline.

This outcome would depend largely on the extent to which physicians participated in the plan. If many physicians chose not to participate and maintained large practices for treatment of privately insured patients, the dual objectives of equal access and cost control would be defeated. The Kennedy-Waxman plan would permit physicians to practice outside the plan, but NHI patients would receive no reimbursement from the plan for services from physicians who accepted *any* private patients. In other words, the bill would require that practices be either fully participating or nonparticipating. Pressure on physicians to participate would obviously be great under this arrangement, but because participation could sharply reduce some physicians' incomes and autonomy, physicians would probably fiercely resist enactment and implementation of an all-or-nothing participation rule. Moreover, because the plan also might inhibit patients' ability to purchase preferential treatment, high-income individuals also might oppose this approach. This opposition makes enactment of the proposed arrangement unlikely.

An alternative arrangement, under which physicians could participate for some of their patients and also serve patients outside the plan, would also probably encourage a high level of physician participation. Given the tax burden inevitable with enactment of the Kennedy-Waxman program, coupled with the progressive income tax system, relatively few patients could afford the luxury of financing care wholly outside the system. This would be particularly true if medical expenses were no longer tax deductible. Thus, even if physicians could operate both outside and inside the plan, outside practice would probably be relatively small.

Strong inducements for participation in the plan would not in themselves end pressures for fee inflation. For example, physicians, once bound by a unified system, would doubtless press to make fees reasonably generous. Serious efforts toward de facto or de jure unionization of providers of medical care might be expected (particularly in light of the negotiations expected to set fees), with possible threats of physician strikes against the system. These threats might persuade the government to make substantial payment concessions in order to avoid disruption or widespread disaffection with the program. The system's objectives would also be threatened if side payments to physicians for preferential treatment became commonplace. If queue jumping through supplementary payments were to become an accepted, though illegal, procedure, objectives of equal access would be defeated.

Even if most physicians were to agree to accept government rates of payment, physicians' responses to fee constraints could impede cost containment. Unlike most providers of goods or services, physicians can influence to some degree the demand for their own services, particularly when their patients face zero prices. If, in response to reduced fees, physicians could increase the volume of services they provided in order to maintain their real incomes, it would become more difficult for fee controls to limit total expenses.

The Kennedy-Waxman plan would respond to this problem by setting annual budgets for physicians' services and by tying the rate of increase in the fee schedule to targets for increases in the annual budgets. In the Kennedy-Waxman plan, as in individual practice association HMOs, physicians would be paid on a fee-for-service basis, but the total funds available for physicians' services would be established in advance. Note that the amount available for all physicians' services would be capped; individual physicians' earnings would not be directly limited. Caps on individuals' incomes would provide obvious incentives to physicians to cease working, except in emergencies, after they had reached the maximum. While reimbursement for services would be determined by a fee schedule, if total billing exceeded the allocated budget, proportionate reductions in total payments to all physicians would be made. Physicians themselves, not the government, would bear the burden of excessive service provision.

Coupling fixed budgets with fee-for-service reimbursements would present several problems. First, the appropriate amount to be budgeted for physicians' services might be hard to determine. The current level of expenditures for physicians' services would provide poor guidance because it is the dissatisfaction with current experience that created the need for reform. Setting appropriate budget levels for different parts of the country would require not only detailed information on morbidity and utilization patterns, but also informed judgments about the appropriateness of particular utilization patterns that deviate from acceptable norms. That is, as a matter of social equity, high-cost areas should not receive larger budgets than low-cost areas on the basis of higher utilization rates, if those higher rates reflect "excessive" provision of services where physician-population ratios are high. As a practical matter, actual reduction of expenditures in high-cost areas is very unlikely.

Budgeting is probably most feasible if the plan were to simply accept existing expenditure levels in different areas and apply limits to the rates of increase in current expenditures. Once a decision has been reached on a target rate of increase in physicians' incomes for the coming year, fee increases to provide for some share of the increase in incomes would be allowed. The balance of the increase in physicians' incomes would be expected to come from increased service provision and intensity. If utilization increases should exceed the anticipated rate, fees would be constrained even more in the next year. For example, the West German government entered into an arrangement in 1976 under which fees would rise by approximately 2 percent in 1976 and 4 percent in 1977, assuming utilization increased by no more than 6 percent and 4 percent respectively. If utilization should increase at faster rates, fees would be cut so that the target rate of increase in ambulatory service expenditures was not more than 8 percent. Quebec has formally adopted a comparable system. In the rest of Canada, fee increases — both absolute rates of change as well as equalization among specialties — are informally tied to desired changes in incomes.

The second potential problem in fixed budget arrangements is that each physician would have an incentive to overprovide, because an individual could profit if his or her provision exceeded that of other physicians, so that the individual's increased number of fees outweighed the losses from the pro rata reductions. In other words, physicians responsible for excessive provision would be remunerated for those services, while pro rata reductions would apply to all physicians in proportion to total billings. The program or physicians themselves would have to carefully monitor utilization patterns to control unnecessary services and to create equity in physician remuneration. Organizations similar to the Professional Standards Review Organizaton might be strengthened by these incentives. Conversely, failure to monitor the system carefully would probably create resentment toward the program on the part of those physicians who had not abused it.

Lessons from Canada

The systems adopted by the Canadians, comparable in most respects to the Kennedy-Waxman plan, appears to have given the government effective control over fees and "demand creation" by physicians. Table 19 provides data on changes in physicians' earnings, in the populations of physicians, and in expenditures for physicians' services by Canadian provinces before and after enactment of national health insurance. Data cover various years between 1958 and 1976, depending on when national health insurance was implemented in each province. Annual compound rates of growth are presented for four-year intervals, both before and after national health insurance. All financial data are stated in 1970 dollars. In order to eliminate the one-time effect of converting to national health insurance, the transition year was excluded from one set of calculations.

Probably the most striking numbers in this table are the declines in physicians' net real incomes in the post-NHI years. If the transition year is excluded from the calculations, the rates of growth during the period after implementation of national health insurance are negative in every province, ranging from -2.37 percent to -6.56 percent per year.

Section B of the table indicates that the population of active, fee-practice physicians grew at extremely high rates, both before and after national health insurance. Annual increases were between 2 percent and 10 percent per year, with most greater than 5 percent per year. In the United States, by contrast, the physician population grew at between 1 percent and 2 percent per year during the 1960s and early 1970s.

Finally, Section C shows that expenditures for physicians' services grew more rapidly in the pre-NHI years than in the post-NHI period. It also illustrates the major impact of the transition year on calculations of average annual expenditure increases. When the transition year is included, growth rates jumped in some cases by as much as a factor of four or five. It appears therefore that, while expenditures continued to grow at a moderate rate, the increases were caused primarily by the large planned expansion in the number of physicians.[116]

Table 20 provides additional data on expenditures for physicians' services in Canada and the United States. The upper half of the table shows expenditures as a percent of the gross national product in each country. In 1960, the United States spent about 22.6 percent more of its GNP for physicians' services than did Canada (1.14 percent and 0.93 percent, respectively). By 1971, when national health insurance was fully implemented in Canada, the gap between the two countries closed by two-thirds, to 7.6 percent. Following conversion to national health insurance, however, the share of Canadian GNP going to physicians dropped dramatically, from 1.31 percent in 1971 to 1.09 percent in 1976. Over the same time period, the United States, which has neither fee controls nor universal and comprehensive health insurance, increased its spending for physicians' services to 1.75 percent of GNP, or approximately 60 percent more than Canada spent. It also is interesting to note that Canada increased its supply of physicians relative to the United States over the sixteen-year span summarized in table 20.

The early 1970s were a period of rapid general price inflation in Canada, as they were in the United States. During this time, physicians' fees were strictly controlled. Rising prices for supplies, office help, and space, combined with controlled fees, probably helped to erode physicans' net incomes. This effect apparently was reinforced by the extremely rapid rates of growth in the physician population, both before and after NHI implementation in Canada. Thus, whatever ability physicians have had to create demand seems to have been at least partially offset by rising input prices, increases in the number of physicians, and the

111

Table 19

ANNUAL COMPOUND RATES OF GROWTH (PERCENT PER YEAR) IN PHYSICIANS' NET INCOME, POPULATION OF PHYSICIANS, AND REAL EXPENDITURES ON PHYSICIANS' SERVICES, BY CANADIAN PROVINCE, BEFORE AND AFTER IMPLEMENTATION OF NATIONAL HEALTH INSURANCE

(1958-76)

	Alberta	British Columbia	Manitoba	New Brunswick	Newfoundland	Nova Scotia	Ontario	Prince Edward Island	Quebec	Saskatchewan
Date NHI implemented	July 1, 1969	July 1, 1968	Apr. 1, 1969	Jan. 1, 1971	Apr. 1, 1969	Apr. 1, 1969	Oct. 1, 1969	Dec. 1, 1970	Nov. 1, 1970	July 1, 1962
Transition year	1970	1969	1969	1971	1969	1969	1970	1971	1971	1963
A. Net Physician incomes (in 1970 dollars)										
Pre-NHI	4.78%	1.10%	2.97%	2.64%	2.65%	2.24%	2.82%	1.70%	0.55%	-2.42%
Post-NHI										
Includes transition year	-4.90	-1.57	-1.63	-6.41	-2.46	0.80	-5.62	-7.46	-5.77	-2.33
Excludes transition year	-5.70	-2.37	-6.21	-6.56	-3.62	-3.16	-6.15	-5.20	-4.92	-3.74
B. Physician population										
Pre-NHI	9.92	9.62	5.74	10.59	9.92	8.95	7.70	7.20	7.07	2.34
Post-NHI										
Includes transition year	5.52	8.34	5.78	8.96	7.53	8.44	5.71	5.47	8.90	6.30
Excludes transition year	5.10	8.06	4.11	5.77	5.63	6.05	4.70	6.10	5.87	4.05
C. Expenditures (in 1970 dollars)										
Pre-NHI	13.35	8.67	5.89	8.65	-10.31	7.55	9.49	7.56	5.00	N.A.
Post-NHI										
Includes transition year	3.41	6.61	4.57	3.13	5.30	9.11	3.23	0.22	3.42	2.62
Excludes transition year	2.41	5.78	-0.82	0.51	0.93	3.59	1.74	4.46	2.08	2.13

Note: This table shows four-year periods before and after implementation of NHI in each province.

Sources: Health and Welfare Canada, *Earnings of Physicians in Canada*, and unpublished statistics from Health and Welfare Canada.

Table 20

EXPENDITURES FOR PHYSICIANS' SERVICES AS A PERCENTAGE OF GROSS NATIONAL PRODUCT, CANADA AND THE UNITED STATES
(1960-76)

	1960	1965	1970	1971	1972	1973	1974	1975	1976
Expenditures for Physicians' Services as a Percentage of GNP									
Canada	0.93%	0.98%	1.20%	1.31%	1.31%	1.19%	1.12%	1.15%	1.09%
United States	1.14	1.37	1.36	1.41	1.49	1.43	1.41	1.69	1.75
Number of Active Physicians per 100,000 Population									
Canada	81	84	93	99	104	106	110	114	116
United States	137	143	147	154	154	154	156	159	162

Sources: Canadian Medical Association, Statistics, Systems and Economic Research Unit, Quick base (February 1977). DHEW, "National Health Expenditures," *Social Security Bulletin* (selected issues).
Health and Welfare Canada, "Earnings of Physicians in Canada, 1953-1973," and unpublished data. Population data from *Statistics Canada*.
U.S. Department of Health, Education, and Welfare, A Report to the President and Congress on the Status of Health Professions Personnel in the United States, DHEW Publication No. (HRA) 79-93, August 1978. Population data from *The United States Statistical Abstract*, 1978.

tying of fee increases to expenditure objectives under national health insurance.

THE MARTIN PLAN

The Martin Plan would change current methods of reimbursing physicians only for individuals covered under the catastrophic insurance program (CAPP). Reimbursement methods now used by private insurance and Medicaid would not be changed. Except in emergencies, however, CAPP subscribers would have to obtain all services from participating physicans. Participating physicians would be required to accept CAPP reimbursement as full payment for services provided to plan beneficiaries. In general, the Medicare reimbursement method would apply to CAPP, but that plan would pay 100 percent (rather than 80 percent) of Medicare reasonable charges once out-of-pocket limits were reached. Similarly, CAPP would make certain changes to Medicare procedures for the purpose of increasing fees and encouraging participation in the program. CAPP would calculate physicians' fee profiles and prevailing charges more frequently and on more current data than occurs under Medicare. The economic index that Medicare now uses would not apply for CAPP reimbursement. Finally, physicians participating in CAPP could be reimbursed in the same way for their Medicare patients — payment in full at CAPP rates.id general price inflation in Canada, Privately insured individuals should experience no change in the methods of payments their plans employ on their behalf. CAPP could result in upward pressure on physician fees, which would adversely affect privately insured individuals either directly or indirectly through premium increases. The Martin bill would not formally add anything to present constraints on private fees.

Unlike the Carter and Kennedy-Waxman plans, the Martin bill would leave Medicaid untouched. Physician fees would remain at levels determined by the states. Problems of access to private physicians which Medicaid beneficiaries have experienced in many states would probably continue.

Fees paid on behalf of Medicare beneficiaries would on average be higher. Medicare beneficiaries whose physicians did not participate in CAPP would experience no change in their Medicare fees. Medicare beneficiaries with physicians who did participate in CAPP, however, would experience changes in their Medicare reasonable charges. Persons whose physicians now accept assignment would have higher fees paid on their behalf because of the more frequent updating and because the economic index would not be applied to prevailing charges. These beneficiaries would probably have access to more physicians but would also have greater coinsurance payments. The effect on those beneficiaries whose physicians do not now accept assignment would depend on whether the CAPP provisions induced them to accept assignment. Physicians' fees under Medicare would be constrained only by non-indexed prevailing charges. In effect, Medicare prevailing charges would increase. If physicans accepted assignment, beneficiaries would pay higher coinsurance charges but would no longer pay the difference between the physicians' charge and the Medicare reasonable charge. In most cases, beneficiaries would be better off. If physicians did not accept assignment, Medicare prevailing charges would remain at current levels. Physicians would charge their normal fee and beneficiaries would be responsible for the difference between that fee and the Medicare reasonable charge, as is now the case.

The Martin plan would exercise decidedly weaker control over physician fees than would either the Kennedy-Waxman or Carter bills. The Martin plan's probable net effect on physicians' fees would be inflationary. The plan would result in some reduction in first-dollar coverage, which would increase consumer resistance to high fees. Market forces might constrain charges to some degree. Offsetting this, however, would be the use of Medicare payment methods for CAPP services without Medicare's economic index. The continued general absence of formal controls on private insurance fees, coupled with relatively weak controls on Medicare fees for many physicians and on all CAPP fees, should add to the inflationary pressure on physicians' fees.

SUMMARY

Each plan's physician reimbursement policies would affect people's access to medical care and the rate of expenditure increases under national health insurance. The Martin bill would adopt a customary, prevailing, reasonable (CPR) payment system for its public catastrophic plan. The result would be relatively generous levels of payment that should improve access to care for persons not now insured. The bill would offer the same generous rates to physicians treating Medicare patients, most likely improving access to care for Medicare eligibles. The Martin bill would not change fees now paid by Medicaid programs and private insurance plans. Relatively generous payment by CAPP and Medicare, however, would make physicians less willing to treat Medicaid patients. The Martin plan would not directly affect access to care for privately insured persons, but public payment rates would probably become a floor for fees charged privately-insured patients.

Use of the CPR payment method would guarantee that public fees would increase at rates physicians controlled, and public fee increases wound encourage increases in private rates of payment. The Martin bill would allow this fee escalation as a means of improving access to care for the poor and the elderly. The inflationary effects of the bill's CPR payment system would be mitigated but not eliminated by the bill's reforms of employer-provided insurance. As was argued earlier, these reforms would probably increase cost sharing and sensitivity to fees among persons now insured.

Because of the inflationary effects of the CPR payment system, the Carter and Kennedy-Waxman bills instead propose the adoption of fee schedules, which would allow government to control the unit prices for medical care. The Carter bill would adopt a fee schedule only for its HealthCare plan and leave fees paid by private insurance plans untouched. The HealthCare fee schedule would mean higher rates of payment for services delivered to persons now uninsured and for current Medicaid recipients. These higher rates should improve these groups' access to care. The bill's terms of payment might, however, reduce the number of physicians willing to treat the elderly. Since the bill would control fees for public but not private patients, all HealthCare beneficiaries might have more difficulty obtaining medical care than would privately insured persons. A two-class system could be prevented if public fees kept pace with private fees. If private fees increased over time as a result of better insurance and general inflation, increases in physician expenditures would be required to assure continued access to care.

The Kennedy-Waxman plan proposes to avoid this problem by adopting a single fee schedule which would apply to all citizens and legal residents. Adoption of equal rates could equalize access to care for all citizens, regardless of income. The proposed rates would be higher than current Medicaid fees and lower than Medicare fees to physicians who do not accept Medicare's rates as payment in full. They would also be lower than fees paid by private insurance plans. If these fees were adopted, physicians might reject participation in the plan. The availability of non-participating physicians would mean better access to care for high-income persons willing to pay physicians' fees (or private insurance premiums) as well as the plan's mandatory premiums. Few people are likely to make this choice. Alternatively, physicians might wield enough political power to assure that the plan adopted rates higher than those now proposed.

Even if most physicians were to participate in the plan at the proposed rates, fee control would not constitute expenditure control. To control total expenditures, the Kennedy-Waxman bill would have to limit the volume as well as the price of physicians' services. If, in a given year, the volume of services at scheduled fees produced expenditures that exceeded a predetermined total budget, fees would be reduced in the following year. Implementing this arrangement would entail the difficult tasks of determining appropriate total budgets, enforcing budgetary ceilings, and policing the delivery of services by individual physicians. Evidence from Canada suggests, however, that rates of increase in physicians' incomes can be controlled.

VII. HOSPITAL COST CONTAINMENT

Hospital expenditures are the largest and the most rapidly rising component of total national expenditures on acute medical care. Between 1968 and 1978, community hospital expenditures increased at an average annual rate of 15 percent.[117] Expenditures per day of hospital care increased at an average annual rate of 13.4 percent,[118] compared with a rate of 7.2 percent for prices for all services. Hospital expenditures increases reflect changes in the prices of goods and services that hospitals buy and in the nature and volume of services hospitals provide. According to the Congressional Budget Office, the relatively rapid rate of increase can be explained by increases in the rates of admitting patients that exceed the rate of increase (or the rate of aging in the population; by price increases for purchased goods and services that exceed the Consumer Price Index; and by increases in the quantity and sophistication — or intensity — of services provided per patient day.[119]

Rising insurance premiums and public expenditures on hospital care have led people to question whether hospital care is worth its price.[120] Critics have identified substantial waste and inefficiency in the hospital industry — specifically, inattention to prices of purchased goods and services, construction and maintenance of unnecessary beds, duplication of expensive equipment, and excessive — even harmful — service delivery. Even where expenditures are not clearly unnecessary, hospitals have little incentive to compare the benefits and costs of service expansion. To the extent that individuals are insured and insurers pay incurred costs, hospital administrators, physicians, and patients have every reason to seek expansion of services as long as they provide some positive benefit. As a result, the dollars spent on hospital expenditures may exceed the value of benefits derived.

Third-party payment policies have facilitated increases in the volume and intensity of hospital services. Although not everyone is insured against all hospital expenses, anyone with private health insurance is likely to have some protection against hospital bills. In combination, private and public hospital insurance now provide more than 90 percent of hospitals' revenues. Extensive third-party payment reduces consumers' concerns about service costs, simultaneously reducing constraints on hospitals' revenues. If third parties also are unconcerned about costs, hospitals have virtually open-ended access to funds. In practice, third parties have been reluctant to set limits on payments to hospitals and have paid either the costs hospitals incur in delivering care or charges as set by the hospitals. These payment mechanisms have provided hospitals and their medical staffs with the revenues to expand services as they see fit, with little regard to costs.

Both the Carter and the Kennedy-Waxman bills propose new approaches to hospital payment, in which the government rather than providers decides how much to spend on hospital care. Sponsors of both NHI bills, in fact, have joined in support of cost-containment legislation independent of enactment of national health insurance. Although Congress rejected this cost-containment legislation, the Carter administration regarded its separately introduced cost-containment bill as an integral part of its NHI plan. As the next section points out, the bill would set voluntary guidelines for hospital expenditure increases and, if hospitals exceeded guidelines, limits on hospital revenues per admission. Our discussion of this bill is complicated by the fact that national health insurance would change the third-party payment structure on which it now rests. The overall approach is nevertheless distinct from the Kennedy-Waxman proposal, which would replace the current payment system with prospective hospital budgets, set within the plan's overall budget for health care. In contrast to the Carter and Kennedy-Waxman bills, the Martin bill would adopt Medicare's current approach to hospital payment and make no attempt to reduce its recognized encouragement of inflation. This section focuses on these differences among the bills and their implications for hospital behavior.

THE CARTER PLAN

Although widespread hospital insurance means there are now few constraints on the demand for hospital care, the Carter bill's coverage provisions would reduce remaining constraints and provide further revenues to the hospital sector. The Carter bill's HealthCare program would increase insurance coverage among the poor, assuring payment for care delivered to people who previously lacked adequate insurance. The assurance of payment would expand revenues available to hospitals to the extent that newly covered people would seek more care than they do now or that payments under HealthCare either compensated for private hospitals' current bad debts or exceeded payments now made to public hospitals by or for these patients. HealthCare-covered individuals above the income standard would face a $2,500 deductible that would deter some admissions or produce unpaid bills. Yet the promise of payment above the deductible would encourage hospitals to accept these patients more readily than they do now.

The Carter Employer Guarantee would expand payments to hospitals for persons whose insurance coverage before enactment of national health insurance had limitations on days of hospital coverage, benefits per hospital day, and coverage of ancillary services, including physician care. (Medicare beneficiaries would fall into this category.) Information is not available on the way limits on insurance coverage now affect hospitals' treatment of patients. Professional ethics (and the opportunity to pass bad debts on to other payers) would probably ensure that, once admitted, patients would receive the level and duration of care they required, regardless of ability to pay. But limits on insurance coverage might inhibit desirable — if not essential — intensity or duration of service. The costs of treating the very ill already seem to be rising more rapidly than other health care costs. Some critics fear that catastrophic insurance would further skew investment toward life-extending and other sophisticated techniques that are of greater value to the affected individual than to society.[121]

The Carter Cost-Containment Provisions

The Carter plan's hospital cost-containment provisions are intended to limit hospitals' capacity to spend. The cost-containment bill has two parts — voluntary expenditure guidelines and mandatory revenue controls.[122] A voluntary guideline would limit the annual rate of increase in national hospital expenditures. The national guideline would be composed of the actual rate of increase in prices of goods and services that hospitals purchase (the hospital marketbasket), the actual rate of increase in the nation's population, and an increase of at least 1 percent to allow for changes in the intensity of service. If the actual rate of increase in hospital expenses nationwide were less than or equal to the voluntary limit, no mandatory controls would be imposed.

If expenses exceeded the national limit, two further tests would determine the application of mandatory controls. The bill would establish a voluntary guideline for each individual hospital, comprising each hospital's actual rate of increase in nonsupervisory wages, area price increases for the hospital's other goods and services, the rate of increase in the state's population, and the same intensity allowance as in the national guideline. Each hospital's actual rate of expenditure increase would be compared to its guieline. Differences would be tallied for all the hospitals in a state. If the amounts by which some hospitals in the state exceeded their guidelines were offset by amounts below the guidelines for other hospitals, no hospitals in the state would be subject to mandatory controls. (Hospitals would also be exempt from federal controls if their state had in effect its own rate control program that satisfied the specific structural and performance requirements discussed below.) If excess expenditures were not offset, mandatory controls would be imposed only on the hospitals that exceeded their guidelines.

Mandatory controls would set ceilings on the allowable rate of increase in revenues per admission, rather than total expenses. Small, nonmetropolitan hospitals, HMO hospitals, and new hospitals would be exempt from controls. Revenue controls would apply to each payer separately. Under current financing arrangements, that would mean that average payments per admission by cost-payers (Medicare, Medicaid, and, often, Blue Cross), and average charges per admission could each increase by no more than the allowed rate. Unlike the guidelines, the mandatory controls would not apply to outpatient services and would not include an intensity factor in the allowed rate of increase. The allowed rate of increase for each hospital would be set by calculating the increase in each hospital's nonsupervisory wage rates and in area prices for each hospital's other goods and services. The resultant rate would be adjusted for the following: efficiency (a bonus of up to 1 percentage point or penalty of up to 2 percentage points, based on a comparison of each hospital's costs to similar hospitals' costs); the percentage by which expenditures exceeded the guideline (to be subtracted from the percentage allowed under the mandatory controls); and the marginal cost associated with changes in admissions. At a hospital's request, the Secretary of the Department of Health and Human Services could make further adjustments to the allowed rate to account for changes in admissions; changes in case mix; changes in capacity or service (including renovation or replacement) if approved under the provisions of the Health Planning Resource Development Act; unanticipated increases in energy costs or costs for changes made to reduce energy use; and expenses associated with the elimination of unnecessary beds. If the Secretary failed to act within ninety days on a hospital's request for exception, it would be automatically approved.

Hospital Responses

With its two-step approach, the Carter bill would give hospitals a chance to regulate themselves and limit government restrictions on their activities. Roughly three-quarters of hospital beds are in metropolitan areas and potentially subject to revenue controls.[123] These hospitals would probably alter their behavior under the bill's guidelines in response to the threat of mandatory ceilings. As others have noted, hospitals could respond by either increasing or decreasing their costs.[124] Because each year's allowed expenditure increase under Carter plan controls would be a percentage of the previous year's expenditures, hospitals could maximize future allowances by spending up to their guideline each year.[125] Hospitals also might spend over the guideline, expecting others to spend below. If that expectation proves incorrect, hospitals exceeding these guidelines would be penalized by reductions in allowed increases in following years. This penalty would reduce but not eliminate the incentive to overspend. Finally, hospitals approaching their guideline might reduce expenditures to avoid revenue controls. Ideally, hospitals would reduce expenditures related to inefficient operations or to provision of unnecessary services. The bill would encourage the latter reduction by allowing a hospital under mandatory controls to continue to include in its revenue base the revenues for services that have been discontinued on a planning agency's recommendation. In contrast, revenues associated with a service reduction that was not approved would be deducted from the base. This provision would discourage reduction of necessary services, reinforcing some state certificate-of-need prohibitions on service changes without approval.

Despite these incentives, hospitals might find it hard to cut expenditures on services or practices valued by professional or administrative staff. They might therefore reduce, though not eliminate, expenditures on low-revenue producing activities — such as outpatient services. Furthermore, to protect their revenues against future ceilings, they might avoid service delivery to nonpaying or low-paying patients.

Hospitals also could respond to expenditure guidelines as a group, attempting to limit expenditures within a state. The industry's current "Voluntary Effort," initiated in December 1977, is an attempt at self-regulation which appears to have had some effect in slowing cost increases.[126] While noting this effect, the Congressional Budget Office questions whether the group effort can suppress individual hospitals' self-interests in the long run. Peer pressure might be effective in discouraging inefficient or expansionary behavior by one hospital that could threaten regulation of other hospitals in a state, and peer support could include technical assistance in efficient management. Unless the industry can impose sanctions (perhaps on the advancement of an administrator), however, the industry's general interests are unlikely to override a hospital's particular interests over a long period of time. Peer pressure would therefore seem to be insufficient to get some hospitals in a state to spend below their guidelines in order to allow others to spend above.

Hospitals could establish sanctions by supporting a state rate-setting program to substitute for federal revenue controls. Although such a program would mean increased government oversight, hospitals might feel they could more readily control a state-run than a federally-run program. The cost-containment bill would encourage the establishment of state programs while including federal oversight to promote their stringency. To obtain federal approval, a state rate-setting program would have to cover hospital revenues as defined in the federal program, and to limit total state expenditures to a predetermined amount. But limits would have to apply to only 90 percent of hospitals covered by the federal program and the ceiling would be raised 1 percent above the voluntary guidelines. Furthermore, the bill apparently would require only assurances from the governor that the limit would be met; it does not discuss penalties if limits are exceeded. Although there are advantages to allowing state administration, which are discussed later, the opt-out provision as now written, appears to offer hospitals an opportunity to weaken regulatory constraints.

To the extent they apply, federal revenue controls could slow the rate of increase in revenues per admission.[127] Although the imposition of these controls would require considerable data on hospitals' costs, expenditures, and revenues, use of a straightforward formula would simplify the regulatory process and minimize interference in hospital management. Ceilings on revenues per admission would encourage reduction of length of stay and intensity of service, both of which are considered major elements in hospital cost inflation. To prevent gains to hospitals that might inappropriately increase admissions, the bill proposes to pay only the estimated marginal cost of admission increases. Measures of this kind were proposed for Phase IV of the Nixon administration's Economic Stabilization Program as likely to eliminate the incentives associated with average cost reimbursement. The program ended, however, before the measures went into effect.

The relative simplicity and the incentives of the Carter revenue controls should help the policy achieve its objectives, but the program also includes less desirable elements and incentives. First, it would exempt outpatient revenues from controls. Although this exemption could encourage a desirable shift in service delivery to a less costly setting, it would also allow a "pseudo-shift," under which inpatients would be temporarily "discharged" to use particular services. Outpatient departments often have not generated net revenue in the past, but if national health insurance were to change that situation, the exemption could also allow hospitals to subsidize inpatient with outpatient revenues.

A second problem with the Carter bill is its "pass-through" of each hospital's wage increases. The effect would be to eliminate pressure on management to bargain effectively with labor. Furthermore, the pass-through of each hospital's nonsupervisory wage increases would offer hospitals no incentive to reduce what may be excessive staff-to-patient ratios and would allow hospitals to shift to a more expensive mix of employees without exceeding ceilings. Although these incentives would be no worse than the current system's, the plan would not encourage change in labor practices.

A third problem with the proposed controls is their encouragement of undesirable along with desirable changes in hospital behavior. Marginal costs of admissions might be difficult to calculate, and incentives to boost admissions might persist. If their expenditures are constrained by revenue ceilings, hospitals might also avoid nonpaying patients[128] and favor patients who now pay the highest amount per admission (relative to average cost of care). To increase net revenues per admission, hospitals might not only reduce inappropriate duration and intensity of service, but also might avoid admitting patients who need extended care and a lot of service or might begin admitting for short stays people who formerly would have been treated outside the hospital.

Finally, in an effort to fend off criticism of uniform ceilings, the Carter administration included a number of provisions that complicate the bill's operations or undermine its effectiveness. In response to criticism that the formula treated inefficient and efficient hospitals alike, the bill proposes an "efficiency adjustment" to each hospital's individual ceiling. Depending on its costs relative to the costs of similar hospitals, a hospital could receive as much as an additional percentage point in its revenue cap or could lose as much as 2 percentage points. The major problem with this approach is that methods used to classify hospitals as similar are often far too rough to achieve their objectives. To measure relative efficiency, each hospital should be compared with other hospitals that are treating similar patients and illnesses. Methods of adjusting payment to case mix are still in the experimental stage. Hospitals now are commonly classified according to size, urban or rural location, or other features that may bear little or no relation to case mix. Hence the validity of current comparisons to measure efficiency is often questionable. The cost-containment bill would leave the choice of classification method to the Secretary of the DHHS. If the Secretary has the data and technical capacity to make case-mix comparisons, the efficiency incentive may be desirable; otherwise, its utility is questionable.

Other provisions have been included in the Carter bill to minimize disruption and to overcome criticism that a formula fails to respond to legitimate differences among hospitals. In comparing hospital expenditures to the proposed guidelines, the House Commerce Committee's version of the Carter plan would exempt capital expenditures that planning agencies have approved and expenditures related to the expansion of medical teaching programs. Both exemptions would avoid disrupting hospitals' plans, but unless there is an interest in encouraging either type of expenditure relative to other patient care, the exemptions appear to be inappropriate.

Under mandatory limits, exceptions would also be possible, on hospital request, for a variety of reasons. The Senate Labor and Human Resources Committee version of the Carter bill would permit exceptions based on changes in admissions, case mix, planning-agency-approved investments (including renovation or replacement), unusual expenditures on energy or investment to improve efficiency in energy use, and expenditures associated with closing a facility. The House Ways and Means version of the bill would also allow appeals and adjustments to accommodate shifts among classes of payers, increases in service coverage by a cost payer, the needs of tertiary care institutions, the planning-agency-approved preservation of a sole community hospital that would otherwise be insolvent, and expenditures on hospital security. Both House committee versions of the bill would require that the DHHS Secretary assess financial solvency as a factor in granting exceptions but would prohibit the Secretary from considering resources acquired through philanthropy in that assessment.

People generally advocate an exceptions process to provide a safety valve for hospitals that suffered inappropriately or excessively from revenue constraints. But the criteria for exceptions are not subject to precise measurement and exceptions are cumbersome to administer. Exceptions might therefore create a loophole to undermine the entire cost-containment effort. Under the Senate Labor and Human Resources Committee version of the bill, the government would be required to act on a request for review within ninety days, or the exception would be automatically granted. In these circumstances, hospitals are likely to appeal in droves, severely taxing the government's capacity to respond. Hence exceptions may be quite common.

Although the federal government would handle most exceptions, exceptions related to planning agency approval would require state action. Reliance on planning agencies for investment decisions would shift responsibility from hospital management which, under the bill, would face revenue constraints, to state and local agencies which currently face no expenditure constraints. In these circumstances, it is not clear that planners would make more efficient choices than hospitals themselves. Preliminary evidence of planning agencies' limited impact on hospital spending suggests that regulation in the absence of fiscal constraints is unlikely to be effective.[129] For this reason, the Carter administration's national health plan includes, along with its expenditure guidelines and revenue controls, a provision that would limit the total dollar amount that health planning agencies could approve. The bill would require the DHHS Secretary to allocate a maximum dollar amount to each state. Approvals under state planning programs would be limited to this amount. Nothing in the Carter bill would prohibit hospitals from relying on contributions from philanthropy or, presumably, on local or state governments to supplement insufficient revenues in paying operating costs. If a hospital proceeded to make capital expenditures without planning agency approval, however, the federal reimbursement to that hospital would be cut substantially.

126

Although capital expenditure ceilings would encourage cost-effective planning, they do not guarantee it. First, there is no guarantee that ceilings would stick. Planners might not be held politically accountable for exceeding their ceilings, and might be willing to approve hospitals' proposals as long as hospitals had sufficient revenues to support proposed investments. Second, if planners did try to stay within ceilings, they would face several obstacles. Technically, it is difficult to predict capital (and associated operating) expenditures in advance of investment. Because hospitals would have an incentive to underestimate costs, overruns would be very likely. Denials of revenue adequate to cover overruns is politically difficult. The United Kingdom's experience with budgeting for medical care also reveals political obstacles to redistribution. Even though the British government had the authority to give more to areas that had less, until recently resource allocation decisions under the National Health Services tended to perpetuate more than alter existing spending patterns.[130]

Finally, it is important to call attention to the advantages of the Carter bill's provision allowing state rate-setting programs to substitute for federal expenditure and revenue controls. Although the bill's current performance criteria for acceptable state programs may be too lenient, the bill nevertheless would offer states the opportunity to design programs that might be superior to the federal revenue controls. Under the bill, states, for example, would not be required to pass through wage increases; nor would they be required to employ a formula approach. They could, if they chose, evaluate hospitals' particular circumstances and adjust payment accordingly. Although this review process would be complex and time consuming no matter where it was conducted, state governments would be dealing with fewer hospitals and might be more closely attuned than the federal government to local concerns and more readily accessible to affected parties. If the federal government held states to a predetermined expenditure ceiling, as the bill proposes, responsiveness would not endanger expenditure control. Financing arrangements in the Carter NHI plan, in fact, might encourage state sensitivity to costs, overcoming the tendency of regulators to be lenient on the industry they regulate. The advantages to state administration are explored further in the section on administration.

THE KENNEDY-WAXMAN PLAN

By eliminating patient cost sharing, the Kennedy-Waxman bill would stimulate demand for hospital care more than the Carter bill would. The difference between the bills would probably be small, however, since a relatively small proportion of beneficiaries would face sizable deductibles under the Carter plan. Furthermore, increased admissions by people who needed hospital care might be offset by decreases in inappropriate admissions. The Kennedy-Waxman bill's coverage of ambulatory care would reduce the incentive to delay treatment (which necessitates more expensive hospitalization later) or to enter the hospital simply to reduce out-of-pocket expenses. Overall, then, the Carter and Kennedy-Waxman bills would imply roughly equivalent pressures to increase hospital expenditures in response to demand.

The Kennedy-Waxman bill's proposals to deal with hospitals' expenditures differ from those of the Carter bill. Under Kennedy-Waxman, hospital cost containment would be part of a cost-containment strategy for all medical services, implemented through a budgeting process. A national budget for all covered expenditures would be apportioned among states, and newly established state boards would translate expenditure limits into payments to providers. In contrast to the situation under the Carter plan, decisions by either national or state governments to spend money on hospitals would be related to spending decisions on all other services. If total budgets were restricted, pressure to limit hospital expenditures could be greater under the Kennedy-Waxman plan than under the Carter bill. In addition, total budgets would reduce the possibility of inappropriate or excessive shifts of services to outpatient departments or physicians' offices. Technical and political problems raised by the budgeting process are discussed later.

Theoretically, a state could control hospital spending within budgetary limits by setting revenue ceilings, like those proposed in the Carter bill, on individual hospitals. The Kennedy-Waxman bill, however, would eliminate differences in payment methods among third parties and would determine rates according to a newly mandated system. Labeled prospective budgeting, this new system could involve greater government oversight and control over hospital spending than revenue ceilings would entail (unless exceptions came to dominate in ceilings' implementation). At the same time, budgeting would allow greater distinctions among hospitals and an opportunity for flexibility in resource allocation. Finally, the Kennedy-Waxman bill would require states to determine hospital payment. In the Carter bill, the federal government would control payments unless a state chose to implement its own rate-setting system.

The Kennedy-Waxman bill specifies some rules for preparing actual budgets but would leave considerable discretion to state boards in actual allocation decisions. The rules, like the Carter bill, would give special protection to wages for nonsupervisory employees. States would be required to include in each hospital's budget whatever wage and fringe benefit costs resulted from collective bargaining. This requirement implies that states should pass through these costs, without trying to constrain them. Total payroll expenses amounted to almost 60 percent of total expenses in 1977, and roughly one-third of these expenses were subject to collective bargaining.[131] A pass-through could therefore have a significant effect on total costs. In a total budgeting system, it would also affect the availability of resources for other services. States could prevent this outcome by refusing to allow the full nonlabor expenditures of hospitals whose labor costs were excessive. But the inclusion of special protection in the federal law might weaken the position of the state, as well as that of management. Experience in Canada indicates that labor pressure can be very hard to resist. Wage increases reportedly caused Canadian provinces to exceed hospital budgetary ceilings and put pressure on wage increases throughout the health sector and the general economy.[132]

Like the House Commerce Committee version of the Carter bill, the Kennedy-Waxman bill would automatically approve expenditures to support capital investments incurred before the bill's enactment and the cost of facility closure. The Carter and Kennendy-Waxman bills would treat future capital investment differently. Although the Kennedy-Waxman bill would subject capital expenditures (and reductions in service) to planning agency review, it would not establish a separate capital expenditures budget. Within overall budgeting limits, hospitals and state health boards would have to weigh capital investments against costs of operating the current system. The need to choose could enhance considerations of efficiency in the development and approval of spending plans, or it could lead to the deferral of needed investment because of preoccupation with current expenses. This outcome would be of particular concern to older facilities in need of renovation. Alternatively, since planning agencies operate outside the budgetary process and perhaps without regard to overall costs, their recommendations could put pressure on state boards to promote capital expansion. Under the budget limits, these expenditures would have to come at the expense of other service areas such as ambulatory care.

To enable states to evaluate and limit hospital expenditures, the KenendyWaxman bill would require each participating provider to submit to the state health board a proposed budget for anticipated expenditures (indicating operating costs, capital costs, inpatient costs, outpatient costs, and nursing costs) and anticipated revenues by source for each type of expenditure. In addition providers would be required to submit information on proposed service changes and capital investment for two- and five-year periods, on the cost implications of proposed changes, on the volume of health services to be provided, and on expected patient characteristics. Information on services provided and patients served is critical to the evaluation of hospital efficiency, which the budgeting process seeks to address. States that have been engaged in prospective budgeting have had problems obtaining sufficiently accurate and detailed information for this purpose. Variations in hospitals' accounting systems make it especially hard to compare expenditures across hospitals. The Kennedy-Waxman bill would require implementation of a uniform cost reporting system to improve comparability. Similar efforts under Medicare have encountered substantial opposition from hospitals who claim that the regulations impose excessive burdens on hospitals dealing with private as well as public payers. Under the Kennedy-Waxman plan, these burdens would be reduced because all payers would employ the same payment system. State boards might nevertheless face opposition to specific requirements.

Finally, the Kennedy-Waxman bill would require state boards to establish statistical screens to distinguish hospitals whose budgets require detailed review from hospitals whose budgets can be accepted as proposed. The bill does not specify actual screens but indicates that norms might be developed for acceptable versus unacceptable rates of expenditure increase (in total budget, cost per admission, or cost per day), average costs (per patient, per day, per outpatient visit, or educational cost per student), or cost ratios (of administrative costs to total costs or to cost per admission or per day). Presumably the intent of this provision is to limit administrative burdens within reasonable bounds by restricting review to only some hospital budgets in a given year.

It is hard to specify in advance what the state priorities would be in evaluating hospital budgets. Some states might wish to avoid the responsibility altogether, abdicating authority to the national board. Other states might take on budgeting responsibilities but might be reluctant to make choices among hospitals or between expenditures on hospitals and other medical care. These states would probably mandate an allowable percentage increase in expenditure for all services. Even if providers exceeded the allowed percentage and a state exceeded its predetermined budget, that state might prefer to bear the additional costs rather than exercise control over medical expenditures. (The desirability of allowing states to overrun is discussed later.) When this occurs, the Kennedy-Waxman hospital payment system in practice would closely resemble the system proposed by the Carter administration. Other states would undoubtedly prefer control to excess spending and might even seek to redistribute resources among hospitals, areas, or services, as the bill allows. As already noted, reallocation of resources is likely to be highly controversial, and politics would undoubtedly play a part in spending decisions. Under Medicaid and other rate-setting programs, conflict has not prevented efforts to constrain expenditures in some states. These states would probably continue to pursue aggressive policies under national health insurance.

THE MARTIN PLAN

The Martin bill would affect the demand for hospital care and hospital revenues in two distinct ways: First, like the Carter bill, it would assure catastrophic protection to people who now have no health insurance and to many other people, including Medicare beneficiaries, whose coverage now has limits on days of hospital coverage, benefits per day, and payments for ancillary services, including physician care. Expansion of coverage would provide greater revenues to hospitals that now treat all patients, regardless of limitations on their insurance coverage. By eliminating limits on coverage, the Martin plan also would encourage longer hospital stays and greater intensity of service per day, thereby boosting hospital expenditures. The plan might also overcome some hospitals' current reluctance to accept patients without full insurance, since the plan's payment of bills above a predetermined amount would limit hospitals' liabilities.

Like the Carter bill's focus on revenue per admission, the choice of a screen could have considerable effect on provider behavior. Providers who find their revenues adequate would probably prefer to avoid detailed budget review if possible. A hospital could avoid increasing expenditures per day or per admission, but could increase the total number of days or admissions, thereby increasing total expenses. Alternatively a hospital could keep its total budget within predetermined norms by reducing services or changing its patient mix. In the first case, hospital costs would rise but access to care would not be significantly threatened. In the second case, costs might be restrained but access problems could arise.

Hospitals' opportunities to outmaneuver reviewers' standards could be reduced if reviewers employed a variety of efficiency screens and shifted their emphasis among screens from year to year. If policymakers have the flexibility to outmaneuver the hospitals, they are likely to be far more effective than if they are bound by rigid rules. Legal requirements for due process — especially the promulgation of decision rules — would inhibit policymakers' flexibility to some extent. But varying emphasis within a set of rules should withstand judicial review. If all hospital budgets were reviewed periodically, state boards would have an opportunity to evaluate efficiency by a variety of measures and to reward hospitals for factors other than efficiency, including the provision of costly but desirable services to the community. This opportunity is lacking in the Carter bill's federal program.

Once budgets are established, the Kennedy-Waxman bill would leave actual expenditure decisions to provider discretion. This provision would allow hospital administrators independence in day-to-day management and avoid government line-by-line oversight of hospital spending. This independence would be substantially less than that provided by the Carter bill, however, for periodic review would give government continuing influence over hospital behavior. State boards would have the power to penalize hospitals whose overall behavior departed from public priorities. Use of this authority would set limits on hospital management's freedom to disregard state decisions.

Second, the Martin bill could affect demand and revenues for hospital care by reducing the prevalence of first-dollar coverage among the currently insured population. As argued earlier, predicting people's actual response to the Martin bill's incentives is not easy. If employees chose plans with higher cost-sharing obligations than they now face, they might avoid hospital admissions. Alternatively, once they were admitted, they might seek shorter hospital stays and less intensive service (as long as their expenses were below insurance plans' deductibles). Given the important role of physicians in determining hospital use, the effects of cost sharing on consumer behavior are not clear. As noted in chapter 5, there is evidence that the demand for inpatient services is sensitive to price. Avoidance of hospital use seems particularly likely among low-income individuals who might well prefer cash rebates to comprehensive health insurance. If the Martin bill's incentives produced a major increase in the cost-sharing obligations of the insured population, and if those cost-sharing obligations reduced use of hospital services, the bill could introduce some limits to hospitals' capacities to generate revenues.

These limits would not be stringent, however, unless changes were also made in the way public and private insurers pay their share of hospital bills. The payment features of the Martin bill make cost containment unlikely, even with substantial changes in consumer behavior. Unlike the Carter and Kennedy-Waxman bills, the Martin bill proposes adoption of Medicare's "reasonable cost" reimbursement provisions for the catastrophic insurance program (CAPP) while leaving all other payers' current payment practices intact. Because most Medicaid programs follow Medicare reimbursement practices, Medicare, Medicaid, the CAPP would operate under government principles of reasonable costs; Blue Cross, commercial insurers, and self-pay patients would pay on other terms. With this approach to hospital reimbursement, the Martin bill would exacerbate the current reimbursement system's tendency to support increases in hospital expenditures.

Reasonable cost reimbursement has been recognized as inflationary almost from the moment of its adoption by Medicare in 1965.[133] The

132

reasonable cost system tends to pay hospitals the costs they incur in serving program beneficiaries. As long as hospitals can expect full payment for whatever costs they incur, they have little reason to constrain their expenditures. The payment system therefore supports inefficiencies in hospital operations and continual increases in the intensity of hospital services. Under the system, costs are retroactively determined according to explicit rules for defining "allowable costs" and for identifying the share of a hospital's total costs attributable to a program's beneficiaries. For many years of Medicare's operation, these rules offered the only means in the reasonable cost system of distinguishing incurred costs from "reasonable" costs.

Both in practice and in theory, the rules are ineffective in constraining hospitals' capacities to generate revenues. When Medicare began, program officials adopted relatively liberal rules in order to encourage hospital participation in the program and to promote the delivery of "mainstream" medical care to beneficiaries. As a result, hospitals could freely incur costs in the treatment of these beneficiaries with the assurance that costs would be paid. Although the program has tightened its rules over time, the rules themselves are too narrowly focused to constrain hospital spending. Definitions of allowable costs can be used to prevent a program's payment for expenditures not related to its beneficiaries (gift shops, cafeterias, research). They can also restrict payment for particular items (payments to related organizations, franchise fees, interest, depreciation). But they cannot limit expenses on resources used to provide patient care to their beneficiaries. Furthermore, regardless of rules on apportionment of total costs to specific programs, a hospital can use its accounting and charge systems to maximize the share of its costs that are reimbursable on a reasonable cost basis.

Recognition of these limitations to reasonable cost reimbursement led Congress to authorize additional restrictive mechanisms for Medicare in 1972. CAPP would presumably adopt these mechanisms as well. The Section 223 amendments authorized implementation of prospectively set limits on Medicare payment. Although Medicare payment continues to be primarily retrospective, the program has used its authority to set some prospective limits. For this purpose, hospitals are grouped according to number of beds and urban or rural location. Hospitals' routine costs are adjusted to reflect variations in hospital labor costs and differences across states in hospital use (with higher rates allowed for hospitals in states with lower hospital use). A ceiling is then set on payment for daily routine costs to hospitals in the group. The ceiling began as the 90th percentile of costs (with a plus factor) for all hospitals in the group, adjusted forward for inflation. It was subsequently lowered to the 80th percentile (plus 10 percent of the median). Regulations have recently been issued to move the ceiling to the mean plus 12 percent, projected forward for price increases in the hospital's marketbasket. Expenditures on capital, medical education, and ancillary services are excluded from the ceilings.

These ceilings differ from the Carter and Kennedy-Waxman proposals in three ways, all of which substantially limit their effect. First, the ceilings apply only to routine, not total, costs; second, the ceilings affect only program payment rather than payment by all payers; and third, the ceilings themselves are tied to hospitals' expenditures rather than being set independent of hospitals' behavior. The focus on routine costs probably reflects the government's greater willingness to limit hotel-type services in hospitals than the delivery of medical care. Ceilings must affect medical practice, however, if they are to limit the increases in volume and intensity of service that now contribute significantly to rising hospital expenditures. Controls in these areas would be even more necessary given the Martin catastrophic plan's encouragement of longer stays and more services. Controls are also necessary to prevent hospitals from shifting overhead from the regulated to the unregulated area of expenditure. Recognition of these problems led New York to extend its controls to cover ancillary as well as routine costs and has reportedly led to proposals to extend Medicare controls to ancillary services at some time in the future.[134]

With the change, a larger share of hospital costs are likely to exceed the Section 223 ceiling, reducing program liabilities from what they would have been if the ceilings did not exist. But as long as hospitals have access to resources from other payers, these ceilings will do little to constrain the rate of increase in program costs over time or to limit increases in overall hospital spending. Since the Section 223 ceilings affect only some rather than all hospital payers, they will not prohibit hospitals from earning revenues to support continuing expenditure increases. The Section 223 ceiling is itself tied to expenditures (at the average plus 12 percent) and will therefore rise as expenditures rise. Obviously, a ceiling can only effectively limit costs if it is independent of, rather than influenced by, hospital behavior. The Section 223 ceiling does not meet this criterion, so program costs will continue to rise.

Finally, the Section 223 ceilings will have little or no impact on the rate of increase in total hospital costs. The failure to cover all payers allows hospitals to use one payer to subsidize another. In these circumstances, hospitals whose costs are above the Section 223 ceilings are less likely to reduce their expenses than to pass those expenses on to other third-party payers. The ceiling's effects will therefore be to shift the effect of expenditure increases rather than to prevent their occurrence.

The Martin bill proposes to adopt reasonable cost reimbursement despite widespread recognition of the problems outlined here. Clearly, then, the bill places greater importance on expanding insurance coverage than on containing costs. As the history of Medicare demonstrates, policy shaped by this attitude is likely to produce continuing escalation in expenses on hospital care.[135]

SUMMARY

Reasonable cost reimbursement promises to pay hospitals the costs they incur in delivering care to a plan's beneficiaries. Policymakers have long criticized this promise as an encouragement to rising hospital costs. The Martin bill nevertheless would adopt Medicare's reasonable cost reimbursement system for its public catastrophic plan. The Medicare payment system has adopted prospectively set ceilings on some reimbursable costs, reducing program liabilities to some extent. For two important reasons, however, the ceilings will control neither program nor total costs in the long run. First, present ceilings fail to cover ancillary service and capital costs, which are important sources of hospital inflation. Second, ceilings affect only public and not private revenues, so hospitals can shift costs from public to private payers and maintain their access to relatively unconstrained sources of income. Expenditure increases supported by these revenues will cause increases in public as well as private reimbursement, since public programs' ceilings are tied to average hospital costs. Despite its ceilings, then, reasonable cost reimbursement will assure continued increases in public expenditures on hospital care. The Martin bill's adoption of this inflationary reimbursement system would probably compensate hospitals for any reductions in revenues they might experience if the bill promoted higher cost sharing and sensitivity to price among privately insured persons.

The Carter and Kennedy-Waxman bills reject reasonable cost reimbursement and propose substantial administrative controls over hospital revenues. Both bills would limit what hospitals could earn from private as well as public payers and set ceilings on payment that are at least somewhat independent of hospital spending patterns. The Carter bill would authorize a federal program to limit rates of increase in revenues per admission. These limits would apply to individual hospitals only if the nation as a whole and the hospitals in a state exceeded a predetermined guideline for expenditure increases. Under the limits, allowed rates of increase in revenues per admission would be tied to actual increases in labor costs and area price increases for other goods and services hospitals purchase. Limits would apply only to inpatient services. Hospitals would be paid the marginal (not average) cost of new admissions and ceilings could be adjusted for a variety of changes in hospital operations.

The Carter bill's primary objective is to limit hospital cost increases to rates of increase in the costs of goods and services hospitals purchase and to discourage inappropriate increases in the volume and intensity of hospital care. The bill's labor cost pass-through provision would support continued and significant hospital cost inflation, and the bill's relatively simple rules for payment would not guarantee efficiency in the delivery of hospital services. Incentives would be created for hospitals to shift costs from inpatient to outpatient departments, to avoid heavy care patients, and to inappropriately admit patients for very short stays. Despite these problems, the bill offers a potentially mechanistic and therefore relatively administrable approach to restraining increases in hospital spending.

Uniform ceilings on revenue increases, however, have been criticized for failing to promote hospital efficiency, to respond to desirable or necessary differences among hospitals, and to prohibit undesirable hospital behavior. To combat these criticisms, the Carter bill includes an exceptions process that would allow adjustments to ceilings in response to individual hospitals' particular circumstances. Although concern with "fairness" to hospitals is understandable, a federally operated exceptions process might become so complex as to overwhelm administrative capacity or to undermine the bill's constraints on hospital costs. Because states have fewer hospitals to deal with than the federal government, the bill's provisions allowing states to establish hospital payment programs within federally set limits might offer a better means of promoting responsiveness to variations among hospitals while retaining control over total expenditures.

In contrast to hospital payment decisions under the Carter bill, decisions on hospital payment under the Kennedy-Waxman bill would have to be made within a total budget for services covered by the NHI plan. The federal government would establish a fixed budget for each state, and state boards would be required to set hospital payments consistent with those budgets. In determining hospital payments, state boards would have to weigh spending on hospital care against spending on other services, increasing the pressure to constrain hospital costs. The bill would not encourage or require states to regulate actual hospital spending decisions. Instead, state boards would set overall hospital budgets (covering outpatient as well as inpatient services) and allow hospitals to spend as they wished within those budgets. Like the Carter bill, the Kennedy-Waxman plan offers special protection to hospital labor costs, thereby sustaining a potential source of hospital cost inflation.

States could satisfy the Kennedy-Waxman plan's requirements by allowing a uniform rate of increase over each hospital's current revenues — which is essentially the approach of the Carter bill. Some states would undoubtedly find this the simplest approach to take, but the bill would encourage states to undertake more detailed review and evaluation of hospital spending. The bill provides general rules for this process but would leave to states the practical problems of setting goals for hospital performance and reconciling simplicity in administration with responsiveness to differences among hospitals. States whose budgets are tight relative to current spending levels (or who have experience in hospital rate setting) might try to redistribute revenues among hospitals and between hospitals and other medical providers. These efforts would undoubtedly pose both technical and political difficulties. Some states might prefer to avoid these difficulties by abdicating responsibility for budgeting to the federal government or by paying the full cost of expenditures that exceeded federally approved budgets. The current bill would not allow overspending; presumably, a state's future federal funds would be reduced by the amount of any excess. In the following section, we argue that prohibitions on overspending by states may undermine the Kennedy-Waxman bill's constraints on costs. We therefore propose an alternative approach, similar to the one the Canadians use.

VIII. ADMINISTERING PROVIDER PAYMENT POLICIES

The Carter and the Kennedy-Waxman bills propose new regulatory mechanisms to determine provider payment. The Carter bill proposes to treat hospitals differently from other providers. All hospital payment would be subject to regulation by the federal government unless a state established an alternative plan that satisfied federal requirements. For other providers, only HealthCare payments would be subject to government regulation. The federal government would make all payment decisions. The Kennedy-Waxman bill would subject all provider payment to government determination. All medical expenditures would be subject to federally set budgets, within which states would make decisions on rates of payment.

This section analyzes the administrability of the regulatory arrangements for provider payment that the Carter and Kennedy-Waxman bills propose. It pays particular attention to each bill's distribution of authority between federal and state government. Since the Martin plan calls for no major changes in governments' policies toward provider payment (relying instead on the marketplace to contain costs) we will not discuss it here.

THE CARTER PLAN

The Carter plan's heavy reliance on federal payment and regulation is largely a response to dissatisfaction with current administration of the Medicaid program. State Medicaid programs have been criticized for failing to cover many poor people and for failing to set rates of payment that will assure beneficiaries' access to care. The Carter bill addresses these problems by proposing the establishment of national eligibility criteria and by proposing that the federal — not state — government take responsibility for provider payment.

Although equity may require national eligibility criteria,[136] the desirability of removing state responsibility for physician payment is much less clear. Most states have attempted to keep reimbursement rates below private and Medicare fees by employing fee schedules instead of the customary, prevailing, and reasonable charge system. States have been severely criticized for low rates because they inhibit Medicaid recipients' access to care. This problem, however, is not inherent in state rate setting. If states were to set rates for all their citizens, not just the poor, an NHI plan could incorporate states' willingness to constrain provider

139

payment without sacrificing access to care. Some states have already taken this course in regulating hospital rates, proving far more innovative than the federal government in payment design. State innovations undoubtedly reflect the greater fiscal pressures state governments face. State tax revenues do not rise so rapidly as federal revenues, and state constitutions typically constrain government borrowing for operating expenditures. Hence, state governments, more than the federal government, are forced to choose between controlling expenditures or raising taxes and therefore must consider the value of health services relative to their costs. These fiscal stakes are likely to strengthen state administrators' resistance to pressure for generosity from the industry they oversee.

The Carter bill recognizes that national health insurance would do well to capture concern with cost containment, and proposes adoption of a financing formula that would penalize states for rapid rates of expenditure increase under HealthCare. Paradoxically, the bill would give states no authority to influence expenditures by physicians. With this policy, the Carter plan would lose not only the benefit of state fiscal pressure but also the opportunity for experimentation that variations in state policy provide.

These disadvantages to the Carter approach are probably necessary concomitants of the decision to regulate fees for only the public segment of physicians' market. As long as payment regulation applies only to the poor and the elderly, there is reason to prefer federal to state administration, for some states have demonstrated insensitivity to access problems among their disadvantaged citizens.[137] When the Carter plan opted for partial regulation, then, it sacrificed the opportunity for state administration.

The bill makes different choices when it comes to hospital payment. Here regulation would apply to private as well as public payments and states would be encouraged to undertake regulatory responsibilities, subject to federal performance requirements. Although the federal requirements might need some improvement, this approach would harness both state fiscal pressure and innovation to NHI administration. At the same time, it would allow federal administration if a state were unwilling or unable to perform acceptably. Ideally, these advantages would be extended to all types of provider payment.

THE KENNEDY-WAXMAN PLAN

The Kennedy-Waxman bill would apply the same payment rules to all beneficiaries and all providers, and establish a joint federal-state administrative structure to implement these rules. The bill's resource allocation process would represent a major departure from current practices and would probably generate considerable political conflict. If the system can withstand that conflict, it offers a considerable opportunity for effective cost containment.

The Kennedy-Waxman bill calls for annual determination of a national budget for health expenditures. With this budget, the bill would try to correct a major flaw in current decision making on health spending. In the public sector, open-ended financing and retrospective payment mechanisms have allowed expenditures to follow provider and user spending decisions. Similar patterns have evolved in the private sector, largely because current insurance arrangements cushion the effect of price increases on consumers and because consumers and insurers have been too fragmented to exercise effective expenditure control. The budgetary process would change this situation by concentrating authority for expenditure decisions in visible public agencies and by requiring government to decide how much to spend in advance of service use.

The United Kingdom probably provides the best example of a centrally budgeted health care system. While the United States has steadily increased the share of gross national product (GNP) devoted to medical care, the United Kingdom has maintained the share of GNP devoted to health at a relatively low and constant level.[138] The United Kingdom, however, has a far lower GNP per capita than the United States and may therefore be unable to spend more on health care, given other needs. Whether budgeting in the United States would constrain health spending would depend on the availability of resources and the value the political process assigns to health care.

The Kennedy-Waxman bill would try to assure expenditure restraint by prohibiting an increase in any year's budget that exceeded the previous year's budgetary estimates by more than the average rate of increase in gross national product for the preceding three years. The ceiling apparently would not apply to the plan's first year, however. Officials' primary concern in that year might well be to gain public acceptance of the plan and to assure that previously unserved people acquired access to medical care. These goals characterized the implementation of Medicare in this country and of Canada's national health insurance program; in both cases health expenditures increased substantially as the new programs began. If, under the Kennedy-Waxman plan, the government were to delay its budgetary ceilings and changes in provider payment mechanisms, the results would probably be similar. Expenditure controls could be introduced after the first year, but they would then apply to a much higher base. The plan would therefore produce a sizable increase in overall expenditures.

This outcome might be avoided if expenditure controls were introduced before or along with benefit expansion. Limits on the rate of increase in provider revenues would reduce the costs associated with newly delivered services. If increases in provider revenues were constrained, services to people not previously served would be financed in two ways. First, the existence of excess capacity would allow provision of some new services at low marginal cost without sacrificing the delivery of services. Second, services to a new population could come at the expense of services to current users. With universal, comprehensive coverage, providers would have no incentive to distinguish among patients according to ability to pay. More care would probably be allocated according to medical need. As a result, the delivery of "essential" services would increase and less essential or "unnecessary" care would decrease.

Whatever the initial experience under the Kennedy-Waxman bill, the statute's limitation on spending increases would make it difficult for Congress to authorize increases in health spending that exceeded growth in GNP. This legislative hurdle might help Congress resist pressure from provider and consumer constituencies to support more spending. Legislative action to override the ceiling, however, might be desirable in certain circumstances. The use of health services varies countercyclically, rising when economic activity slows.[139] This pattern is related to the lower prices of individuals' time and decreases in health status that accompany unemployment. Although the bill's use of a three-year average increase — rather than a single year's increase — in GNP accommodates this phenomenon to some extent, federal officials might sometimes wish to promote even greater health expenditure increases.

Regardless of how the national budget is set, it is to be allocated among states as a ceiling on per capita state expenditures. Along with the GNP-related ceiling on total budget increases, the bill specifies that increases in each state's budget over the previous year's expenditures are to reflect the state's per capita spending relative to national per capita spending. The lower the state expenditures were relative to national expenditures, the higher would be the state's allowed increase. Except for states with populations explicitly identified as underserved, the allowed increase would be required to range between 80 percent and 120 percent of the previous year's increase in the national budget.

This budgeting process is intended to limit spending on covered services, regardless of their source of financing. With minor exceptions, then, the bill would preclude supplementation of approved budgets by state or local governments whose citizens wished to pay for more or better service. These provisions could be enforced by reducing federal payments to compensate for any state expenditures above budgeted levels. Enforcement probably would engender considerable resistance from the states. States that wanted to spend more than their federally set budgets would probably press Congress to raise budgetary ceilings to accommodate their preferences. To raise ceilings for some states (probably states with higher incomes and higher-priced services) and not all states would create significant inequities in health services across areas. Hence Congress might have to raise ceilings — and federal contributions — for all states if it responded to pressure from some. Congress would therefore face a choice between allowing cost escalation, thereby avoiding political conflict, and holding onto its budgetary limits in the face of considerable state opposition. Since all states would have something to gain from higher expenditures, Congress would probably sacrifice cost containment to maintain political peace.

If, instead, the bill were to allow state supplementation, Congress might be able to control costs and minimize conflict. The Canadians have taken this course, fixing the federal government's contributions to expenditures in each province and allowing the provinces to supplement federal contributions as they see fit. States might spend above budgetary ceilings, pressing the national program to cover the excess. But, overall, allowing supplementation would probably produce less pressure on Congress than prohibition would engender. Telling states they could not spend could generate opposition to the entire NHI plan. Telling states they could spend if they wanted to might leave them dissatisfied but less hostile. Although supplementation raises the possibility that richer areas would have more and better services than poorer ones, designing federal contributions to vary with state income could mitigate this effect. Furthermore, if Congress were to stick to its budgetary ceilings, states' inclination to supplement might well decline over time.

Supplementation aside, using budgets to redistribute resources would pose substantial political and technical problems. As indicated earlier, experience in Britain suggests that budgeting is more likely to reflect than to alter current spending patterns. Efforts to limit total expenditure increases would probably generate considerable controversy in themselves; further efforts to restructure the system might generate more pressure than politicians and administrators would tolerate.

Resource allocation also is a formidable technical task. It requires definition of medical service areas, estimates of need for medical care (a function of population characteristics — such as age, sex, race, income, occupation, morbidity, and mortality — and environmental characteristics like density and climate), of the mix and volume of services appropriate to meet this need, and of the cost of providing those services. Obviously, many data are needed to perform this task effectively. Furthermore, behavior cannot be guided solely by need and cost estimates. Value judgments will be necessary to decide to support one area's need for physicians over another area's need to renovate its hospitals, to decide how much to penalize an area for inefficiency, or to decide what constitutes an acceptable versus an unacceptable level of service.

To make these judgments, the Kennedy-Waxman bill would establish a fairly elaborate administrative structure, involving both federal and state governments. The bill not only would make states responsible for allocating expenditures within budgets; it also would mandate a specific structure for state decision making and subject state decisions to federal rules. The bill would require each state to charter a "state health insurance corporation," and each governor to appoint a five-member board of directors. Appointments to the board would be subject to approval by the national board, and terms would be staggered. As indicated in discussions of provider payment, state boards would have to follow payment rules set by the national board.

The structure is new, untested, and charged with massive responsibilities. Since the Kennedy-Waxman plan would eliminate patient cost sharing, the full burden for cost containment would rest on the state boards. Given this considerable responsibility, the plan's proposal to share authority between federal and state governments seems desirable. The Kennedy-Waxman bill would strike a compromise between federal and state administration. Through budgets and oversight, the bill would hold state boards accountable to the federal government for some aspects of their performance. At the same time the boards would have considerable discretion in payment and resource allocation. In exercising this discretion, the boards would be accountable to the citizens of their state. Although the boards would not be directly accountable to the governor, as they would be if put within a state agency, they would be similar to independent rate-setting commissions, which have apparently responded to state budgetary concerns by limiting payments.[140]

This mechanism would capture the state's sensitivity to fiscal pressures, since state residents' premiums would vary with state health expenditures. (Sensitivity would be even greater if the bill allowed state supplementation for which state residents would bear the full costs of expenditures above budgets.) State discretion in budgeting also would allow states the freedom to reflect state residents' practices and preferences, thereby encouraging desirable and instructive variation across states. (A state unable to perform budgeting tasks could presumably allow the national board to allocate funds on its behalf.) At the same time, the equal application of payment rules to all citizens (reinforced by federal oversight) would reduce the likelihood that state administration would lead to discrimination against the poor.

144

There is, of course, no certainty that these arrangements would limit health expenditures. The people within a state might favor more spending and seek federal relief as costs rose. If Congress responded by approving higher health budgets, national health expenditures would continue to increase. The bill nevertheless would establish a mechanism that encouraged conscious choices about health spending and benefits and therefore represents a major, if controversial, improvement over the current system.

IX. NATIONAL HEALTH INSURANCE
AND CITIES

This chapter examines each bill's implications for cities. Local governments play an important role as health care providers and financiers. Recent changes in the Medicaid and Medicare programs have increased the importance of the medical care that local governments provide to many of their residents, particularly low-income persons.[141] Demand is growing, however, just as cities are also facing increasingly stringent budgets. Taxpayer revolts, high unemployment, and cuts in federal aid have all contributed to budgetary pressures. Thus, for many cities, national health insurance may be both a method of providing more medical care to their residents and an important form of fiscal relief. This chapter first reviews the role of cities as providers and financiers of medical care. Then we analyze the three bills' implications for coverage, income redistribution, employment, and payment and resource allocation.

Choosing to focus on cities poses two problems. One is simply deciding what we mean by cities. For example, the Bureau of the Census identified 18,517 municipalities with a total population of 137 million people in 1972.[142] However, 18,125 of these municipalities had populations less than 50,000; the remaining 392 cities had a total population of about 72 million people. About 300 of these cities are also designated as the central cities of Standard Metropolitan Statistical Areas (SMSAs). In 1976, these central cities had a total population of almost 60 million people. Even within this group, however, financial condition, poverty populations, and medical care delivery systems vary widely.

The second problem that arises is the lack of some current data specifically defined for cities. In general, the most complete source of data is the 1970 Census, which is now ten years old. More recent data are available for selected variables for all central cities of SMSAs and for the central cities of the twenty largest SMSAs. Almost no data on health insurance coverage or medical care use are available for individual cities.

Theoretically, it might be ideal to structure this analysis along several clear-cut lines: urban versus rural, metropolitan versus nonmetropolitan, large cities versus small cities, central cities versus suburban rings, or poor cities versus rich cities. Data limitations make it impossible to follow such analytical frames thoroughly. Instead, we maintain a dual focus throughout much of the chapter. Our goal is to indicate how the

NHI plans might affect cities with different fiscal and population characteristics. Evidence therefore is provided for all central cities in order to contrast their populations with noncentral city portions (suburban fringes) of SMSAs and, to a lesser extent, with nonmetropolitan residents. Because central cities vary widely in their economic and social characteristics, we also use a second set of data for selected cities from among the twenty largest SMSAs. To select these cities, we ranked central cities by their percentage of population below the poverty level in 1976. The five cities with the highest percentages of poverty populations plus New York, which ranked seventh, were grouped together and are referred to as high-poverty cities. Similarly, the five with the lowest percentages of poverty populations were combined into a low-poverty group.

Table 21 lists the individual cities and SMSAs and reports their poverty populations and family income distributions. Not surprisingly, the central cities have larger poverty populations than the SMSAs for both groups,[143] but the differences are much greater for the high-poverty group. Data on the distribution of families by income reinforce this conclusion. More than 16 percent of families in high-poverty central cities had incomes below $5,000. By contrast, fewer than 10 percent of families in low-poverty central cities, and fewer than 7 percent of families in noncentral cities, were in this class.

LOCAL GOVERNMENTS AND PUBLIC MEDICAL CARE

Local governments have long been an important source of medical care for the poor. The most visible part of this system of care is the urban public hospital, which in many cities serves as a major employer, a tertiary care center, and a primary source of ambulatory care. Local governments also support care for the poor through payments to private hospitals, and, often in conjunction with federal grants, the operation of free-standing clinics and special care programs — maternal and child health centers or drug treatment facilities.

The ability of many local governments to take up the slack created by recent changes in the Medicare and Medicaid programs has been constrained by the urban fiscal crisis — shrinking populations and tax bases and limited revenue-raising options. Current economic conditions reduce cities' prospects for obtaining direct fiscal relief from the state or federal government. Ultimately, in the absence of revenue increases, cities have these options: to reduce services, to encourage private providers to take on more responsibility for caring for the poor, or to do both.

Table 21

POPULATION, PERCENTAGE BELOW POVERTY LEVEL, AND PERCENTAGE DISTRIBUTION OF FAMILIES BY INCOME AND PLACE OF RESIDENCE, SELECTED CITIES AND SMSAs (1976)

A. Population and Percentages Below Poverty

	Central Cities		SMSAs (total)	
	Population (000s)	Percentage Below Poverty Level	Population (000s)	Percentage Below Poverty Level
High-Poverty				
St. Louis	413	25.4%	2,187	9.3%
Philadelphia	1,781	23.2	4,734	11.7
Chicago	3,077	21.9	7,130	11.3
Boston	469	21.6	2,358	8.1
Detroit	1,224	20.4	4,065	9.4
New York	7,073	17.5	10,953	13.4
Low-Poverty				
Dallas	805	13.0%	1,647	11.2%
Houston	1,246	11.5	2,188	11.8
Pittsburgh	385	10.1	2,447	6.7
Minneapolis-St. Paul	740	9.2	1,936	4.8
Anaheim-Santa Ana-Garden Grove	494	9.1	1,760	5.2

B. Percentage Distribution of Families by Income and Place of Residence

	High-Poverty SMSAs		Low-Poverty SMSAs	
Income Level	In Central Cities	Outside Central Cities	In Central Cities	Outside Central Cities
Under $3,000	4.8%	0.9%	2.6%[a]	3.6%
3,000-4,999	11.5	2.6	5.5	2.5
5,000-6,999	11.1	4.5	6.2	5.1
7,000-9,999	11.9	8.2	10.8	9.5
10,000-14,999	30.3	15.2	21.2	17.8
15,000-19,999	17.6	20.3	17.5	20.5
20,000-24,999	10.9	16.7	14.6	17.0
25,000+	13.8	31.6	21.6	24.8
Number of Families (000s)	3,617	4,606	932	1,709

a. Data not available for Pittsburgh for this income class.

Sources: Part A — U.S. Department of Commerce, Bureau of the Census, *Characteristics of the Population below the Poverty Level: 1976*, series P-60, no. 115, July 1978; Part B — U.S. Department of Commerce, Bureau of the Census, *Money Income in 1976 of Families and Persons in the United States*, series P-60, no. 114, July 1978.

149

This policy may produce what the news media and congressional hearings have recently labeled the "financially distressed hospital." In a survey of hospitals in the nation's 100 largest cities, the American Hospital Association found two hundred hospitals — almost 20 percent of all hospitals — in a deficit position in 1978.[144] Individual hospitals deficits ranged from 0.1 percent to 40 percent of revenues. The total exceeded $200 million. Some hospitals and communities facing these deficits have asked for federal assistance to prevent service reductions, bankruptcy, and closure; this behavior suggests local government's unwillingness or inability to sustain service provision.

Responsibility for public medical care at the local level varies from area to area. Three levels of government, city, county, and special district, may either divide or share the financing and management of the public system. Arrangements typically vary by region of the country. In the northeast, the city government usually has primary responsibility for both hospital and ambulatory care, while in other regions, hospital care frequently comes under county or special district jurisdiction. According to data from the 1976-77 *Census of Governments*, local governments spent a total of $14.3 billion, about 12 percent of national medical expenditures, for medical services and medical vendor payments in 1976.[145] Counties accounted for 50 percent of the total, cities for 33 percent, and special districts for the remainder. Almost 60 percent ($8.5 billion) was spent for public hospitals, with the remainder evenly split between other health activities and medical vendor payments (including payments to private hospitals). New York City accounted for almost half of all medical vendor payments by local governments.

Since spending for public hospitals constitutes the largest share of local governments' medical care expenditures, it is useful to detail the characteristics of these hospitals. According to American Hospital Association data, local governments (cities, counties, and special districts) owned 1,688 short-term general hospitals in 1976.[146] Recent publicity about the plight of large, financially distressed public hospitals such as Metropolitan in New York, Homer Phillips in St. Louis, Cook County in Chicago, Philadelphia General, and D.C. General create the impression that these institutions are typical of all public hospitals. In reality, only 111 public hospitals have 300 or more beds, while 1,298 have fewer than 100 beds. However, these 111 large hospitals accounted for almost half of total expenditures by local public hospitals.

Another important factor distinguishing public hospitals from each other is teaching status. Again according to American Hospital Association data, 155 hospitals owned by state and local governments were affiliated with medical schools.[147] Public teaching hospitals differ significantly from other public hospitals in their sources of revenue. In

1978, public teaching hospitals received 21 percent of their revenues from Medicaid, 22 percent from Medicare, and about 18 percent from government grants and appropriations.[148] In contrast, other public hospitals obtain only about 8 percent of their revenues from Medicaid, 2 percent from government appropriations and grants, and 34 percent from Medicare.

Finally, public hospitals differ in terms of the share of their expenditures raised from patient billings. In particular, hospitals owned by special districts, which accounted for almost 30 percent of total hospital expenditures by local governments, raised about 90 percent of their expenses from current charges.[149] City and county hospitals, on the other hand, raised only about 40 percent of their expenses from patient charges. It appears, then, that large public teaching hospitals, particularly those owned by cities and counties rather than by special districts, are heavily dependent on local government resources. An NHI plan that would aid these institutions would also aid their owner governments.

Separate data on governments' medical care expenditures are not available for the central cities of SMSAs and their suburban rings. Data by size of city and size of county, however, clearly show that the bulk of local governments' health spending occurs in the most populous jurisdictions.[150] Counties and cities with more than 300,000 people accounted for more than 50 and 70 percent, respectively, of total medical spending for the two types of governments. Per capita spending is also strongly correlated with size, ranging from about $65 in cities of 1 million or more population to just over $10 in cities of 50,000 or smaller population. At the county level, jurisdictions of 300,000 or more population spent about $40 per capita, compared to $28 for counties of 100,000 or smaller population.

Table 22 reports data on medical care spending for the high- and low-poverty cities identified earlier in this chapter. These eleven cities (and their respective counties) spent almost $3.5 billion for medical services in 1976. This was approximately 25 percent of total spending for medical care at the local level. It is interesting to note first the differences in organization of the public medical care system in the two groups. None of the city governments in the low-poverty group has jurisdiction over a public hospital. This responsibility is taken by either county governments or special districts. Conversely, in four of the six high-poverty areas, the city governments have full responsibility for public health services. The two groups do not differ markedly in terms of the share of local governments' budgets devoted to medical care. (Counties and special districts are merged with cities in these and the per capita calculations, as appropriate.) The high-poverty areas spent 18.2 percent of their budgets on medical care, compared with 14.5 percent for the low-poverty areas.

151

Table 22

LOCAL GOVERNMENTS' HEALTH EXPENDITURES, SELECTED AREAS (1976-77)

	Expenditures for Public Hospitals ($ millions)		Expenditures for Other Health Activities ($ millions)		Total per Capita Public Health Spending, All Jurisdictions[a]	Public Health Expenditures as a Percentage of Total Budgets, All Jurisdictions[a]	Percentage of Revenues from Total Own Sources, All Jurisdictions[a]	Percentage of Health Expenditures Received from State, All Jurisdictions[a]
High-Poverty Cities	City	County or Special District	City	County or Special District				
St. Louis	$ 47.0	N.A.	$ 8.4	N.A.	$105	20.6%	71.1%	24.2%
Philadelphia	54.2[b]	N.A.	65.9	N.A.	66	11.0	67.4	37.9
Chicago	1.9	163.1	53.5	11.2	39	13.3	67.6	8.2
Boston	70.8	N.A.	7.5	N.A.	123	10.0	64.7	4.6
Detroit	51.2	113.0	35.7	40.6	95	18.6	46.6	21.0
New York	690.0	N.A.	1,739.1[b]	N.A.	325	19.9	52.6	5.3
Average per Area[c]	—	—	—	—	167[d]	18.2	55.2	8.3
Low-Poverty Cities								
Dallas	0.0	68.2	4.5	2.8	54	19.4	83.6	2.0
Houston	0.0	59.4	16.1	6.6	42	12.9	85.1	5.1
Pittsburgh	0.0	28.7	0.3	34.3	42	16.0	53.8	37.0
Minneapolis	0.0	40.3	6.1	22.8	76	15.5	49.2	8.5
Anaheim-Santa Ana-Garden Grove	0.0	8.9	0.0	30.2	23	9.6	58.3	30.2
Average per Area[c]	—	—	—	—	52	14.5	67.0	14.2

a. City, county, and special district populations, expenditures, and revenues are combined as relevant.

b. Includes $1,358 million for medical vendor payments.

c. Weighted by areas' populations.

d. $92 per capita if New York's medical vendor payments are excluded.

Sources: U.S. Department of Commerce, Bureau of the Census, *City Government Finances in 1976-77*, *County Government Finances in 1976-77*, and *Finances of Special Districts, 1977*.

Much more striking, however, is the difference between the two groups in the per capita burden of local public medical care, $167 in the high-poverty areas and $52 in the low-poverty ones.[151]

To some extent, medical expenditures in high-poverty areas are already subsidized by state and federal governments. This is shown by the share of total revenues raised from own sources. Not surprisingly, the low-poverty areas were less dependent on outside funds, raising 67 percent of their revenues locally, compared with 55 percent for the high-poverty areas. If one examines state transfers earmarked for health and hospital spending, the picture somewhat reverses. The high-poverty areas received a smaller share of their medical care budgets from state governments than did low-poverty areas, 8.3 and 14.2 percent, respectively.

Despite these subsidies, local revenues support more than half the medical expenditures made at the local level. Any national health insurance plan which would expand insurance coverage for the poor and shift the burden of financing care from local to national sources would therefore provide some measure of fiscal relief for local governments. The data just reviewed suggest that most of this relief would be distributed to the largest cities and counties, particularly those with large poverty populations. These areas tend to have the largest share of aggregate medical care spending at the local level as well as larger per capita burdens. The amount and exact nature of an NHI plan's effects depend on each plan's implications for coverage, financing employment, and payment and resource allocation. These areas are analyzed in the following section.

IMPLICATIONS OF NATIONAL HEALTH INSURANCE FOR COVERAGE IN CITIES

This section investigates the distribution of the now uncovered population by place of residence and the extent to which the Carter and Martin plans' coverage provisions would differentially affect city residents. (The Kennedy-Waxman bill is not discussed here because it leaves no significant coverage gaps.) Table 23 reports data from the 1976 Health Interview Survey on the distribution of the population by health care coverage and place of residence. Eleven percent of the population, more than 23 million people, reported no health care coverage of any kind. Rural residents were least well covered (14.1 percent), followed by central city residents (11.7 percent) and suburban residents (8.1 percent). Of those without coverage, 40 percent lived outside standard metropolitan statistical areas (SMSAs) while 31 percent were central city residents, and

Table 23

DISTRIBUTION OF THE POPULATION, BY TYPES OF HEALTH CARE COVERAGE AND RESIDENCE
(1976, '000s of people)

Residence	Private Hospital Insurance, Medicare, or Both		Medicaid Coverage Only		Other Plans or Programs Only		Private Hospital Insurance; Don't Know Coverage		No Other Insurance; Don't Know If Covered by Private Hospital Insurance		No Health Care Coverage	
	(No.)	(%)	(No.)	(%)	(No.)	(%)	(No.)	(%)	(No.)	(%)	(No.)	(%)
SMSAs	116,328	80.7%	8,992	6.2%	3,302	2.3%	1,129	0.8%	639	0.4%	13,837	9.6%
In Central Cities	46,109	75.1	6,008	9.8	1,409	2.3	425	0.7	292	0.5	7,168	11.7
Outside Central Cities	70,219	84.8	2,983	3.6	1,892	2.3	704	0.9	347	0.4	6,669	8.1
Outside SMSAs	51,385	77.4	3,171	4.8	1,783	2.7	495	0.8	222	0.3	9,363	14.1
Nonfarm	46,354	77.4	3,069	5.1	1,676	2.8	463	0.8	213	0.4	8,106	13.5
Farm	5,031	76.9	102	1.6	107	1.6	32	0.5	9	0.1	1,257	19.2
All Persons	167,713	79.6	12,162	5.8	5,084	2.4	1,624	0.8	861	0.4	23,200	11.0

Source: U.S. Department of Health, Education, and Welfare, National Center for Health Statistics, *Advancedata*, DHEW Publication no. (PHS) 79-1250, September 20, 1979, p. 60.

29 percent were noncentral city residents. Another 5.8 percent of the population had no coverage other than Medicaid. Almost half of these people lived in central cities. Thus, 16.8 percent of the entire population had no coverage or Medicaid-only coverage. However, 20.5 percent of central city residents were in this category, compared with 11.7 percent of surburban residents, and 18.9 percent of rural residents. Finally, a smaller percentage of central city residents, 75.1 percent, reported having private hospital insurance and/or Medicare coverage than did residents of any other place.

These data show that on average, central city residents have less insurance coverage and are much more likely to depend on Medicaid than are other SMSA residents. More detailed data on the kind and quantity of care received by place of residence are available from a 1976 household survey.[152] Table 24 reports selected findings from this study. Central city residents were most likely to have no regular source of care and least likely to be covered by a private group insurance policy. Furthermore, those central city residents with insurance were less likely to be covered for hospital, surgical, or major medical services than other insured SMSA residents. In spite of these apparent differences in coverage, actual use of services was fairly similar in all areas. The percentage seeing a physician within a year varied little by place of residence, and central city residents had somewhat more physician visits per person and a higher proportion of hospitalization. However, they also reported more disability days per person than residents of other places, which suggests that use relative to need is fairly similar across places of residence. It appears then that although private insurance is less prevalent and less comprehensive in central cities, Medicaid and locally provided free care helped compensate for possible adverse effects on the use of services.

Comparable data for selected individual central cities are not available from published sources. Thus, it is not possible to observe directly the extent to which individual central cities deviate from national averages. One can, however, examine data on several population characteristics (age, income, and employment status) associated with insurance coverage. These are reported in Table 25. By and large, differences between central city and other portions of the selected SMSAs are small. The one striking exception is the proportion of families in the lowest income class. The number of families with incomes below $5,000 is more than four times larger in the central cities of the high-poverty SMSAs than in their surburban rings. Differences in income distribution are less dramatic in the low-poverty SMSAs.

These tables indicate that central cities would benefit more than surburban areas by the expansion of public insurance protection to cover at least all families and individuals with incomes below 55 percent of

Table 24

SELECTED DATA ON HEALTH INSURANCE COVERAGE AND MEDICAL CARE USE, BY PLACE OF RESIDENCE (1976)

	SMSAs		
	In Central Cities	Outside Central Cities	Rural, Nonfarm
Percentage of Population by Regular Source of Care			
Particular physician/osteopath	71%	77%	84%
No particular physician/osteopath	14	10	6
No regular source	15	13	10
	100	100	100
Percentage of Population with Private Insurance, by Type			
Group	62%	70%	67%
Individual	8	9	10
Percentage of Insured Population, by Types of Coverage			
Hospital	85%	90%	88%
Surgical	84	89	86
Outpatient physician visits	60	57	52
Major medical	54	60	52
Percentage of Population Seeing a Physician Within a Year	77%	78%	75%
Number of Physician Visits per Person per Year[a]	6.01	5.02	5.03
Percentage of Population with One or More Hospitalizations a Year	13%	10%	12%
Disability Days per Person[a]	12.55	10.76	11.05

a. Adjusted for age and sex differences.
Source: LuAnn Aday, Ronald Andersen, and Gretchen Fleming, *Health Care in the U.S.; Equitable for Whom?* (Beverly Hills, Calif.: Sage Publications, 1980), various tables.

poverty level, especially in high-poverty cities. Furthermore, it appears that much of the benefit to central cities would be in the form of fiscal relief, to government and to private providers rather than in the form of sharp increases in medical care consumption, since residents already use services at rates comparable to other areas. As was suggested earlier, however, the Carter plan might still leave substantial coverage and medical care financing problems for those just above HealthCare's low-income threshold. Table 26 explores this issue by examining the distribution of people at various proportions of the poverty level. Although the data are from the 1970 census, the relative distributions are unlikely to have changed dramatically. The upper portion of the table clearly shows that central cities would benefit more than other areas from expanded coverage for the very poor. Central cities appear to have almost twice as large a proportion of their population under 50 percent of the poverty level as other areas do. Furthermore, more than half of these people are either individuals or in male-headed families. Many of them might not be eligible under current Medicaid eligibility criteria, particularly in states where two-parent families do not qualify for cash assistance.

The bottom half of table 26, on the other hand, indicates fairly clearly that the remainder of the poor and the near-poor — who are not covered by HealthCare — also constitute a substantial proportion of central cities' residents: 19 percent in the high-poverty cities and 17.5 percent in the low-poverty cities. There are three times as many people between 50 and 150 percent of the poverty level as are in the very poor category, which would be automatically covered by the Carter plan. Again, more than two-thirds of these people are either individuals or in male-headed families, and are unlikely to be included in HealthCare through categorical eligibility criteria.

These data have important implications for city budgets and urban hospitals. If many physicians were to deny access to individuals above the low-income standard who are eligible for HealthCare only through the spend-down mechanism, these individuals would probably end up receiving care from public hospitals serving as providers of last resort. These hospitals would receive payment from HealthCare only after the spend-down liability had been met. If the hospital could not collect that liability from the individual, the hospital incurs a deficit and the city budget, a burden.

The Martin bill's catastrophic insurance plan (CAPP) would automatically cover everyone who was not otherwise covered by a qualified public or private plan and who incurred more than a specified income-related amount for uninsured medical expenses. Although coverage would be universal, this plan might provide less relief for central cities than other places of residence because a disproportionate share

Table 25

VARIOUS POPULATION CHARACTERISTICS, SELECTED METROPOLITAN AREAS (1970 and 1976)

	High-Poverty SMSAs		Low-Poverty SMSAs	
	In Central Cities	Outside Central Cities	In Central Cities	Outside Central Cities
Total Population (000s)	15,985	16,700	3,786	5,390
I. Age				
18-24 years	11.5%	10.2%	8.8%	10.3%
II. Family Income (1976)				
Total Families (000s)	3,617	4,606	932	1,709
Less than $5,000	16.3%	3.5%	8.1%[a]	5.2%
$5,000-9,999	23.0	12.7	17.0	14.7
$10,000-14,999	30.3	15.2	21.2	17.8
$15,000+	30.4	68.6	53.7	62.2
III. Employment Status				
Civilian, noninstitutionalized population, 16+ years (000s)	11,687	11,324	2,660	3,612
Employed	54.8%	57.8%	59.5%	56.9%
Unemployed	2.7	2.0	2.4	2.1
Self-employed	3.5	4.7	4.4	4.6
Not in Labor Force	42.3	39.4	37.9	40.5
IV. Weeks Worked				
Employed, civilian work force, 16+ years (000s)	7,384	7,632	1,855	2,394
50-52	58.2%	59.5%	57.2%	60.6%
27-49	26.1	22.5	24.5	21.5
# 26	15.7	17.9	18.4	17.8

a. Data not available for Pittsburgh for this income class.

Sources: U.S. Department of Commerce, Bureau of the Census, *1970 Census of Population: General Population Characteristics,* various state volumes, tables 24, 85, and 88 (Sections I, III, and IV); U.S. Department of Commerce, Bureau of the Census, *Money Income in 1976 of Families and Persons in the United States,* series P-60, no. 114, July 1978.

Table 26

POVERTY STATUS BY PLACE OF RESIDENCE,
SELECTED SMSAs
(1970)

	High-Poverty SMSAs		Low-Poverty SMSAs	
	In Central Cities	Outside Central Cities	In Central Cities	Outside Central Cities
Total Population (000s)	15,760	16,387	3,724	5,311
Percentage below 50 Percent of Poverty Level				
All Persons	6.3%	2.5%	5.2%	2.9%
Persons in Families with Male Heads	2.0	1.0	1.7	2.9
Persons in Families with Female Heads	2.5	0.7	2.0	0.8
Individuals	1.8	0.8	1.5	0.8
Percentage between 50 and 150 Percent of Poverty Level				
All Persons	19.0%	8.1%	17.5%	12.7%
Persons in Families with Male Heads	10.0	5.0	10.4	7.7
Persons in Families with Female Heads	5.6	1.6	3.9	3.4
Individuals	3.4	1.5	3.2	1.6

Source: U.S. Department of Commerce, Bureau of the Census, *1970 Census of Population: General Population Characteristics,* various state volumes, tables 207 and 208.

of low-income persons reside in central cities. The ratio of the plan's maximum out-of-pocket payment for low-income families ($500 for families with income less than $4,000 and $500 plus 25 percent of income between $4,000 and $10,000 for other families with income less than $10,000) to family income attains its minimum (.125) at $4,000 of income. The ratio increases rapidly as income either falls or rises (for example, .166 at $3,000 and, .150 at $5,000). Consequently, one would expect many very low-income families to continue to seek free care from public sources. But fiscal relief would clearly be provided to local governments and private providers for large medical expenses not now covered by insurance.

Based on these data, the following inferences appear warranted. The Carter plan would clearly expand coverage and relieve cities of much of the fiscal burden associated with care for the very poor. Coverage gaps are likely to remain, particularly among the near-poor, and these gaps would be more of a problem for central cities than for suburbs. Medical spend-down provisions coupled with mandatory coverage of catastrophic, maternity, and infant care would close part of the gap. Difficulties with applying the spend-down and the magnitude of the deductible required before one is qualified for catastrophic protection would nevertheless impose disproportionate hardships on this segment of the population.

Similarly, the Martin plan's CAPP program would relieve cities of a portion of their responsibilities for providing care, namely payment for bills exceeding the income-related ceiling on personal out-of-pocket expenses. These ceilings would remain high, however, and would do little to alleviate coverage problems for ambulatory care services.

IMPLICATIONS OF NATIONAL HEALTH INSURANCE FOR FINANCING AND INCOME REDISTRIBUTION

An NHI plan's financing scheme would redistribute income not only among persons in different income classes, but also among places of residence. As chapter 3 showed, the three bills under consideration would have very different implications for the distribution of NHI benefits and costs among people in different income classes. In considering alternative bills' effects on cities, it is important to note the significant differences in the distributions of income among cities, suburbs, and nonmetropolitan areas.

Information on the distributions of benefits and costs by place of residence under the existing system is very limited. Some data on expenditures for medical care by source of payment are available from a 1970 household survey.[153] There appear to be no data on the distribution of tax burdens or insurance premiums by place of residence. As a result, it is possible to make only indirect inferences about the three bills' income redistribution implications for cities. Our analysis, therefore, is based on applying national estimates of net benefits by income class to data on the distributions of families by income class in each place of residence. In addition, the assessment of the Martin plan examines data on differences in the distributions of "catastrophic" expenditures.

160

Table 27 reports the distribution of incomes for all families by place of residence. About 27 percent of families reside in central cities of metropolitan areas. Comparing income distributions by place of residence shows that the distribution in central cities is fairly similar to that in nonmetropolitan areas, and that both differ markedly from income distribution in suburban areas (metropolitan, outside central cities). About 17.8 percent of families in central cities reported incomes below $6,000, while 27.8 percent had incomes of $20,000 or more. The corresponding percentages for families in suburban areas are 8.9 percent below $6,000 and 39.9 percent above $20,000. (Since the distributions are similar for large and small metropolitan areas, subsequent tables will report data for all central cities combined.)

Table 28 reproduces estimates of net benefits under the current system and three NHI bills (see chapter 3). The estimates for the current system and the Martin plan are averages based on all families within the four income classes. The intermediate (CHIP) and comprehensive (HSA) plan estimates, which are used as analogs to the Carter and Kennedy-Waxman plans, are calibrated to a family of four with one full-time wage earner at each of the specified income levels. Thus, the two pairs of estimates are not precisely comparable.

As can be readily seen, each of the three bills would increase the amount of income redistribution to the lowest-income families. Families just above the poverty line appear to do worse under the intermediate plan than under the other two proposals, but better than under the current system. Finally, highest-income families fare the best under the intermediate plan, since the net transfers to the rest of the system under this plan would be lower than those under the Martin or comprehensive plans.

Given the data on the distributions of families by income and place of residence, it appears that central cities would gain the most under the Kennedy-Waxman plan. This is not surprising, since coverage would be universal and the financing relatively progressive. Perhaps more surprising is the finding that cities might receive larger income transfers under the Martin plan than under the Carter plan. (This conclusion must be treated as highly tentative, since the Carter financing plan, while similar to the intermediate bill's plan, is not identical to it.) The best explanation for this result lies in the way the two bills define catastrophic expenditures. The Martin bill relies on income-related expenditure limits while the Carter and intermediate plans specify a fixed-dollar maximum ($2,500 for the Carter bill). Table 29 shows that the distribution of family outlays varies significantly under the two definitions. Only 1 percent of families with incomes below $2,000 in 1970 (equivalent to an income of about $1,000 in 1980) had outlays in excess of $1,000. But 38

Table 27

PERCENTAGE DISTRIBUTION OF FAMILIES, BY INCOME AND PLACE OF RESIDENCE
(1976)

Family Income Level	All Metropolitan Areas		Metropolitan Areas of:				All Nonmetropolitan Areas
			1,000,000 or More		Less than 1,000,000		
	In Central Cities	Outside Central Cities	In Central Cities	Outside Central Cities	In Central Cities	Outside Central Cities	
0-$2,999	4.6% } 17.8	2.4% } 8.9	4.7%	2.0%	4.6%	3.0%	5.0% } 17.1
3-5,999	13.2	6.5	13.8	5.9	12.0	7.3	12.1
6-8,999	12.7	9.6	13.2	9.1	12.2	10.3	14.0
9-11,999	11.8	10.0	11.6	8.5	11.9	12.2	14.3
12-14,999	12.2	11.3	11.6	10.0	12.8	13.0	13.3
15-19,999	17.9 } 45.7	20.6 } 60.5	17.1	20.4	18.9	20.5	18.4 } 40.6
20-24,999	12.3	15.4	5.3	16.2	12.6	14.1	10.5
25 and over	15.5	24.5	16.0	27.8	15.0	19.6	11.7
Total Number of Families (000s)	(15,529)	(22,426)	(8,144)	(13,492)	(7,384)	(8,934)	(18,755)

Source: U.S. Department of Commerce, Bureau of the Census. *Social and Economic Characteristics of the Metropolitan and Non-Metropolitan Population: 1977 and 1970*, Special Study P-23, no. 75.

Table 28

ESTIMATES OF NET BENEFITS PER FAMILY BY INCOME CLASS, UNDER CURRENT SYSTEM AND THREE ALTERNATIVE NHI BILLS (1975)

Number and (%) of Families (000s)		Income Class (All Families)	Current System	Minimal (Martin)
6,766	(12%)	Less than $5,000	$ 99	$234
11,920	(21)	5,000- 9,999	-37	12
12,561	(22)	10,000-14,999	-363	-377
25,310	(45)	15,000+	-876	-987
56,245	(100%)			

Number and (%) of Families (000s)[a]		Income Class (Family of Four with One Full-Time Worker)	Intermediate Plan (CHIP)[b]	Comprehensive Plan (HSA)[c]
172	(2%)	$ 3,000	$ 400	$ 960
409	(4)	6,000	-40	740
821	(8)	9,000	-90	480
1,198	(12)	12,000	-140	250
1,598	(16)	15,000	-190	-10
2,487	(25)	20,000	-300	-450
		⎰30,000	-580	-1,170
3,255	(31)	⎱40,000	-910	-2,020
180	(2)	50,000	-1,270	-2,930
10,122	(100%)			

a. Four-person, husband-wife families; data are for income intervals implied by column 2 income levels.

b. 1973 Comprehensive Health Insurance Plan, very similar to Carter Plan.

c. Health Security Act, very similar to Kennedy-Waxman plan.

Source: Estimates of net benefits under CHIP and HSA are from Mitchell and Schwartz, *The Financing of National Health Insurance*, p. 12.

Table 29

PERCENTAGES OF FAMILIES THAT INCURRED CATASTROPHIC EXPENDITURES, BY INCOME AND PLACE OF RESIDENCE (1970)

Family Income	Outlay[a] is $1,000 or More[b]	Outlay[a] is 15 Percent or More of Pretax Family Income
Under $2,000	1%	38%
2,000- 3,499	4	25
3,500- 4,999	6	13
5,000- 7,499	13	14
7,500- 9,999	12	4
10,000-14,999	28	3
15,000+	37	4
Poverty Status		
Above Poverty Level	93	34
Below Poverty Level	7	66
Residence		
SMSA, Central City	23	27
SMSA, Outside Central City	47	26
Rural, Nonfarm	16	26

a. Outlay, as defined by Andersen et al. (p. 278), includes the difference between health insurance premiums and benefits paid, as well as out-of-pocket medical expenses. (Medicaid and other free care are treated as insurance benefits.) If premiums exceed benefits, then the difference is added to out-of-pocket costs.

b. $1,000 in 1970 is equivalent to almost $2,000 in 1980.

Source: Ronald Andersen, Joanna Lion, and Odin Anderson, *Two Decades of Health Services,* (Cambridge, Mass.: Ballinger Press, 1976), p. 91-3.

percent of those families spent more than 15 percent of their incomes on medical care. These figures are almost exactly reversed for families in the highest income class. Because of the differences in income distributions by place of residence, 47 percent of suburban families, who on average have higher incomes than central city families, spent more than $1,000, compared with 23 percent of central city families. Using the income-related criterion, however, eliminates differences by place of residence in the proportion of families with catastrophic expenditures; about one-quarter of families in each area spent more than 15 percent of their incomes on medical care.

Thus, the more progressive a plan's overall financing scheme, the more cities stand to gain in terms of income redistribution. Clearly, when plans that emphasize protection against catastrophic expenditures are compared, cities would find advantageous a plan that defines *catastrophic* as a percentage of family income rather than a plan that sets a specific dollar limit. Under the latter type of plan, a smaller proportion of city residents would qualify for aid, since the poor generally have lower absolute outlays. As a result, much of the cost of free medical care would still be financed by local revenues rather than shifted to more progressive federal revenues.

IMPLICATIONS OF NATIONAL HEALTH INSURANCE FOR EMPLOYMENT IN CITIES

Both the negative and positive employment effects associated with national health insurance would vary by place of residence. The current health care financing system displays wide variations across industries both in the number of employees covered and in employers' premium contributions. Differences among places of residence in the relative importance of various industries would lead to differential allocations of unemployment increases. At the same time, however, growth in health sector employment might also be unevenly distributed among places of residence because of differences in the bills' effects on the demand for medical care. As in chapter 4, this section focuses chiefly on the Carter and Kennedy-Waxman plans, because the Martin bills' employment effects would be minimal.

The differential impact on unemployment would depend mainly on differences by place of residence in the distributions of employees by industry and between firms which now do and do not offer health insurance plans. Distribution of employees by industry is relevant primarily to the Carter plan, which would have very different effects on unemployment in various industrial sectors. The distribution between firms with and without coverage is pertinent to the Kennedy-Waxman plan, which would place most of the increased premium burden on firms not now providing coverage for their employees. Unfortunately, no data are available for the latter by location.

Table 30 reports data on the total number of employed persons and their distribution by industry in central cities and in metropolitan counties outside of central cities. Compared with areas outside central cities, central cities have 3.4 percentage points more of their workers in service industries; about the same percentages in public utilities, wholesale and retail trades, and finance; lower percentages of workers in agriculture,

165

Table 30

PERCENTAGE DISTRIBUTION OF EMPLOYED PERSONS 16 AND OLDER, BY INDUSTRY IN METROPOLITAN AREAS
(1977)

Industry	All Metropolitan Areas		All Metropolitan Areas of 1,000,000 or More		Metropolitan Areas of Less than 1,000,000	
	In Central Cities	Outside Central Cities	In Central Cities	Outside Central Cities	In Central Cities	Outside Central Cities
Total (000s)	24,593	36,088	12,725	22,263	11,869	13,825
Agriculture, Forestry, and Fisheries	0.6%	2.0%	0.3%	1.1%	0.8%	3.4%
Construction	4.4	5.6	4.0	5.5	4.9	5.6
Manufacturing	20.8	23.4	21.2	22.8	20.5	24.4
Transportation, Communication, and Other Public Utilities	6.9	6.6	6.7	6.9	7.1	6.3
Wholesale and Retail Trade	21.4	21.5	20.4	21.8	22.5	21.1
Finance, Insurance, and Real Estate	7.0	6.2	7.7	6.8	6.3	5.3
Services[a]	32.0	28.6	33.0	29.0	30.9	28.1
Other[b]	6.9	6.0	6.7	6.1	7.1	5.9

a. Includes business and repair services, personal services, entertainment and recreation services, professional and related services.

b. Includes public administration and mining.

Source: U.S. Department of Commerce, Bureau of the Census. *Social & Economic Characteristics of the Metropolitan and Non-Metropolitan Population: 1977 and 1970*, Special Study P-23, no. 75.

construction, and manufacturing. These distributions are very similar for both large and small metropolitan areas. It appears, then, that interarea differences in industrial composition are unlikely to cause large differences in induced unemployment by place of residence.

Positive effects on health sector employment, on the other hand, might very well be stronger in central cities than in other areas. By historical accident more than any other reason, many health care institutions, particularly hospitals, tend to be located in or near cities' poverty areas. (See figure 3 for two examples.) As a result, the health care industry might be a particularly important source of employment, income, and upward mobility for residents of cities' poverty neighborhoods.

Table 31 reports data on health sector employment for selected high- and low-poverty SMSAs in 1970. The health industry accounted for 6.1 percent of central city employment, compared with 5.3 percent of employment outside central cities. Slightly more central city health workers were employed in hospitals, about 70 percent compared to about 62 percent outside central cities. Much more striking, however, are the differences in employment by race. The proportion of black and Hispanic health workers in central cities was about four times larger than the proportion outside central cities. Furthermore, this difference was approximately the same in both the high- and low-poverty SMSAs.

Thus, both bills should expand health sector employment, and a major share of this employment increase would probably occur in central cities. Furthermore, if the bulk of the increase in demand were by the poor, much of the additional employment would occur in institutions either now serving poor populations or in new offices and clinics established in or near poverty areas. Since the Kennedy-Waxman bill would have a larger aggregate impact, its effects on aggregate and cities' health sector employment should be larger than the Carter bill's effects. In both bills, the employment increases would partially offset short-run unemployment caused by mandated employer contributions, as well as draw workers from other industries (particularly in nonhealth occupations).

IMPLICATIONS OF NATIONAL HEALTH INSURANCE FOR PAYMENT AND RESOURCE ALLOCATION IN CITIES

The final section of this chapter focuses on how each NHI plan's provisions for payment and resource allocation might differentially affect cities relative to other places of residence. This topic encompasses three major elements: cost containment through the marketplace (price competition among insurers and reliance on patient cost sharing), physician

Figure 3

LOCATION OF HEALTH CARE INSTITUTIONS AND POVERTY AREAS BUFFALO AND CLEVELAND

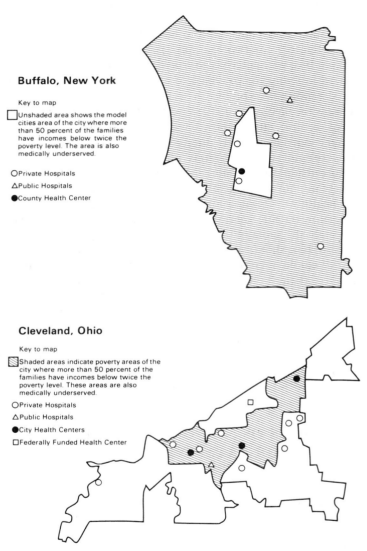

Buffalo, New York

Key to map

☐ Unshaded area shows the model cities area of the city where more than 50 percent of the families have incomes below twice the poverty level. The area is also medically underserved.

○ Private Hospitals

△ Public Hospitals

● County Health Center

Cleveland, Ohio

Key to map

▨ Shaded areas indicate poverty areas of the city where more than 50 percent of the families have incomes below twice the poverty level. These areas are also medically underserved.

○ Private Hospitals

△ Public Hospitals

● City Health Centers

☐ Federally Funded Health Center

Source: General Accounting Office, "Outpatient Health Care in Inner Cities: Its Users, Services, and Problems," Report to the Congress, MWD-75-81, June 6, 1975.

Table 31

HEALTH SECTOR EMPLOYMENT, SELECTED SMSAs
(1970)

Category	High-Poverty SMSAs		Low-Poverty SMSAs	
	Central Cities	Noncentral Cities	Central Cities	Noncentral Cities
Total Employment	6,402,252	6,540,826	1,583,128	2,054,624
Total Employment (Health Occupations)[a]	255,300	253,333	65,249	72,830
By Race and Sex				
Whites (Total)	60.4%	90.9%	76.5%	93.3%
Female	38.9	60.7	55.6	68.4
Male	21.5	30.2	20.9	24.9
Blacks (Total)	36.3	7.9	19.6	4.3
Female	30.5	6.7	17.0	3.7
Male	5.8	1.2	2.6	0.6
Hispanics (Total)	3.3	1.2	3.9	2.3
Female	2.1	0.7	2.6	1.6
Male	1.2	0.5	1.3	0.7
Occupations				
Physicians and Dentists	20.3%	26.0%	17.3%	19.9%
Other Professions and Technicians[b]	41.6	40.8	42.1	45.2
Health Service Workers	38.2	33.2	40.6	34.9
Total Employment (Health Industry)				
By Sector and Race				
Hospitals	284,254	214,883	67,176	63,107
Blacks	39.6%	10.4%	24.3%	5.7%
Hispanics	5.3	1.4	4.4	2.5
Other Health Workers[c]	105,257	140,549	30,085	38,183

a. Employment in health occupations is smaller than total health industry employment because the latter includes nonhealth occupations (janitors, secretaries, clerks, etc.).

b. Includes nurses.

c. Breakdown by race not available.

Source: U.S. Department of Commerce, Bureau of the Census, *1970 Census of Population: General Population Characteristics,* various state volumes, tables 86, 87, 93, 94, 99, and 100.

169

reimbursement, and hospital payment and cost control measures. Cities clearly would benefit, along with the rest of the nation, from any plan that improved resources allocation and helped bring costs under control. Thus cities have a stake in attaining the common goal of an efficiently organized national health system. Specific effects on cities and city residents, however, would depend on the particular mechanisms each plan used to achieve the common goal. This section identifies those mechanisms and attempts to identify the approaches to payment and resource allocation that would be most beneficial for cities.

Market Competition

Each of the three plans would rely on aspects of market competition to encourage efficiency and cost containment. The plans differ, however, in the relative importance of market mechanisms. At one extreme is the Martin plan, which would not require employers to offer group insurance to their employees, would encourage people to buy plans with high cost sharing or other cost-saving features, and would create a catastrophic-only public insurance plan to cover people not otherwise protected from large expenditures. Promoting consumers' sensitivity to prices of both insurance and medical care is the Martin plan's only mechanism for cost containment. At the other extreme is the Kennedy-Waxman bill, which would explicitly eliminate cost sharing and set a maximum insurance premium that would depend on income and the community's (state's) overall average per capita medical care expenditures. Despite these restrictions on price competition, the Kennedy-Waxman bill nevertheless would encourage competition among insurers through premium rebates to subscribers, with the size of the rebate dependent on the insurer's ability to keep costs down for its subscribers. The Carter plan falls between the other two. It would retain patient cost sharing as an element of its market strategy and would offer incentives for employees to select lower-cost health insurance policies. But the Carter plan's incentives are not as strong as those in the Martin bill. (There is no limit on the amount of employer contribution that would be tax deductible and any insurance premium rebates received by an employee would be fully taxable.)

As was noted earlier, central cities tend to have poorer and older residents than their suburban rings do. In 1977, 15.8 percent of the population in central cities had incomes below the poverty level, and 11.4 percent were 65 and older.[154] The corresponding proportions for suburban residents were 6.9 and 8.4.[155] Central city residents also appear to have greater health problems. According to the 1974 Health Interview Survey, 11.2 percent of central city residents reported only a limited ability or an inability to carry on their major activity because of chronic illness, compared with 8.9 percent of suburban residents.[156] Central city residents also reported more disability days per person per year, 12.55 compared to 10.76 for suburban residents.[157] Because of these characteristics, city residents will fare worse under a plan that emphasizes insurer competition with experience-rated premiums and high-cost sharing. In such a system, high-risk city residents would face higher premiums. Low-income residents who chose high cost-sharing policies would face a greater financial burden and a deterrent to the use of care. Although Medicaid and free care provided by city hospitals would reduce cost sharing to zero, taxpayers would still bear a major share of the cost of this care through state and local taxes.

The main disadvantage of insurer competition with experience-rated premiums is that high-risk individuals will be charged higher premiums. People who could not or did not buy private insurance could purchase coverage in a public program under the Carter plan and would be automatically covered under the Martin plan. But in both plans, public programs would probably be residual programs whose beneficiaries might find it hard to obtain care on the same terms as people covered by private insurance. Although the Kennedy-Waxman plan also would encourage insurer competition through rebates and more generous benefits, persons with high medical risks would bear less of the cost of cream skimming because the maximum personal premium would be limited by personal income and community experience. "Good" risks might receive higher rebates but, to the extent that good health is correlated with income and employment, these people would also pay higher premiums than "bad" risks.

Physician Reimbursement and Access

Both the Carter and the Kennedy-Waxman plans propose to pay physicians under fee schedules. But the fee schedule would apply only to HealthCare beneficiaries under the Carter plan, while it would act as a maximum payment for all physicians' services regardless of insurance carrier under the Kennedy-Waxman plan. The Martin plan proposes the least change to existing reimbursement procedures. As noted earlier, it would require physicians participating in CAPP to accept that program's fees as payment in full; the fees would be set at 100 percent of the relevant Medicare reasonable fees. Thus, CAPP fees would embody all of the existing variations in Medicare reasonable fees and, as a further incentive for physician participation, would not be limited by Medicare's Economic Index.

The general effects of the Carter plan's fee schedule, as discussed earlier, would apply to city residents. Government would have greater control over the price of services and would therefore be better able to

171

control expenditures under the HealthCare program. Because the fees would apply only to HealthCare, however, the access of HealthCare's beneficiaries to private providers would — as evidence from Medicare and Medicaid programs suggests[158] — worsen if the difference between HealthCare and private fees grow. HealthCare is designed to replace Medicaid, which is most important to central city residents. But barriers to access faced by current Medicaid eligibles would probably persist. In addition, growing refusal of private providers to participate would shift much of the financial responsibility for care back onto locally supported clinics and hospitals.

A second potential problem for cities concerns the setting of the HealthCare fee schedule, which could be either on a statewide or an area-specific basis. As already noted, fee schedules have the effect of making fees more uniform among physicians within an area. Fees in urban areas now tend on average to be higher than rural fees.[159] Thus, a fee schedule that made fees uniform across a state would benefit (or do less harm to) rural physicians relative to urban physicians. The likely result is that rural physicians' incomes would increase relative to urban physicians' incomes, which in turn would cause some urban physicians to migrate to rural locations.[160] Thus, it would be in the interest of cities to press for urban-rural fee differentials. Statewide fee schedules could also increase the disparity between private and public fees in urban areas and affect HealthCare participation of urban physicians.

The implications of the Kennedy-Waxman plan for cities can also be divided into the general and the specific. In general, cities should benefit from increased access and cost containment. By eliminating incentives for physicians to treat individuals and families differently, access of the urban poor to care should increase. At the same time, control over aggregate rates of increase in physician expenditures would help control urban residents' costs.

More specifically, two possible problems could be of concern to cities. Efforts to redistribute health spending between urban and rural areas could cause difficulties for cities. Redistribution within an overall expenditure cap could mean lower real spending for cities. Physicians' incomes are higher in urban areas than in rural areas despite higher physician-to-population ratios because of higher fees, higher incomes, and broader insurance coverage among the general population in urban areas.[161] The high levels of expenditure on physicians' services in urban areas do not appear to result from high utilization of physicians' services by the urban poor. But it might be difficult to reduce the budgets for spending on physicians' services in urban relative to rural areas without cutting back on physicians' services to the urban poor. If the budget allocated to physicians' services were clearly low, physicians would probably refer patients to other providers, most likely hospital inpatient and outpatient departments. Because hospital budgets would also be limited, hospitals would resist taking large numbers of referred patients. The result could be continued limited access to private hospitals for the poor. City public hospitals would continue to be needed as the source of care of last resort, following enactment of the Kennedy-Waxman bill. If budgets allocated to public hospitals were inadequate to support delivery of this care, cities would have to supplement NHI to finance these services. Thus cities would have an interest in maintaining urban-rural disparities in spending, or, failing this, in having a voice in the allocation of hospital and physician budgets within the city.

Whether these problems arise depends on two factors. First, although the total budget for physicians' services would be fixed, it probably would be higher in the short run under the Kennedy-Waxman bill than the levels of spending for physicians' services under the existing system. If increased spending in rural areas were to come out of new money added to the system, then cities would not be any worse off. As demands for care grew over time, however, an urban-rural conflict over distribution of the fixed budget would undoubtedly sharpen. Thus, the second factor affecting how cities fare is their bargaining strength in the budgeting process. Cities have the advantage of being tertiary care centers and the location of most medical schools. Rural areas, however, have traditionally had disproportionate political power within state legislatures. Under these circumstances, it is not possible to make a clear-cut prediction of how successful cities would be in capturing an appropriate share of the budget for physicians' services.

Finally, the Martin plan does little to alter existing methods of physician payment. Medicaid fee restrictions would remain intact. If fees continued to grow at high rates, then Medicaid eligibles' problems of access to private physicians would also continue. Medicare beneficiaries, conversely, would have somewhat better access than they do under the current system if physicians choosing to participate in CAPP also agreed to treat all of their Medicare patients on assignment. (The incentive is payment at the CAPP rate which would be higher than the corresponding Medicare rate.) In sum, the Martin bill probably would not profoundly change current conditions.

Hospital Payment and Cost Control

To city residents in general, like all citizens, hospital cost containment would offer some potential relief from rapidly rising hospital costs and related increases in insurance premiums. Cost-containment policies also raise two particular concerns for city governments and their low-income residents: (1) How would cost-containment policies affect access to care and the need for public facilities? and (2) How would cities, particularly inner cities, fare in the allocation of funds among hospitals?

To the extent that cost-containment policies encouraged discrimination or patient dumping (the alleged practice of transferring uninsured or nonpaying patients to public hospitals) by private hospitals, they would exacerbate the demand for publicly provided care. Under the Carter bill, a hospital approaching its guideline would probably try to avoid delivering services for which it would not be reimbursed or for which reimbursement would be below costs. Hospitals constrained by revenue ceilings or wishing to increase net revenues would probably also avoid delivering free care. Hospitals therefore would probably discriminate against patients whom the Carter bill left without insurance coverage or with only limited coverage. Because the Carter bill would allow differences in payment levels among third parties, private hospitals might also discriminate against relatively low-paying patients. Furthermore, hospitals under revenue ceilings have an incentive to avoid patients needing particularly intensive care or extensive stays. Public hospitals would be needed as a last resort for these patients. The demand for care from public hospitals would increase further if the HealthCare program's restrictions on physicians' fees reduced private physicians' willingness to serve HealthCare beneficiaries.

Different versions of the Carter cost-containment bill have included various provisions to discourage patient dumping or to protect hospitals that provide last-resort care. The House Ways and Means Committee version, for example, proposed that expenses on care for which hospitals are not compensated should not count toward expenditure guidelines and that charges not collected should not count as revenues under mandatory revenue ceilings. The expenditure exemption would prevent the guidelines from exacerbating private hospitals' current tendency to avoid treating nonpaying patients, for expenditures on nonpaying patients would not trigger the imposition of revenue ceilings. Similarly, the focus on collected rather than billed charges under revenue ceilings would maintain access to revenue sources for hospitals treating nonpaying patients. These provisions would be particularly valuable to public hospitals, for without them, cost containment could constrain whatever capacity these hospitals now have to earn patient revenues.

These provisions would be hard to administer and might offer some hospitals an opportunity to evade expenditure or revenue constraints in unintended ways. Furthermore, the provisions would not eliminate the incentives of hospitals seeking revenues to prefer paying to nonpaying patients. Nor would they prevent discrimination against heavy-care patients by hospitals under revenue ceilings. Despite the Ways and Means provisions, dumping will continue to occur and public hospitals will be called upon to provide care.

Other versions of the Carter bill adopt a different approach to prevent dumping, simply prohibiting hospitals from reducing their current proportions of "uninsured, low-pay or unusually costly patients" and from refusing admission for emergency care. Enforcement proceeds both through periodic administrative oversight and through investigation of complaints from institutions or individuals. The Secretary of DHHS could exclude any hospital that violated the rules from future participation in public programs or could reduce public reimbursement owed the hospital by $2,000 for each rejected patient.

Although the objective of these provisions is admirable, it is not clear that they could effectively prevent patient dumping. It is difficult and time consuming to document intentional changes in admissions practices, and the task is likely to be further complicated by hospitals' administrative and judicial appeals. Equally important, penalties may not be effective. Denying a hospital the right to participate would exacerbate rather than eliminate access problems. Government is unlikely to employ such a drastic measure. A penalty that is not likely to be used has little value in deterring undesirable practices. Fines would only encourage the admission of patients to the extent that rejections were detected and that fines exceeded the costs of care to rejected patients. The costs of care for such patients might well exceed the fines actually levied. These problems raise questions about the effectiveness of prohibitions on patient dumping, and suggest that protecting the hopsitals that treat nonpaying patients may be more important.

The Kennedy-Waxman bill would reduce but not eliminate the likelihood of patient dumping. Because all patients except illegal aliens would be insured and all third parties would pay hospitals on the same basis, hospitals would have very little reason to discriminate among patients. Hospitals with limited budgets, however, might try to avoid heavy-care patients, just as they would under the Carter bill. Oversight through the budgetary process could discourage this behavior, but it surely will not eliminate the need for "last resort" care.

Because the Martin bill would not constrain hospital revenues, it is unlikely to promote an increase in patient dumping. Instead, its primary effect would be to pay for patients who are not now covered by insurance, but who would qualify for CAPP. The availability of catastrophic insurance, however, might force major changes in the structure of public institutions. Because CAPP would limit bad debts associated with care to the poor, private hospitals would probably become more willing to accept these patients for inpatient care. Public hospitals might then face a reduced demand for inpatient services. Unless public hospitals reduced their capacity, low occupancy rates would increase their routine costs, perhaps putting them above the Section 223-type ceilings of CAPP, Medicare, and Medicaid. Local governments would be called upon to finance the resulting deficits.

Local governments faced with fiscal pressure might try to avoid these burdens by closing public hospitals or shifting their ownership or control to the private sector. Several localities have taken this course in recent years.[162] Closures or shifts, however, might mean a reduction of outpatient as well as inpatient services. Since the Martin bill would impose substantial cost-sharing requirements, public outpatient facilities would continue to be the only source of ambulatory care for many poor people. Reorganization of public facilities would therefore be preferable to closure if access to care is to be maintained.

Both the Carter and the Kennedy-Waxman bills would require explicit decisions on resource allocation to hospitals. Because the Carter bill operates primarily by formula, explicit allocation decisions would be limited to the granting of exceptions to expenditure or revenue ceilings and to the treatment of capital expenditures. Exceptions to federal expenditure and revenue controls are handled by the federal government and are not subject to an overall ceiling. In contrast, capital expenditure allocations are handled by state governments and local health systems agencies, subject to a nationally determined expenditure ceiling. This difference may be important to public and inner-city hospitals. In the payment exceptions process, hospitals do not compete against each other, but appeal for recognition of their particular circumstances. The federal government might be willing to recognize a hospital's availability to treat a low-income population with little or no insurance coverage as a circumstance deserving particular protection. The federal government's recent interest in assisting "financially distressed" urban hospitals might persist under national health insurance. Hence the Carter bill's assurance of access to the federal government might be valuable in providing resources to inner-city hospitals.

With respect to capital expenditures approval, however, hospitals are dependent on state decision making. To date, capital expenditure review has not been subject to an expenditure ceiling. The Carter bill would impose a ceiling, forcing choices among investments at both the state and local levels. Inner cities would be competing for resources with suburbs and rural areas. Federal priorities for resource allocation to maintain health and safety standards would offer all hospitals some protection in the allocation process. But other decisions would be influenced by the political power of different areas and hospitals. Many inner-city hospitals are important teaching and tertiary care institutions, whose value to the city and state goes beyond their services to the poor. These hospitals should fare well in the resource allocation process, but others might have difficulty. State governments' responsiveness to hospitals whose primary function is serving the poor will probably vary from state to state.

The same considerations would apply to broader state responsibility for resource allocation, either under the Carter bill's state rate-setting option or the Kennedy-Waxman bill's mandated state budgeting. Pressure to choose among hospitals and among areas would be greater under the Kennedy-Waxman bill, for its fixed budget would affect not only hospitals but also all other medical services. Under either bill, city governments and residents would have a considerable stake in assuring that the resource allocation process operated according to explicit, publicly promulgated criteria, and that it allowed for participation by affected parties.

The Martin bill proposes no explicit allocation process, and thus implicitly adopts the current system's allocation procedures. As argued in chapter 5, however, the bill would encourage continued escalation of hospital costs and public expenditures. If efforts to reduce taxes or limit the federal budget proved successful, these expenditures would have to come at the expense of other public expenditures, whether in health or other areas. Reductions in other federal expenditures might adversely affect programs that inner cities and their low-income residents value. The Martin bill's avoidance of payment constraints therefore would pose a major risk to cities' positions in the broader resource allocation process.

SUMMARY

Cities now spend substantial sums (almost $5 billion in 1976) for medical care because of their disproportionate share of the nation's poor and a long tradition of local public hospitals. The continual conflict between the demand for such care and the ability to pay for it is strongest in the older, declining cities of the northeast and north central regions of the country. Thus national health insurance could be particularly important to cities. It could help eliminate the remaining barriers to the use of care and medical services by the poor and medically needy, and it could provide significant fiscal relief to strained city budgets and public medical care institutions. This chapter has examined the implications of the three alternative NHI plans for cities, focusing on four broad areas: coverage, financing and income redistribution, employment, and payment and resource allocation.

Data on the current pattern of insurance coverage show that more than

20 percent of central city residents either have no insurance coverage or are covered by Medicaid only. (Almost half of the approximately 12 million people reporting Medicaid-only coverage are central city residents.) However, the actual use of services varies little by place of residence after adjusting for differences in the need for care. This suggests that existing gaps in coverage for city residents, particularly poor ones, are partially filled by locally provided free care. Clearly, the Kennedy-Waxman plan would eliminate almost all coverage gaps, since all persons except illegal aliens would be enrolled in the same plan. The Carter and Martin plans also would improve insurance coverage for many, but would also leave some with inadequate coverage and relatively high out-of-pocket financial burdens. These people would remain primarily the responsibility of local public medical care systems.

Data on the distribution of families by income and place of residence show that central cities (and nonmetropolitan areas) have substantially higher proportions of low-income residents than suburban areas do. It follows directly then that the more progressive the financing of an NHI plan, the more the cities would gain in terms of income redistribution. The Kennedy-Waxman plan, which would rely on the federal income tax and income-related insurance premiums to raise revenues and would eliminate cost sharing as a condition for use of services, clearly would be more progressively financed than the other two bills. Another important finding is that cities would benefit much more under a plan that defined catastrophic medical expenses as a percentage of income rather than a fixed dollar amount. Consequently, cities might prefer the Martin plan to the Carter plan on this count, although the former still would impose a relatively high maximum out-of-pocket payment obligation, $500 for families with incomes at or below $4,000.

Differences between cities and other places of residence in unemployment induced by employer-mandated premium financing should be small. City and suburban residents are distributed across industries in approximately the same way. Thus, the national estimate of a 0.5 percentage-point increase in short-term, private, nonfarm unemployment induced by the Kennedy-Waxman plan should apply to cities, as should the 0.25 percentage-point increase estimated for the Carter plan. (The Martin bill should have minimal impact on employment.) There would also be permanent increases in health sector employment generated by higher medical care expenditures under national health insurance. The Kennedy-Waxman bill should have about twice the job-enhancing impact the Carter bill would have, since the former would stimulate expenditure increases of about 17 percent and the latter of about 8 percent. Expanded health sector employment should be particularly beneficial for low-income, minority, and female workers who make up disproportionate shares of health workers, especially in central cities.

Finally, the impact of payment and resource allocation policies on cities also differs among the three bills. Both the Carter and Martin plans would rely heavily on cost sharing and insurer competition to encourage efficiency. Cost sharing, however, is generally more burdensome to the poor than to the rich, and insurer competition and experience rating might raise premiums for high-risk persons. The Kennedy-Waxman plan would prohibit cost sharing, would provide the same basic coverage to all people, and would not link premiums to medical risk or insurability. These features should be more beneficial to city residents than would coverage provisions of the other two bills.

The impact on cities of the bills' provisions for physician reimbursement and hospital cost containment are more diffuse and thus more difficult to ascertain. The Martin bill would adopt the inflationary Medicare method for physician payment with only minor changes and has no options for directly controlling physicians' fees or hospital costs. Both the Carter and Kennedy-Waxman bills would establish mechanisms for setting physicians' fees and limiting payments to hospitals. The Carter approach is more patchwork (fee schedules would apply only to services financed by HealthCare; hospital cost containment would be adminstered separately from other aspects of the plan) than the Kennedy-Waxman approach (a network of budgeting and planning boards at various levels of government). Unfortunately, the evidence on whether these systems would work is unclear. How cities would fare under each approach is even less predictable. For example, statewide fee schedules and hospital budgeting could drain resources from cities if political power in the allocation process lies with surburban and nonmetropolitan areas. At this time, however, such a conclusion would be merely conjecture.

Overall, it seems fairly clear that any of the three NHI plans considered would leave cities better off than they are under the current system. Which of the three bills would be most beneficial to cities is less clear cut. The Kennedy-Waxman bill has several advantageous features, but it also would be the most expensive initially, and it would rely on a method of budgeting and resource allocation without precedent in the American system. If this system could be made to work efficiently and equitably, then the approaches embodied in the Kennedy-Waxman bill would probably provide the greatest benefits for cities and city residents.

X. NATIONAL HEALTH INSURANCE: CONCLUSIONS

How can the United States expand health insurance and control the pressure on spending that more insurance would entail? This question has become the central issue in the political debate over national health insurance. Roughly 20 million Americans have neither public nor private health insurance and millions of other Americans have insufficient insurance to protect them against the potentially catastrophic costs of illness. Legislation to expand health insurance, however, could speed the increases in public and private spending for medical care that policymakers and the public already find unacceptable. Strong pressures to constrain government spending and fears that more coverage will mean more inflation impede enactment of national health insurance. And yet fundamental changes in health financing may well be necessary to constrain the rapid inflation induced by current financing arrangements. The challenge, then, is to design a national health insurance plan that can simultaneously expand access and contain costs.

Whether any plan can do both is critical, both to its economic success and to Congress's political willingness to enact it. This paper assesses the effects on access and costs of three alternative approaches to national health insurance:

- Public catastrophic insurance for all Americans, with minimal changes in existing public or private financing arrangements (the Martin bill).
- Catastrophic insurance and a new federal program to cover the poor and the elderly, with partial reform of provider payment mechanisms to limit costs (the Carter administration bill).
- A unified system of comprehensive coverage for the entire population, with government control over all provider payment and resource allocation (the Kennedy-Waxman bill).

We have asked four basic questions of each proposal:

- Would the bill provide adequate protection against the costs of illness?
- Would it reduce the regressivity of the current health care financing system?
- Would it avoid unacceptable increases in labor costs and unemployment?
- Would it encourage efficient allocation of health care resources and control medical expenditures?

181

Our purpose has been not to recommend any particular bill but to emphasize that any bill must satisfactorily answer these questions. Existing proposals naturally have their strengths and weaknesses. Our analysis identifies the strengths that many NHI plans could incorporate and the weaknesses any plan should avoid. The following summary highlights our findings about each proposal's effects on coverage, income distribution, employment, and resource allocation. These findings have led us to formulate a set of principles that any equitable and efficient NHI plan should follow.

SUMMARY OF NATIONAL HEALTH INSURANCE BILLS

The Martin Bill (The Medical Expense Protection Act)

The Martin bill would focus on closing a major gap in our current health financing system — coverage of catastrophic expenses — while changing that system as little as possible. The bill would provide catastrophic insurance to low-income people now ineligible for Medicaid, to people who cannot obtain health insurance through employment, and to the employed population. Protection would be automatically available to all individuals through a federal Catastrophic Automatic Payment Plan (CAPP) financed through general revenues. Under CAPP, catastrophic expenses would be defined in proportion to income, with the proportion rising as income rises. Private insurance would continue to provide catastrophic and other protection to employees whose employers chose to offer qualified plans. Employees whose employers offered qualified plans would have a ceiling of $2,500 on out-of-pocket expenditures. For employer-offered coverage, the bill would allow income tax exemptions only for contributions of up to $120 a month to qualified health insurance plans. Employees choosing qualified plans that cost less than the employer contribution would receive rebates that were partially tax deductible. Medicaid would remain untouched and Medicare would be amended to reduce cost-sharing requirements and to establish a limit on beneficiaries' out-of-pocket payments.

By providing catastrophic protection to people who now lack insurance and to people whose insurance is now limited, the Martin bill would significantly reduce this gap in current health insurance coverage. Gaps and inequities would nevertheless persist. Poor people not eligible for Medicaid would face substantial cost-sharing requirements, a minimum of 12.5 percent of their incomes. Poor people who met Medicaid's family status, age, or disability eligibility requirements would be better insured than other poor people. In addition, employees of firms offering qualified plans would have access that others would lack to comprehensive insurance at relatively low prices. Employees in low-risk occupations and low-cost areas would get more coverage per premium dollar than employees in high-risk occupations and high-cost areas. And individuals who lost their jobs because of illness would have to pay more for first dollar coverage than their former coworkers. These features of the Martin bill would mean continued barriers to receipt of medical care (or continued bad debts) by low-income people and continued inequities in out-of-pocket payments for medical care.

The Martin bill's use of general revenues to finance catastrophic expenditures and its limit on tax-deductible premiums would make financing more progressive than it is under the current system. But reliance on premium financing and on cost sharing means that the bill's overall impact would be regressive. That is, low-income people would spend a larger percentage of their incomes on medical care than people with higher incomes would spend.

Because the bill would not require employers to increase the coverage they offered or the proportion of premiums they paid, the Martin bill would have no direct impact on labor costs or employment.

The Martin bill's primary innovation with respect to resource allocation would be to promote choice and competition in the market for private health insurance. Proponents of this approach believe that competition would favor higher cost sharing and expansion of health maintenance organizations and other closed panel plans. Both of these outcomes would be expected to bring more efficient use of medical services, and therefore, to control costs. The Martin bill would set a ceiling on the premiums that are tax exempt, would encourage employers to offer employees a choice of plans, would require employers to make the same dollar contribution to employees regardless of the plan chosen, and would provide employees rebates — partially exempt from taxes — if their premiums were lower than the employer's contribution. These provisions would give employees an incentive to choose relatively low-cost insurance plans — that is, high deductible, traditional insurance, or, if comprehensive coverage is desired, HMOs or other closed panels. Because premium subsidies would remain high and some taxes on rebates would persist, however, the incentives to choose a low-cost plan would be weak and likely to affect primarily low-income employees. Preferences for comprehensive coverage and fee-for-service medicine are likely to be strong and other obstacles to growth of closed panels would persist. The bill is therefore unlikely to induce massive shifts to closed panels or substantial increases in patient cost sharing. Furthermore, any changes in cost sharing would probably have only a limited impact on service use. Low-risk individuals are more likely than high-risk individuals to choose high cost-sharing plans. Since the low-risk population uses fewer services anyway, this change would do more to shift insurance costs from the well to the sick than to alter the use and price of services.

The Martin bill proposes no direct intervention in mechanisms for paying providers. As is true today, private insurers would be free to adopt whatever payment methods they choose. CAPP, Medicare, and most Medicaid programs would continue to pay hospitals on a reasonable cost basis, and CAPP and Medicare would pay physicians according to their customary, prevailing, and reasonable charges. Reinforced by the increased demand for high-cost services that the bill's catastrophic coverage would probably produce, these payment methods would assure that medical costs would continue to increase rapidly. Emphasis on catastrophic rather than first-dollar coverage might also exacerbate the current disproportionate allocation of resources toward life-extending and high-technology medicine and away from primary care.

The Carter Bill (The National Health Plan)

Like the Martin bill, the Carter bill focuses on gaps in coverage. At the same time, however, the bill tries to reform the current payment and resource allocation process. The Carter bill would require employers to provide maternal, infant, and catastrophic coverage to their employees; would provide catastrophic coverage to Medicare beneficiaries; would offer maternal, infant, and catastrophic coverage to individuals not covered through employment; and would provide comprehensive coverage to all persons whose incomes are below 55 percent of the federal poverty standard (or whose medical expenses caused them to "spend down" to that level). Individuals not covered through employer plans and current beneficiaries of Medicare and Medicaid would be covered in a single, federally run HealthCare plan. The Carter bill defines catastrophic expenditures as out-of-pocket expenses exceeding $2,500. For employed individuals, the $2,500 is a limit that would be reached through whatever structure (if any) of deductibles and coinsurance employers and employees chose in the mandated private plans. For individuals not covered through employment, the $2,500 would be a deductible that could not be separately financed through private insurance policies. Employers would be required to pay at least 75 percent of premiums for qualified plans and to offer employees a choice between a qualified traditional insurance plan and all federally qualified HMOs in the area. Employees who chose qualified plans that cost less than the employer's fixed dollar contribution would receive a rebate, but that rebate would be subject to federal taxes.

By requiring all employers to provide their employees with catastrophic coverage, by amending Medicare, by replacing the Medicaid program with a national program for all low-income people (not just the "categorically" eligible aged, blind, or disabled), and by offering catastrophic coverage to individuals above 55 percent of the poverty line but not covered through employment, the Carter bill would substantially improve the population's protection against the cost of illness. But the plan's fixed-dollar definition of catastrophic coverage and different treatment of different segments of the population would perpetuate a major gap and inequity. Specifically, individuals whose incomes are relatively low but too high to qualify them as "poor" would, at best, acquire coverage only after spending a major share of their incomes (25 percent of a $10,000 pretax income, for example) on medical care. For both employed and unemployed individuals, such sizable cost-sharing obligations would pose continued deterrents to service use or continued likelihood of bad debts to providers.

The Carter bill would reduce the regressivity of the current financing system because HealthCare would eliminate out-of-pocket expenditures for a part of the poor population that are now uncovered. The plan's continued reliance on cost sharing and premiums, however, would perpetuate a system in which nonfederally covered low-income people spend a larger proportion of their incomes on medical care than people with higher incomes do. In other words, the Carter bill's overall financing system would be regressive.

The requirement that employers provide catastrophic coverage and pay 75 percent of premiums would increase labor costs and therefore might encourage some additional short-term unemployment (an estimated increase of 0.2 to 0.3 of a percentage point) — particularly among part-time workers. Although the bill would subsidize employers' premiums if they exceed 5 percent of the payroll, this provision is not likely to eliminate the unemployment effect. Very few employers would have premiums high enough to qualify for the subsidy. An inflationary economy, however, reduces the duration of the additional unemployment. If current conditions were to continue, the unemployment increases would dissipate in less than six months. In addition, higher total expenditures induced by the bill would expand health sector employment by about 8 percent.

With respect to resource allocation, the Carter bill proposes several innovations, but few of them would be likely to contain costs. First, the bill would require employers to offer employees a choice of insurance plans and to pay an equal dollar amount toward each plan offered. Employees would receive rebates (in salary or fringe benefits) of any difference between the employer contribution and the premiums of the plans they chose. The objectives of this approach are, in general, to encourage employees to consider the costs of a plan in relation to its benefits and, in particular, to encourage the selection of HMOs. Given the benefits (especially catastrophic and maternity benefits) the Carter plan requires of traditional insurance plans and the bill's failure to alter the tax status of employer contributions or employee rebates, the opportunity for choice would probably not produce either a major expansion of HMOs or a substantial increase in the cost-sharing obligations of traditional plans. Provisions to encourage HMO enrollment of HealthCare beneficiaries also would probably have limited impact. Overall, then, the Carter bill's efforts to change service use through changes in insurance structure would probably be ineffective.

The Carter plan also proposes direct measures to change methods of paying providers. The most extensive intervention would apply to hospital payment. Separately introduced cost-containment legislation (purportedly a part of the Carter administration's overall plan), would impose mandatory ceilings on hospital revenues per admission (if hospital expenditures exceeded predetermined guidelines). Although imposition of the ceilings would be administratively complex and subject to a variety of loopholes and exceptions, it nevertheless would offer a potential for some reduction in the rate of hospital cost increases. Particularly advantageous is the opportunity the bill would offer states to develop their own hospital cost-containment mechanisms, acceptable as long as state expenditures remained within federal limits.

For physicians, the Carter bill proposes less extensive change, with far less potential for containing medical costs. The bill proposes that the federal government establish fee schedules to pay physicians treating HealthCare patients. Physicians would have to agree to accept assignment for HealthCare patients, that is, accept government-established fees as payment in full. Private insurance plans would be encouraged but not required to use HealthCare fee schedules. The proposed uniform fee schedule, set at current Medicare levels, would mean higher payments to physicians on behalf of the poor, and thus expanded access by HealthCare beneficiaries to private physicians, at least at first. Fee levels would not change for current Medicare beneficiaries, but mandatory assignment might reduce physicians' willingness to treat elderly patients.

Fee schedules would offer government greater control over the price and volume of services that beneficiaries use and therefore represent an improvement over the federal government's current reliance on the customary, prevailing, and reasonable approach to payment. But use of the fee schedule only for HealthCare beneficiaries would effectively undermine the government's capacity to simultaneously control costs and to assure access to care. Since private fees would not be controlled, they would probably rise more rapidly than public fees; this situation would reduce physicians' willingness to accept HealthCare patients. The government would either have to accept reduced access for its beneficiaries or raise public fees, thereby sacrificing its cost-containment objective. To simultaneously control inflation and maintain access for HealthCare beneficiaries, the plan would ultimately have to control private as well as public fees.

The Kennedy-Waxman Bill (Health Care for All Americans)

Rather than simply address current gaps in coverage, the Kennedy-Waxman bill proposes a total reform of current insurance arrangements and provider payment mechanisms. All citizens and legal residents (except Medicare beneficiaries) would automatically receive comprehensive insurance coverage — with no cost sharing — by enrolling (or being enrolled) in one of three types of qualified insurance plans: a Blue Cross-Blue Shield plan, a commercial insurance carrier plan, or an HMO. Employed individuals would join plans through their employers. Other individuals would enroll independently in the same plans. Medicare beneficiaries would receive comprehensive coverage through the existing public program. Coverage would be financed through general revenues, continued use of the payroll tax and beneficiary premiums for Medicare, and income-related premiums. To allocate resources and control expenditures, the Kennedy-Waxman bill would establish an annual national health services budget, which would set the total amount that could be spent on covered services in the coming year. Budget increases would be limited to the average rate of increase in GNP over the preceding three-year period. The national budget would be allocated among the states; the states would then determine prospective budgets for their hospitals and other institutions and maximum fee schedules for physicians.

With its universal, comprehensive coverage, the Kennedy-Waxman bill would absorb the currently uninsured population, along with everyone else, into the same NHI plan. Because it would leave no differences among the poor or between the poor and the better-off, the bill would eliminate inequities in coverage. The elimination of cost sharing and reliance on general revenues and income-related premiums would also make the proposed plan's financing both less regressive than current arrangements and progressive overall.

The bill would require many employers to significantly expand insurance coverage for their employees and to pay at least 65 percent of the premiums for mandated coverage. Labor costs, and therefore unemployment, would rise in the short run because of increased fringe benefits. Additional premium payments would amount to about 1.5 percent of firms' labor bills (roughly three times the increase of the Carter plan). But, the impact on unemployment would be mitigated by two factors: the premium would be related to an individual's income and thus would not distort hiring decisions; all firms that do not now offer plans and experience profit declines would be eligible for subsidies equal to one-half of their premium costs above 3 percent of payroll in the first year of the plan. It is estimated that short-term unemployment would increase by about 0.45 and 0.55 of a percentage point with the adverse effects lasting less than six months.

There would also be a permanent increase in health sector employment. By expanding total spending for health care by about 17 percent over current levels, the bill would add almost 1 million new jobs to the health sector. This expansion would be particularly beneficial to women and blacks, who make up disproportionate shares of the health labor force.

To make these changes compatible with efficient resource allocation and cost containment, the Kennedy-Waxman bill proposes an entirely new system of insurer organization and provider payment. All private insurers would be required to participate in one of the five national consortia: Blue Cross-Blue Shield plans, commercial insurance carriers, prepaid group practice HMOs, individual practice association HMOs, and self-insurers. Individuals could choose among all plans available in their area. Plans could compete for enrollees by offering benefits not covered by the NHI plans and, if costs were less than premiums, by offering tax-exempt rebates to enrollees. Since the bill would eliminate all cost sharing, plans could not compete by varying cost-sharing amounts. The purpose of these arrangements is to encourage insurance plans to compete by controlling utilization and provider payments and operating efficiently. The bill would try to prevent insurers from competing for favorable risks by basing payments to insurers on enrollees' risk categories (actuarially determined) and by encouraging insurers to police each other in the distribution of premium income. Risk selection might nevertheless continue to occur. If so, competition would reduce insurance costs (premiums minus rebates) for the healthy and increase costs for the sick. Because of ceilings on individual premiums, however, high-risk individuals would not bear the full burden of such market segmentation, if it were to occur.

It seems unlikely that competition would encourage changes in service price and use for two reasons: (1) competition could not focus on cost-sharing obligations, since there would be none; and (2) competition would probably not reduce costs and use of services, given the regulatory constraints the bill could apply to the entire system. The Kennedy-Waxman bill would impose a budget to constrain all payments to health care providers. Insurers could pay less but not more than the hospital budgets and physician fee schedules that state governments would negotiate within federally determined limits according to federally established rules. This proposed budgeting mechanism offers a strong potential for cost containment. Unlike the current system, in which most insurance expenditures follow provider/patient decisions on service use, hospital budgets and negotiated fee schedules would allow governments to determine in advance what they were willing to spend. Since the plan would pay the same rates for all people, it would eliminate the current incentives for providers to discriminate against patients who pay lower rates.

Whether the Kennedy-Waxman bill could realize its potential for cost containment, however, is open to question. A desire to make the program acceptable to providers and to the public might lead officials to delay imposing expenditure controls until after the program's first year. The result would be a massive increase in health expenditures. Even if officials could resist initial pressure to increase spending, it would be hard to impose budgetary ceilings. The bill's limit on health budget increases to rates of increase in the gross national product would be a political obstacle — but not a prohibition — to greater expenditure increases. Congress or program administrators might allow health expenditures to increase faster than the GNP for a variety of reasons. First, federal policymakers might want to accommodate the greater demand for medical care that would accompany a decline in the GNP or a change in the population. Second, officials might respond to political pressure from states whose citizens wished to spend more on health. The bill would not allow states or communities to spend more than their nationally allocated budget, even from their own funds. The states' only alternative, then, would be to press Congress to raise the national ceiling. Third, Congress or administrators might respond to pressure from providers that budgeted rates were inadequate to support their participation in the program. Budgets for physician expenditures would be particularly hard to set, given initial data limitations. Federal officials might prefer to pay higher rates than to risk physician dissatisfaction or resistance. Finally, the federal government might respond to complaints from the general public as well as providers that budgets were inadequate to support universal access to quality care.

Whether the Kennedy-Waxman bill would successfully expand access and contain costs, therefore, depends on a variety of political decisions yet to be made. Regardless of the outcome, however, the bill would require government to make decisions on how much to spend, and it offers mechanisms to enforce those decisions. The current system lacks both these elements of an efficient resource allocation process.

189

PRINCIPLES FOR NATIONAL HEALTH INSURANCE

As stated at the outset, each of the three bills analyzed here would improve the current system somewhat but each has some financing or organizational problems. The following set of principles indicates the ways in which each plan (or other plans) could be modified to promote greater equity and efficiency.

First, national health insurance should provide benefits adequate to protect all citizens and legal residents against the cost of illness. The services that constitute adequate coverage are not controversial in NHI politics, and all the plans would cover similar types of services. In contrast, the share of medical expenses covered varies from plan to plan. In order to assure adequate protection, any national health insurance plan should set a limit on personal liabilities for medical care and that limit should be set in relation to income.

Second, people in equal circumstances should be treated equally by a national health insurance plan. The current Medicaid program allows differences in eligibility criteria across states and provides no protection to low-income people who do not meet categorical eligibility criteria. The current private insurance system provides better coverage at lower rates to employees in large firms than to employees in smaller firms, the self-employed, or unemployed. National health insurance should eliminate inequities of this kind.

Third, a NHI financing scheme should take into account individuals' ability to pay. Therefore, a plan should not take a greater share of income from the poor than from the better-off. Cost sharing that is related to income can be a major component of the financing scheme for an equitable NHI plan. If premiums are income related, they too can be an equitable source of financing. Income-related premiums are preferable to fixed-dollar premiums not only because of the direct limits they place on insurance costs for low-income individuals, but also because they equalize the impact of premiums-as-labor-costs across employees. This effect reduces the likelihood that higher premium costs would lead to disproportionate unemployment among low-income and part-time workers. The probability of any increase in unemployment due to national health insurance could also be reduced with subsidies, financed through general revenues, to employers whose premiums exceed a specified percentage of payroll. Because any unemployment due to higher premiums would be of short duration — particularly in a period of general inflation — subsidies should be phased out over time.

A fourth principle is that NHI administration should be responsive to variations in individuals' or communities' preferences and should encourage innovation. None of the principles enumerated previously is inconsistent with an NHI system that would operate through many separate plans. Decentralization would be preferable to establishment of a single, federally administered plan covering the entire population. Except for administering certain functions (e.g., income-related cost sharing or a national pool for financing and administering a catastrophic program for high-risk persons), the federal government's primary function should be to set the rules — as for eligibility and benefits (including cost sharing) — within which plans would operate. States and private insurers could comply with these rules while offering considerable variety in the organization of care delivery and in benefits beyond the minimum (including the supplementation of cost sharing). The result would be to allow considerable individual choice and an opportunity to learn from diversity, while maintaining equity through federal oversight.

Fifth, if national health insurance were to encourage choice among multiple plans, the tax system should be as neutral as possible toward insurance purchases. The most neutral system would be to eliminate all tax subsidies for insurance. If these tax subsidies are retained, rebates of amounts by which employer contributions exceeded premiums should also be fully tax exempt.

Sixth, competition should not interfere with the risk spreading that insurance aims to provide. Encouragement of choice among multiple plans therefore would require measures to protect against the adverse effects of cream skimming or market segmentation that separate the high- from the low-risk individuals. The likelihood of cream skimming or market segmentation could be reduced in two ways: (1) by requiring community rating and open enrollment or (2) by allowing experience rating, with public subsidies for premiums adjusted to reflect purchasers' actuarial risk categories. Neither system would prevent insurers from avoiding high-risk enrollees. If multiple plans were used, the government would have to have the authority to require insurers to share the costs of high-risk individuals or would have to establish a government back-up plan for the high-risk population.

The final principles involve payment and resource allocation. To assure efficient resource allocation, public expenditures under national health insurance should reflect consideration of benefits in relation to costs. Market mechanisms — including income-related cost sharing and competition among insurance plans — could play a useful role in expenditure determination, encouraging consumers to weigh costs and benefits. But ceilings on cost sharing would limit its effects and the impact of competing insurance plans is uncertain and would be slow in coming. Government should therefore set maximum payment rates for providers.

To assure equitable treatment of all people in a system with multiple payers, all payers should be required to pay providers no more than the rates set by public plans. Individuals or providers could reject participation in national health insurance on these terms, but they would then have to lose most or all of the payments the NHI plans would otherwise make on their behalf. Without equal payment requirements, providers would favor enrollees in better-paying plans. To maintain access for their enrollees, public plans would have to raise the rates they pay, and therefore would have limited ability to control the allocation of resources to medical care.

To further ensure efficiency, the level of government that sets rates must bear the financial costs of its rate-setting decisions. To satisfy this requirement while allowing spending to vary with local and state preferences, national health insurance should adopt financing arrangements (similar to Canada's) that give states incentives and authority to control costs. (States with limited administrative capacity could let the federal government set rates on their behalf.) The federal government should determine annually the amount it is willing to spend to support medical care and allocate that amount among the states. (Allocation could reflect several criteria — including income redistribution if desired.) State governments would then negotiate rates of provider payment consistent with the federal allocation and whatever supplementation from their own resources they deemed necessary or desirable. Costs that exceeded revenue projections would be borne by the state that incurred them. This method would provide state governments a considerable incentive to contain their costs while allowing states to pursue different preferences for resource allocation to health. Since state-determined rates would apply to all people in the state, problems of discrimination against the poor, as have occurred under Medicaid, would be unlikely to arise.

These principles address the basic elements of a national health insurance plan, leaving considerable latitude for variation in specific plan design. Plans that are consistent with these principles have the potential to expand access to medical care while controlling expenditures.

CHARTS SUMMARIZING NATIONAL HEALTH INSURANCE PROPOSALS

Appendix Chart 1

MARTIN BILL: THE MEDICAL EXPENSE PROTECTION ACT OF 1980
INTRODUCED FEBRUARY 4, 1980, AS H.R. 6405

Subject	Provisions
General Concept and Approach	The proposal would establish a Catastrophic Automatic Protection Plan (CAPP) which would pay a share of medical expenses once an individual or family incurs medical expenses in excess of a specified deductible and would cover *all* medical expenses once out-of-pocket expenses are incurred equal to a specified percentage of family income.
	Employers are not required to offer a qualified health care plan, but full-time workers whose employers do offer a qualified plan would have the option of joining the private plan or CAPP.
Coverage of the Population	**CAPP**
	All U.S. citizens and legal resident aliens would be eligible.
	CAPP is designed primarily to cover the working poor, the self-employed, part-time and seasonal workers, the unemployed, and their dependents.
	Employer Plans
	Most full-time workers would continue to be covered under private health insurance plans provided by employers. Employees who choose not to join a private plan would be eligible for CAPP, but would face a higher deductible.
	If an employee's income-related deductible as calculated under CAPP were less than the $2,500 deductible required under a qualified health plan, the employer would be required to pay the interim costs incurred by the employee. CAPP would then reimburse the employer for these expenses, plus administrative costs.

194

MARTIN BILL (continued)

Subject	Provisions
Administration	The Department of Health and Human Services (DHHS) would administer and process claims for CAPP essentially as in Medicare, including use of private insurers and other organizations as fiscal intermediaries. The Internal Revenue Service and other state and federal agencies would assist DHHS in determining eligibility and in income verification.
Relationship to Other Government Programs	Medicare: Would be amended to eliminate hospital coinsurance under Part A and there would be no limit on hospital days Medicare Part B benefits would be expanded to include prenatal care, well-baby care through age one, and immunizations without regard to the current Part B deductible. Medicare eligible would be allowed to receive CAPP benefits (including certain outpatient drugs) after they insure out-of-pocket medical expenses equal to their income-related deductible. Medicaid: Would not be affected except a maintenance of effort provision would prevent states from reducing or eliminating services now provided under state Medicaid programs.
Financing	CAPP would be financed through general revenues deposited in a Social Security trust fund established for this purpose. Employer plans would continue to be financed through existing private arrangements. Medicare and Medicaid would continue to be financed through existing arrangements.
Standards for Providers of Services	Services would be paid for under CAPP only if delivered by "participating providers," except in emergencies. Participating providers would have to accept reimbursement from CAPP as payment in full for services provided to CAPP beneficiaries.

195

MARTIN BILL (continued)

Subject	Provisions	
	CAPP	**Employer Plans**

Benefit Structure

CAPP

Covered services would be essentially the same as those under Medicare with these changes:

1. Instead of Medicare's 190-day lifetime limitation for inpatient psychiatric hospital services, CAPP would provide 45 days of care in a calendar year.

2. CAPP would cover prenatal and well-baby care through age one, and immunizations.

Cost-Sharing — CAPP would set up a series of income-related deductibles, co-insurance rates, and "stop loss" limits applied to benefits under the program. The schedule proposed is as follows:

Family Income	Out-of-pocket deductible	Coinsurance rate (percent)	"Stop-loss" limit
Not over $4,000	$300	10	$500
Over $4,000 but not over $10,000	$300, plus 29 percent of income over $4,000	15	$500, plus 25 percent of income over $4,000
Over $10,000	$1,500, plus 20 percent of income over $10,000	20	$2,000, plus 25 percent of income over $10,000

Employer Plans

After the $2,500 deductible for out-of-pocket expenses has been reached by an employee, qualified health plans would have to cover all services covered by CAPP.

Employers would not be required to offer a health insurance plan. If a qualified plan were offered, an employer would be required to contribute 50 percent of the premium for the least expensive plan offered.

For federal tax purposes, an employer would be permitted to deduct as business expenses only contributions to a *qualified* plan and employees could exclude only contributions to *qualified* plans from their taxable income. Employer contributions above $120 would be treated as taxable income of employees.

If an employee enrolled in a qualified plan which cost less than the employer's fixed contribution, the employer would be required to pay a rebate equal to at

MARTIN BILL (continued)

Subject	Provisions		
	CAPP		Employer Plans

Benefit Structure (continued)

CAPP: Income-related deductible would be used to determine CAPP eligibility. Once deductible has been reached, CAPP would pay for covered benefits, with the individual or family paying a percentage of additional expenses as coinsurance. When total out-of-pocket expenses reach a "stop-loss" limit, the individual or family would pay no additional amount. Deductible amount would be based on family income during the preceding calendar year.

Employer Plans: least 75 percent of the difference between the employer contribution and the cost of the selected plan. If the employer contribution was below the $120 limit, up to $8.33 per month of the rebate would not be taxable income to the employee.

Reimbursement for Providers of Services

Hospitals: As in Medicare, on a reasonable cost basis.

Physicians: As in Medicare, on a reasonable charge basis, but CAPP would pay 100 percent of allowable reasonable charges rather than Medicare's 80 percent. More frequent updating of fees is provided for than is currently done, and the economic index which currently restrains fee increases in Medicare is eliminated.

CAPP and Medicare fees would be raised to the 75th percentile of prevailing charges for physicians in shortage areas (rather than at the 50th percentile under current law).

Delivery and Resources

Proposal would authorize study and demonstration projects with respect to (1) adding a long-term care program to Medicare or CAPP over time; (2) consolidating Medicaid into CAPP; and (3) devising strategies for providing alternatives to Medicare and Medicaid based on consumer choice.

Chart 2

CARTER NATIONAL HEALTH PLAN (PHASE 1) INTRODUCED SEPTEMBER 24, 1979, AS S.1812

Subject	Provisions
General Concept and Approach	The program would encompass two components:
	HealthCare — a public plan providing comprehensive coverage to the aged, the disabled, the poor, and the near-poor, and offering catastrophic coverage to those individuals and firms unable to obtain such insurance in the private sector; and
	Employer Guaranteed Coverage — a program requiring employers to provide full-time employees, their spouses, and dependent children with health benefits meeting uniform federal standards. Employers would be required to pay at least 75 percent of the premium for health insurance.
Coverage of Population	**HealthCare**
	All those now eligible for Medicare plus any person over age 65 whose income is less than 55 percent of the federal poverty standard
	All persons currently eligible for cash assistance and others whose income is less than 55 percent of the federal poverty standard
	Any person whose medical expenses cause a "spend down" to 55 percent of the federal poverty standard
	Employer Guaranteed Coverage
	All-full time employees, their spouses, and dependent children

CARTER PLAN (continued)

Subject	Provisions
	HealthCare
Coverage of Population (continued)	Any other person or group who pays a specified premium (coverage subject to $2,500 deductible)
	(Eligibility levels are intended to rise to the full poverty standard in a later phase of the plan.)
Benefit Structure	Institutional Services:
	Hospitals
	Skilled Nursing Facilities: 100 days per year
	Mental Hospitals: 20 days per year
	Personal Services:
	Physicians
	Diagnostic Services
	Home Health Services (200 visits per year)
	Outpatient Mental Health Care: $1,000 per year
	Medical Equipment
	Laboratory and X-ray
	Other Services and Supplies:
	Prenatal care, delivery, and preventive and acute health care in the first year of life
	Family Planning
	Immunizations
	(Drug benefits, well-child care up to age 6, and preventive care for all persons are proposed as future additions to the Phase I plan.)

CARTER PLAN (continued)

Subject	Provisions
Benefit Structure (continued)	**Cost Sharing** No cost sharing for people with income below 55 percent of the federal poverty standard. Aged and disabled: Cost sharing similar to Medicare's, but subject to a ceiling of $1,250 per year in out-of-pocket costs Other eligibles: Deductible of $2,500 in HealthCare Maximum deductible of $2,500 in employer plans; after deductible has been met, plans must offer all benefits available under HealthCare and may offer broader coverage. No cost sharing on prenatal services, delivery, and prevention and acute care in child's first year of life. (Deductibles are to be replaced with coinsurance and out-of-pocket limits to be lowered in a later phase of the plan.)
Administration	The federal government would administer HealthCare through fiscal agents, as it does in Medicare, and it would regulate private plans. Private insurers would market and underwrite qualified insurance plans for most current beneficiaries and add new beneficiaries through Employer Guaranteed Coverage.
Relationship to Other Government Programs	Medicare and Medicaid would be consolidated under HealthCare with standardized eligibility benefits and reimbursement policies. Medicaid would continue for noncovered services.

200

CARTER PLAN (continued)

Subject	Provisions
Financing	Hospital insurance portion of the Social Security tax, premiums paid by nonpoor aged and disabled enrollees equivalent to Medicare Part B premiums, state government revenues, and federal general revenues.
	Premiums by individuals and employers will finance insurance plans (at least 75 percent by employers; up to 25 percent by employes).
Standards for Providers of Services	Similar to Medicare
Reimbursement of Providers of Services	Under HealthCare, hospital services would be reimbursed as they are under Medicare, but in both HealthCare and private plans payment would be limited according to hospital cost containment legislation, separately introduced.
	Physicians and other providers of ambulatory services to HealthCare patients would be reimbursed under fee schedule. All physicians who accepted HealthCare claims would have to accept fee schedule amount as payment in full. After first year of implementation, alterations in schedule would be developed by negotiation between HealthCare and physician representatives.
	Under private plans these fee schedules may or may not be used, but plans would furnish enrollees with lists of physicians in states who accepted a particular plan's reimbursement as full compensation for their services.
Delivery and Resources	Dollar limit on changes in hospital capital expenditures a state can approve through certificate of need.
	Proposes to encourage HMOs in HealthCare through adoption of advance capitation approach and, in the employer plans, by requiring multiple choice with equal employer contributions to all offered plans.
	Expansion of PSRO activities.

201

Chart 3

KENNEDY-WAXMAN BILL: HEALTH CARE FOR ALL AMERICANS ACT
H.R. 5191, 96th CONGRESS, INTRODUCED SPETEMBER 5, 1979

Subject	Provisions
General Concept and Approach	Would provide comprehensive health care benefits by mandating enrollment in a private health insurance plan, either through an employer or on an individual basis. Premiums would vary with income, with government paying in full for the poor. Premiums and payments to providers would be negotiated within a predetermined NHI budget.
Coverage of Population	All U.S. citizens, permanent resident aliens, legal nonpermanent aliens employed by a foreign embassy or international organization, and foreign visitors whose governments make agreements with the U.S. government.
Benefit Structure	Benefits with no limitations, except as noted: Institutional Services: Hospital inpatient and outpatient services (with limits on services for mental illness) Skilled Nursing Facilities: 100 days following hospitalization of three days or more Personal Services: Physician services (with limits on services for mental conditions) Home health services: 100 visits per year Preventive services including basic immunizations, pre- and postnatal maternal care and well-child care (up to age 18) Other Services and Supplies: Medical and other health services, includes x-ray and laboratory, medical equipment, prosthetic devices, etc. Outpatient drugs only for Medicare eligibles and only for chronic illness

KENNEDY-WAXMAN BILL (continued)

Subject	Provisions
Benefit Structure (continued)	**Other Services and Supplies:** (continued) Outpatient physical, speech, and occupational therapy Mental Health day care services: 2 days a year for each day of allowed inpatient psychiatric benefits Audiological exams and hearing aid coverage: 1 exam per year; 1 hearing aid every 3 years
Administration	**Federal Government:** National Health Board, to be newly established by this program, would be responsible for establishing national policy guidelines and overseeing the program's implementation, computing national and state NHI budgets, and setting rules for paying for services within the budgets. **State:** State governments would nominate members of newly created State Health Boards, which, under contract with the National Board, would be responsible for negotiating prospective budgets and fee schedules for payment of providers, overseeing insurance enrollment, and guaranteeing provider payment. State governments would administer residual Medicaid and certificate-of-need programs. **Private Insurers and HMOs:** Would establish national consortia that collect and distribute premiums and participate in provider payment negotiations. Individual plans would enroll members and pay providers.
Relationship to Other Government Programs	**Medicare:** The bill would — Make payroll tax applicable to all employment Remove limitations on days of hospital coverage Remove deductible and coinsurance requirements for inpatient hospital services and posthospital extended care services Extend automatic eligibility to all persons ages 65 +

KENNEDY-WAXMAN BILL (continued)

Subject	Provisions
Relationship to Other Government Programs (continued)	Medicare: (continued) Delete Part B deductible and 20 percent coinsurance requirements (except for treatment for mental conditions) Mandate Part B enrollment Add drug benefits to list of covered services Medicaid: Federal government would pay 90 percent of administrative costs of residual Medicaid programs if state programs meet federal standards.
Financing	Program financing would be from seven primary sources: Premiums on wage income and premiums on substantial amounts of nonwage income (premiums calculated as a percentage of income); state payments on behalf of AFDC and state institutional populations; federal payments on behalf of SSI beneficiaries and federal institutional populations; voluntary payments on behalf of U.S. residents who are employees of foreign governments or of international organizations; Medicare taxes and premiums; and general revenues.
Standards for Providers of Services	Similar to Medicare's, with authority to apply more stringent conditions for coverage of specified high-risk, high-cost, elective, or overutilized services
Reimbursement of Providers of Services	Hospitals, Home Health Agencies, Neighborhood Health and other Health Centers, and Skilled Nursing Facilities: Would be reimbursed based on prospective rates consistent with approved budgets. Physicians: Fee schedules subject to overall budget limits HMOs: Capitation payments

KENNEDY-WAXMAN BILL (continued)

Subject	Provisions
Delivery and Resources	**Health Planning:** National Health Board would establish national health care improvement and planning objectives. The board would prepare and annually update a 5-year plan describing national health care needs. The national plan would be based on state 5-year plans, prepared and annually updated by governors at the national board's request.

PSRO: Would review all covered services

Health Resources Distribution: Under this plan $500 million would be authorized for the first year of benefits (rising in each successive year) to be used by the national and state boards for a variety of purposes, including conversion or closure of underutilized facilities, provision of services in shortage areas, stimulation and support of HMOs and other cost-effective delivery systems, start-up programs of continuing educational and professional development through PSROs or other private agencies, and other purposes appropriate to achieving quality, accessibility, and other objectives for health care under the program.

Health Education: State boards would carry out program to educate all residents on health, self-care, effective use of health care system, and rights and privileges under the NHI program.

Personal Care Services: National Health Board would be required to carry out a demonstration program in the organization, delivery, and financing of personal care services. The board would make grants to assist in the development of community programs which seek to maintain people in their homes who, without personal care services, would require institutionalization. |

205

APPENDIX B
TABLES AND FIGURES

Appendix Table 1

TAXES AND TAX RATES, OASDHI TAX
(1969)

Earnings Class	Number of Earners (in Millions)	Total Earnings (in $ Billions)	Taxable Earnings (in $ Billions)	Tax (in $ Billions)	Tax Rate[a] (Percent)
Under $3,000	36.44	$ 45.11	$ 45.11	$ 4.245	9.41%
3,000- 3,600	5.06	16.64	16.64	1.566	9.41
3,600- 4,200	5.04	19.60	19.60	1.844	9.41
4,200- 4,800	4.77	21.41	21.41	2.015	9.41
4,800- 6,600	12.29	69.52	69.52	6.542	9.41
6,600- 7,800	6.90	49.53	49.53	4.661	9.41
7,800- 9,000	6.48	54.26	51.01	4.778	8.81
9,000-12,000	8.82	90.35	70.79	6.565	7.27
12,000-15,000	3.28	43.60	27.20	2.482	5.69
15,000+	3.72	92.62	33.40	2.933	3.17
Total	92.80	$502.64	$404.21	$37.631	7.49%

a. Ratio of tax to total earnings.
Source: John Brittain, *The Payroll Tax for Social Security* (Washington, D.C.: The Brookings Institution, 1972), table 4-3.

Appendix Table 2

DISTRIBUTION OF TAX SAVINGS FROM THE EXCLUSION OF EMPLOYER CONTRIBUTIONS TO EMPLOYEE HEALTH INSURANCE PLANS
(1977)

Expanded Income Class	Number of Taxpayers in Income Class (in thousands)	Total Tax Savings for All Taxpayers in Income Class (in $ millions)	Average Tax Savings per Taxpayer in Income Class	Percentage Total Tax Savings to Taxpayers in Income Class	Percentage of All Taxpayers in Income Class
Less than $ 5,000	24,727	$ 91	$ 4	1.6%	27.8%
5,000- 10,000	19,300	494	26	8.9	21.7
10,000- 15,000	15,145	814	54	14.6	17.0
15,000- 20,000	12,022	1,028	86	18.5	13.5
20,000- 30,000	11,891	1,547	130	27.8	13.4
30,000- 50,000	4,433	882	199	15.9	5.0
50,000-100,000	1,182	456	386	8.2	1.3
100,000 and over	297	248	835	4.5	0.3
All Returns	88,997	$5,560	$ 62	100.0%	100.0%

Source: U.S. Congress, Congressional Budget Office, *Tax Subsidies for Medical Care: Current Policies and Possible Alternatives* (Washington, D.C.: U.S. Government Printing Office, January 1980), p. 8.

Appendix Table 3

DISTRIBUTION BY INCOME LEVEL OF TAX SAVINGS FROM THE MEDICAL EXPENSE DEDUCTION

Expanded Income Class	Number of Returns with			Percentage of All Returns in Income Class with Medical Deduction	Total Tax Savings from the Deduction for Taxpayers in the Individual Income Class[c] (in $ millions)	Average Tax Increase per Claimant if the Deduction Were Repealed[d]	Percentage of Tax Savings from the Deduction Received by Taxpayers in the Indicated Income Class	Percentage All Tax Returns Filed with Expanded Income in Income Class
	Either Medical Expense Deduction[a] (in thousands)	Separate Deduction for Health Insurance Premiums (in thousands)	Separate Deduction for Extraordinary Medical Expenses[b] (in thousands)					
Less than $5,000	309	238	282	1.4%	$ 10.0	$ 64	0.4%	26.2%
5,000- 10,000	1,650	1,382	1,472	8.8	162.8	103	6.4	21.7
10,000- 15,000	2,978	2,529	2,261	21.5	350.8	117	13.8	16.0
15,000- 20,000	3,425	2,975	2,291	29.5	415.1	122	16.3	13.1
20,000- 30,000	5,424	4,900	2,918	41.9	685.1	127	26.9	14.6
30,000- 50,000	3,408	3,215	1,299	58.8	541.3	162	21.2	6.5
50,000-100,000	856	819	205	60.5	251.4	310	9.9	1.5
100,000-200,000	162	156	22	61.2	105.8	748	4.1	0.3
200,000 and over	42	40	3	65.1	27.5	829	1.1	0.1
All Returns	18,253	16,255	10,754	20.4%	$2,549.8%	$143	100.0%	100.0%

a. All returns with either a deduction for insurance premiums, a deduction for extraordinary medical expenses, or both.

b. Qualifying medical expenses over 3 percent of adjusted gross income.

c. Calculated as the increase in taxes resulting from repeal of the deduction under 1979 law at 1978 income levels.

d. Estimate for calendar year 1979 at 1978 income levels.

Source: U.S. Congress, Congressional Budget Office, *Tax Subsidies for Medical Care: Current Policies and Possible Alternatives* (Washington, D.C.: U.S. Government Printing Office, January 1980), pp. 28-29.

Appendix Table 4

PERCENTAGE OF NONSUPERVISORY EMPLOYEES EARNING THE MINIMUM WAGE ($1.60) OR LESS, BY INDUSTRY (1970)

Industry	All Firms	Private, Nonfarm Industries		
		Firms Covered by FLSA[a] Prior to 1966	Firms Covered by FLSA as of 1966	Firms Not Covered by FLSA
Contract Construction	0.5%	0.5%	—	—
Manufacturing	0.1	0.1	—	—
Transportation and Public Utilities	0.3	0.3	—	—
Wholesale Trade	0.3	0.3	—	—
Retail Trade	19.2	1.7	20.1%	35.8%
Finance, Insurance, and Real Estate	2.1	1.5	—	—
Services	15.8	2.5	21.2	20.8

a. Fair Labor Standards Act.

Source: U.S. Department of Labor, Employment Standards Administration, "Wages and Hours of Work of Nonsupervisory Employees in all Private Nonfarm Industries by Coverage Status Under the Fair Labor Standards Act," 1972.

Appendix Table 5

MEAN PREMIUMS AND EMPLOYER SHARES OF GROUP INSURANCE POLICIES BY INDUSTRY
(1977-78)

Type of Industry	Individual Policies			Family Policies			Average Payroll per Employee 1977	Ratio of Employer Share to Average Payroll per Worker (%)	
	Total	Employer	Employer Share %	Total	Employer	Employer Share %		Individual Policy	Family Policy
Construction	$498	$418	84%	$ 981	$602	61%	$12,386	3.37%	4.86%
Transportation, Communication	745	693	93	1,122	921	82	13,900	4.98	6.59
Wholesale Trade	369	314	85	857	621	73	12,987	2.42	4.78
Retail Trade	456	388	85	735	453	62	6,473	5.99	7.00
Manufacturing	405	360	89	884	728	82	12,736	2.83	5.72
Service	379	330	87	970	605	62	8,612	3.83	7.03
TOTAL	$404	$356	88%	$ 917	$667	73%	$10,453	3.41%	6.38%

Note: Mean premiums and employer shares computed as weighted averages from data on distributions of employees over premium classes and employer shares. The percentage of employees in each class were used as weights. Midpoints were used to represent premium or employer share intervals. The open-ended premium interval, greater than $1,500, was arbitrarily set at $1,600.

Sources: Average payroll per employee from U.S. Department of Commerce, Bureau of the Census, *County Business Patterns, 1977, United States* (Washington, D.C.: U.S. Government Printing Office, 1979), p. 1.

All other data from Malhotra et al., "Employment Related Health Benefits: A Survey of Establishments in the Private Nonfarm Sector," Draft Final Report, vol. 2 (Seattle, Wash.: Battelle Human Affairs Research Center, 1980), pp. 52-55.

Appendix Figure 1

DISTRIBUTION OF FINANCING COSTS BY FAMILY INCOME

A. Pure Financing Methods

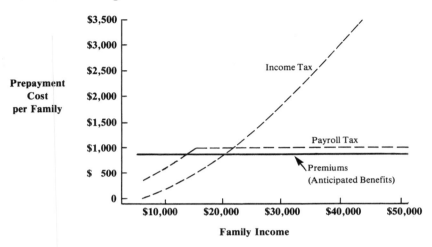

B. Combined Financing Methods

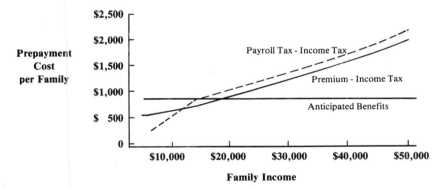

Source: Bridger Mitchell, "Basic Elements of Financing National Health Insurance," Rand Paper P-5610 (Santa Monica, Calif.: The Rand Corporation, March 1976), pp. 5, 10.

NOTES

1. For a description of bills, see U.S. Congress, House of Representatives, Subcommittee on Health of the Ways and Means Committee, "Summaries of Selected Health Insurance Proposals and Proposals to Restructure the Financing of Private Health Insurance," Committee Print 96-74, February 11, 1980.

2. Other bills receiving attention include a catastrophic bill — similar to President Carter's — drafted by Senator Long and the Senate Finance Committee, and a variety of "competitive" bills, similar to Congressman Martin's. We have focused here on those bills most prominent at the time of writing.

3. Because of space limitations and the limits of our own expertise, we have not assessed the bills' implications for quality of care, consumer satisfaction, geographic and time accessibility or consistency with the current health planning system.

4. Robert M. Gibson, "National Health Expenditures, 1979," *Health Care Financing Review* 2 (Summer 1980): 16-17, tables 1 and 2A.

5. Robert M. Gibson and Marjorie Smith Mueller, "National Health Expenditures, Fiscal Year 1976," *Social Security Bulletin* 40 (April 1977):14.

6. U.S. Executive Office of the President, Council on Wage and Price Stability, "The Problem of Rising Health Care Costs," Staff Report, April 1976, p. 7.

7. U.S. Executive Office of the President, Office of Management and Budget, *Special Analyses, Budget of the United States Government, Fiscal Year 1975*, Special Analysis J, "Federal Health Programs," p. 136.

8. *Economic Report of the President*, transmitted to Congress January 1980, p. 285.

9. Gibson, "National Health Expenditures, 1979," pp. 25 and 27, table 5.

10. These data are from those publications of the U.S. Department of Commerce, Bureau of the Census, *City Government Finances in 1976-77, County Government Finances in 1976-77*, and *Finances of Special Districts* (Washington, D.C.: U.S. Government Printing Office, 1978). It is important to consider county governments here since in many areas the county in which a city is located will have primary responsibility for public health care. Cook County in Illinois is probably the best known example of this arrangement.

11. For an explanation and elaboration of cost estimates, see chapter 3.

12. This provision does not apply to Medicare eligibles who continue to obtain coverage through the federally administered Medicare program. Although these beneficiaries can choose between fee-for-service providers and qualified health maintenance organizations, the federal government remains their insurer.

13. U.S. Congress, Congressional Budget Office, *Profile of Health Care Coverage: The Haves and Have-Nots* (Washington, D.C.: U.S. Government Printing Office, 1979). Much of this chapter's discussion of current insurance arrangements is based on CBO's useful analysis of the 1976 Survey of Income and Education, conducted by the U.S. Bureau of the Census.

14. Suresh Malhotra, Kenneth McCaffree, John Wills, and Jean Baker, "Employment Related Health Benefits: A Survey of Establishments in the Private Nonfarm Sector," Final Report, vol. 2 (Seattle, Wash.: Battelle Human Affairs Research Center, 1980), tables 1 and 2.

15. Ibid., tables 2 and 3.

16. Ibid, table 35.

17. Dorothy R. Kittner, "Changes in Health Plans Reflect Broader Coverage," *Monthly Labor Review* 101 (September 1978):57-59.

18. Malhotra et al., "Employment Related Health Benefits," table 51.

19. Judith M. Feder, "Private Health Insurance and the Health Care System: Problems and Solutions," Government Research Corporation, R-359, September 15, l975, Appendix, pp. 10-11.

20. U.S. Congress, Congressional Budget Office, *Profile of Health Care Coverage*, p. 23, based on Daniel N. Price, "Health Benefits for Laidoff Workers," *Social Security Bulletin* 39 (February 1976):40-45.

21. Marjorie Smith Carroll and Ross H. Arnett III, "Private Health Insurance Plans in 1977: Coverage, Enrollment, and Financial Experience," Health Care Financing Review 1 (Fall 1979):22, table 12.

22. U.S. Congress, Congressional Budget Office, *Profile of Health Care Coverage*, p. 16, table 4.·

23. Ibid., pp. xi, 26.

24. For a review of Medicare coverage and its gaps, see Judith Feder and John Holahan, *Financing Medical Care for the Elderly: Medicare, Medicaid, and Private Health Insurance* (Washington, D.C.: The Urban Institute, 1979).

25. States have three options: they can provide Medicaid benefits to all persons eligible for federal SSI payments; they can provide Medicaid benefits to persons eligible for state SSI supplements; or they can limit Medicaid eligibility to persons meeting standards used by the states on January 1, 1972, before the federal SSI program was established.

26. U.S. Department of Health, Education and Welfare, *Data on the Medicaid Program: Eligibility, Services, Expenditures, 1979* (Baltimore, Md.: Health Care Financing Administration, 1979), pp. 61-62.

27. U.S. Congress, Congressional Budget Office, *Profile of Health Care Coverage*, p. 16, table 4.

28. Ibid., p. 25, table 8.

29. Ibid., p. 16, table 4.

30. Ibid., p. 21, table 6.

31. For an analysis of problems in implementing Medicaid's spend-down, see Urban Systems Research and Engineering, "Evaluation of Medicaid Spend-down," Final Report, Contract No. SRS 74-58, February 15, 1976.

32. Data are from U.S. Department of Health and Human Services, Health Care Financing Administration, Health Care Financing Trends 1 (Fall 1979):5; and *Economic Report of the President, 1980* (Washington, D.C.: U.S. Government Printing Office, 1980), p. 226.

33. Malhotra et al., "Employment Related Health Benefits," estimated from table 33.

34. Lynn Paringer, "Determinants of Work-Loss and Medical Care Utilization," Ph.D. dissertation, University of Wisconsin, 1978.

35. Gordon R. Trapnell Associates, "A Comparison of the Cost of Major National Health Insurance Proposals-Executive Summary," prepared under Contract No. DHEW-OS-74-138 for the Department of Health, Education and Welfare, September 1976, table C-2.

36. Ronald Andersen et al., Expenditures for Personal Health Services, DHEW Publication No. (HRA) 74-3105 (Rockville, Md.: Health Resources Administration, 1973), p. 12.

37. Much of the material in this section is from Bridger M. Mitchell and William B. Schwartz, *The Financing of National Health Insurance*, Rand Publication No. R-1711-HEW (Santa Monica, Calif.: Rand Corporation, 1976).

38. John A. Brittain, *The Payroll Tax for Social Security* (Washington, D.C.: The Brookings Institution, 1972), table 4-3.

39. U.S. Congress, Congressional Budget Office, *Tax Subsidies for Medical Care: Current Policies and Possible Alternatives* (Washington, D.C.: U.S. Government Printing Office, 1980), p. 8.

40. Ibid., pp. 28-29.

41. Personal communication from Richard Froh, professional staff member of the Subcommittee on Health and Scientific Research of the Senate's Committee on Labor and Human Resources, May 19, 1980.

42. Maximum payments will be about $800 for individuals and $1,900 for families. Personal communication from Richard Froh, May 19, 1980.

43. U.S. Congress, Congressional Budget Office, *Tax Expenditures: Current Issues and Five-Year Budget Projections for Fiscal Years 1981-1985* (Washington, D.C.: U.S. Government Printing Office, 1980), p. 33.

44. Bridger M. Mitchell and Ronald J. Vogel, "Health and Taxes: An Assessment of the Medical Deduction," Rand Publication No. R-1222-OEO, (Santa Monica, Calif.: Rand Corporation, 1973), p. 31.

45. Ibid., p. 26. Mitchell and Vogel estimated that in 1970, 50 percent of medical expenses in excess of 15 percent of adjusted gross income (AGI) was incurred by families with AGIs below $7,000. Families with AGIs above $20,000, on the other hand, incurred less than 3 percent of total excess medical expenses.

46. Private insurance appears to take on a much more significant role in Kennedy-Waxman than in the Health Security Act. However, it must be remembered that the former in effect makes private insurance a quasi-public authority through creating the health insurance consortiums which collect premiums, the vesting of the power to set premium rates in the hands of public authorities, and the mandating of income-related premium payments. Thus, the Kennedy-Waxman bill is similar to the Health Security plan in that about 85 percent of the funds are channeled through public or quasi-public agencies. It differs markedly in administrative structure, however.

47. These estimates are extremely crude for three reasons. First, individuals are excluded from the calculations. Since many of the elderly who are heavy users of services would be classified as individuals, these data understate the amount of transfers to low-income persons. Second, data for various parts of the table are from different sources. Thus, comparability of the underlying populations is likely to be small. Third, definitions of care and payments vary across the underlying studies as well.

48. Under the Martin plan, families with an income of $5,000 would have a 15 percent maximum liability. Families below $5,000 would have a lower percentage limit while those with incomes above $5,000 would have a higher limit. However, families covered by qualified employer plans also have a $2,500 maximum liability, which means that such families with incomes greater than $16,666 would also face percentage limits lower than 15 percent. Thus, the lower-middle-income range of the distribution would receive fewer benefits, while the lowest-, middle-, and upper-income ranges would receive greater benefits than are implied by a uniform 15 percent limit.

49. Mitchell and Vogel, p. 26.

50. In 1970, families were estimated to account for about 60 percent of total expenditures. Individuals would bear a disproportionate share of catastrophic expenditures, however.

51. S. Long and M. Cooke, "Financing National Health Insurance," unpublished discussion paper, NHI Financing Team, U.S. Department of Health, Education, and Welfare, January 6, 1978, p. 26.

52. Mitchell and Schwartz, pp. 9-13.

53. See Bridger M. Mitchell and Charles E. Phelps, "National Health Insurance: Some Costs and Effects of Mandated Employee Coverage," *Journal of Political Economy* 84 (June 1976):559. Much of the material in the first section of this chapter is based on their paper.

54. Ibid., p. 560.

55. U.S. Department of Labor, Bureau of Labor Statistics, *Handbook of Labor Statistics* (Washington, D.C.: U.S. Government Printing Office, 1976), table 34.

56. Ibid.

57. Malhotra et al., "Employment Related Health Benefits."

58. Ibid., p. 17. A small proportion of these workers are covered through union-sponsored insurance plans, which were not included in the 1978 survey. Plans jointly administered by a union and firms are included in the survey as "employer-provided" plans.

59. Ibid., p. 32.

60. Ibid., p. 27.

61. Averages were computed by inflating 1979 premiums to 1980 by the increase in the medical care component of the Consumer Price Index, and by assuming that 80 percent of covered workers have family policies. See Appendix B, table 5, for separate data for family and employee-only policies.

62. U.S. Congress, Congressional Budget Office, *Profile of Health Care Coverage*, p. 36.

63. Personal communication from Gordon Trapnell, Actuarial Research Corporation, June 12, 1980.

64. Mitchell and Phelps, p. 562.

65. Ibid., pp. 561-62.

66. Their study included agricultural firms, which had the highest cost increases of all sectors. Thus, their estimates for private, nonfarm industries would be somewhat lower.

67. Charles Phelps, "National Health Insurance by Regulation: Mandated Employee Benefits," in Mark V. Pauly, ed., *National Health Insurance: What Now, What Later, What Never?* A conference sponsored by the American Enterprise Institute, 1980), pp. 59-64.

68. A staff memo prepared by the Department of Labor estimated that the unemployment effect of an income-related premium is about half that of a capitation premium set to raise the same amount of revenue. U.S. Department of Labor, Office of the Assistant Secretary, "Wage Based Premiums vs. Capitation Premiums," memo from Robert Copeland to Joe Onek and Nelson Ford, April 7, 1978.

69. Phelps, "National Health Insurance by Regulation," p. 56.

70. National Commission for Manpower Policy, *Employment Impact of Health Policy Developments*, Special Report No. 11 (Washington, D.C.: U.S. Government Printing Office, October 1976), pp. 19-24.

71. U.S. Department of Labor, Bureau of Labor Statistics, *Handbook of Labor Statistics* (Washington, D.C.: U.S. Government Printing Office, 1977), p. 59.

72. Ibid., p. 25.

73. Victor Fuchs, "The Earnings of Allied Health Personnel — Are Health Workers Underpaid?" *Explorations in Economic Research* 3 (Summer 1976): 412.

74. Philip E. Enterline et al., "The Distribution of Medical Services Before and After 'Free' Medical Care — The Quebec Experience," *New England Journal of Medicine* 288 (May 31, 1973):1174-78.

75. There may be some double counting of office-based physicians who are employees of other physicians, but this should not distort these estimates.

76. The estimated regression was $LEMPL = 11.015 + .999*LEXP$, $R^2 = .99$, t-statistic = 30. (LEMPL = natural log of employment, LEXP'natural log of medical care expenditures measured in constant dollars.)

77. U.S. Congress, Congressional Budget Office, *Tax Subsidies for Medical Care*, pp. 7-9.

78. For a review of the 1979 bills, see U.S. Congress, Congressional Budget Office, *Controlling Rising Hospital Costs* (Washington, D.C.: U.S. Government Printing Office, 1979). In 1980, bills were introduced by Congressmen Martin, Jones, Gebhardt and Stockman. The Gebhardt-Stockman bill (H.R. 7527) most closely resembles the Consumer Choice Health Plan developed by Alain Enthoven at the request of then-DHEW Secretary Joseph Califano. Enthoven's plan is developed in Alain Enthoven, *Health Plan: The Only Practical Solution to the Soaring Cost of Medical Care* (Reading, Mass.: Addison-Wesley, 1980).

79. A discussion of the differences between these points of view was presented as part of "A Conference on Health Care—Professional Ethics, Government Regulation, or Markets?" September 25-26, 1980, sponsored by the American Enterprise Institute, Washington, D.C.

80. On physician opposition, see Clark C. Havighurst, "Professional Restraints on Innovation in Health Care Financing," *Duke Law Journal* (May 1978). Other problems are noted by Alain Enthoven in "Supply Side Economics of Health Care and Consumer Choice Health Plan," paper presented at "A Conference on Health Care," pp. 24-25.

81. Karen Lennox and Judith Feder, "Employers' Implementation of Dual Choice," Working Paper 1261-1 (Washington, D.C.: The Urban Institute, June 1979).

82. For a discussion of employer attitudes, see Judith M. Feder, "Private Health Insurance and the Health Care System: Problems and Solutions," Report R-359, Government Research Corporation, Washington, D.C., September 15, 1975.

83. Jon Kingsdale, "Labor and Management-Sponsored Innovations in Controlling the Cost of Employee Health Care Benefits," Council on Wage and Price Stability, *Federal Register*, September 17, 1976, pp. 40298-40326.

84. U.S. Congress, Congressional Budget Office, *Controlling Rising Hospital Costs*, p. 71.

85. Malhotra et at., "Employment Related Health Benefits," p. 83, table 50.

86. U.S. Congress, Congressional Budget Office, *Controlling Rising Hospital Costs*, p. 72.

87. This discussion is based on Harold S. Luft, *Health Maintenance Organizations: Dimensions of Performance* (New York: Wiley-Interscience, forthcoming); Harold S. Luft, "How Do Health Maintenance Organizations Achieve Their 'Savings'?: Rhetoric and Evidence," *New England Journal of Medicine* 298 (June 15, 1978):1336-43; and Harold S. Luft, "Health Maintenance Organizations, Competition, Cost Containment, and National Health Insurance," in Mark V. Pauly, ed., *National Health Insurance: What Now, What Later, What Never?*, pp. 283-306.

88. Luft, "Health Maintenance Organizations, Competition, Cost Containment and National Health Insurance," p. 287.

89. The presence of a maximum contribution — 75 percent of premiums — can mean lower contributions for lower-cost plans.

90. Jack A. Meyer, "Health Care Competition: Are Tax Incentives Enough?" paper presented at "A Conference on Health Care," p. 23.

91. Harold S. Luft, "Health Maintenance Organizations, Competition, Cost Containment and National Health Insurance," pp. 300-305, reviews evidence on the competitive impact of HMOs. The University of California experience he reviews was analyzed in Dyan Piontkowski and Lewis H. Butler, "Selection of Health Insurance by an Employer Group in Northern California," *American Journal of Public Health* 70 (March 1980): 274-76. The Minneapolis experience was analyzed in Jon B. Christianson and Walter McClure, "Competition in the Delivery of Medical Care," *New England Journal of Medicine* 301 (October 11, 1979):812-18.

92. Christianson and McClure, "Competition in the Delivery of Medical Care."

93. Luft, "Health Maintenance Organizations, Competition, Cost Containment and National Health Insurance," p. 300-305.

94. Christianson and McClure, "Competition in the Delivery of Medical Care."

95. Luft, "Health Maintenance Organizations, Competition, Cost Containment and National Health Insurance," p. 287.

96. For a discussion of the possibly negative effects of IPA growth under national health insurance, see Harold S. Luft, Judith Feder, John Holahan and Karen D. Lennox, "Health Maintenance Organizations," chapter 3 in Judith Feder, John Holahan and Theodore Marmor, eds., *National Health Insurance: Conflicting Goals and Policy Choices* (Washington, D.C.: The Urban Institute, 1980).

97. Luft, "Health Maintenance Organizations, Competition, Cost Containment and National Health Insurance," p. 303.

98. Ibid., pp. 304-305.

99. Enthoven, *Health Plan*, p. 91, p. 132-33, p. 137.

100. U.S. Congress, Congressional Budget Office, *Rising Hospital Costs*, p. 70, n. 11.

101. Factors affecting choice are discussed in Luft, "Health Maintenance Organizations, Competition, Cost Containment, and National Health Insurance," pp. 294-96.

102. U. S. Congress, Congressional Budget Office, *Controlling Rising Hospital Costs*, p. 71, n. 12.

103. The bill requires that benefits be added in the following order: (1) reduction in premiums associated with preventive services not covered by HealthCare, (2) reduction in premiums attributable to cost sharing, (3) reduction in premiums for noncovered services to the lowest level charged any enrollee, and (4) further reduction in premiums for (or addition at no extra premium of) noncovered services.

104. Karen Davis, *National Health Insurance: Benefits, Costs and Consequences* (Washington, D.C.: The Brookings Institution, 1975).

105. Enterline et al., "The Distribution of Medical Services," pp. 1174-78.

106. Joseph Newhouse, Charles E. Phelps and William B. Schwartz, "Policy Options and the Impact of National Health Insurance," *New England Journal of Medicine* 290 (June 13, 1974):1345-59.

107. Other bills introduced in 1979 and 1980 offer different configurations of tax exemptions and rebates. The Martin bill's provision allowing the employer to retain a portion of the difference between contributions and actual premiums is an incentive to employers to offer low-cost plans. If, instead, the plan were to give employees the full rebate, the bill would have to offer employers other incentives or require that they offer a low-cost plan in order to have the same effect.

108. U.S. Congress, Congressional Budget Office, *Catastrophic Health Insurance* (Washington, D.C.: U.S. Government Printing Office, January 1977), p. 55, tables A-1 and A-2.

109. Analyses in this section are more fully developed in John Holahan, "Physician Payment," chapter 2 in Feder, Holahan and Marmor, eds., *National Health Insurance.*

110. Robert Lee and Jack Hadley, "Physicians' Fees and Public Medical Care Programs," Health Service Research (forthcoming, 1981).

111. Frank A. Sloan and Bruce Steinwald, "The Role of Health Insurance in the Physicians' Services Market," *Inquiry* 12 (December 1975):275-99; John Holahan, "Physicians' Availability, Medical Care Reimbursement and the Delivery of Medical Services: Evidence from the Medicaid Program," *Journal of Human Resources* 10 (Summer 1975):378-402.

112. Karen Davis and Cathy Schoen, *Health and the War on Poverty* (Washington, D.C.: The Brookings Institution, 1978).

113. Jack Hadley, "Physician Participation in Medicaid: Evidence from California," *Health Services Research* 14 (Winter 1979):266-280.

114. Jay Helms, Charles E. Phelps, and Joseph Newhouse, "Copayments and the Demand for Medical Care: The California Medicaid Experience," *Bell Journal of Economics* 9 (Spring 1978):192-208.

115. Jack Hadley and Robert Lee, "Toward a Physician Payment Policy: Evidence from the Economic Stabilization Program," *Policy Sciences* 10 (1978-1979): 117.

116. Jack Hadley, John Holahan, and William Scanlon, "Can Fee-for-Service Reimbursement Coexist with Demand Creation," *Inquiry* 16 (Fall 1979):247-58.

117. U.S. Congress, Congressional Budget Office, *Controlling Rising Hospital Costs*, p. 5.

118. Expenditures per patient day calculated from data compiled by the American Hospital Association from the Annual Survey of Hospitals, reported in Robert M. Gibson, "National Health Expenditures, 1978," *Health Care Financing Review* 1 (Summer 1979), p. 36, table 9, and, for 1978, American Hospital Association, *Hospital Statistics*, 1978 ed. (Chicago: American Hospital Association, 1978).

223

119. U. S. Congress, Congressional Budget Office, *Controlling Rising Hospital Costs*, pp. 2-5. Hospital wage rates increased at rates comparable to rates for all private sector wages.

120. For a more detailed discussion of concerns, see Judith Feder and Bruce Spitz, "Hospital Payment," chapter 6 in Feder, Holahan, and Marmor, eds. *National Health Insurance.*

121. U.S. Congress, Congressional Budget Office, *Catastrophic Health Insurance*, p. 55, table A-1, and discussion pp. 44-46. For a comprehensive discussion of issues related to catastrophic coverage, see Clark C. Havigurst, James F. Blumstein, and Randall Bovbjerg, "Strategies in Underwriting the Costs of Catastrophic Disease," *Law and Contemporary Problems* 40 (Autumn 1976):122-95.

122. This description is based primarily on S.570 as developed by the Health Subcommittee of the Senate Committee on Labor and Public Welfare. Its features are reported in "Summary of Committee Print of S.570. Hospital Cost Containment Act of 1979," July 11, 1979.

123. American Hospital Association, *Hospital Statistics*, 1978 edition.

124. U.S. Congress, Congressional Budget Office, *Controlling Rising Hospital Costs*, p. 44.

125. As the CBO analysis indicates, the House Ways and Means Committee version of the bill included a provision to allow hospitals to carry forward to future years half the unused but allowed increase. This provision would reduce but not eliminate the incentive to spend up to the guideline.

126. See U.S. Congress, Congressional Budget Office, *Controlling Rising Hospital Costs*, chapter 2.

127. For evidence on the effectiveness of rate setting in the absence of national health insurance, see ibid.; and Bruce Steinwald and Frank A. Sloan, "Regulatory Approaches to Hospital Cost Containment: A Synthesis of the Empirical Evidence," paper presented at "A Conference on Health Care," American Enterprise Institute, September 25-26, 1980.

128. The House Ways and Means Committee version of the bill has provisions related to bad debts and charity care that would mitigate the effect of ceilings on hospitals treating nonpaying patients. See chapter 7.

129. David S. Salkever and Thomas W. Bice, *Hospital Certificate-of-Need Controls: Impact on Investment Cost, and Use* (Washington, D.C.: American Enterprise Institute, 1979).

130. On the U.K. experience, see Michael H. Cooper, *Rationing Health Care*, (New York: John Wiley and Sons, 1975); Michael H. Cooper, "Health Costs and Expenditures in the United Kingdom," in Teh-Wei Hie, ed., *International Health Costs and Expenditures*, DHEW, Public Health Service, National Institutes of Health, DHEW Publication No. (NIH): 76-1067, 1976; and Alan Maynard, "Health Care Planning in the United Kingdom," prepared for a Conference on Policies for the Containment of Health Care Expenditures, Fogarty Center, DHEW, May 1976.

224

131. On payroll expenses, see Mark S. Freeland, Gerard Anderson, and Carol Ellen Schendler, "National Hospital Input Price Index," *Health Care Financing Review* 1 (Summer 1979):43. An estimated 700,000 of 2.25 million hospital workers were in unions in 1977. Roger Feldman and Richard Scheffler, "Unionization and Hospital Compensation," *Industrialization and Labor Relations Review*, forthcoming.

132. Lewin and Associates, Inc. "Government Controls on the Health Care System: The Canadian Experience," unpublished paper, Washington, D.C., (January 1976, pp. 3-41—3-46; and personal communication with Canadian official. For further discussion, see Judith Feder and Bruce Spitz, "Hospital Payment."

133. For a history and critique of Medicare's reimbursement policy, see Judith M. Feder, *Medicare: The Politics of Federal Hospital Insurance* (Lexington, Mass.: Lexington Books, 1977).

134. Personal communication with HCFA officials, May 1980.

135. Judith Feder, *Medicare*.

136. Data from 1976 indicate that some states continue to cover extremely small proportions of the poor, despite a decline in variations in per capita spending across all states since 1970. These findings and the discussion in the text are elaborated in Judith Feder and John Holahan, "Administrative Choices," chapter I in Feder, Holahan, and Marmor, eds., *National Health Insurance*.

137. Ibid.

138. The shares of total personal income devoted to expenditures for the National Health Service were 6.1 percent in 1971 and 6.3 percent in 1978. Central Statistical Office, *Social Trends* (London: Her Majesty's Stationary Office, 1974), p. 203 and *Social Trends* (1980), pp. 134, 166.

139. Frank A. Sloan and Judith D. Bentkover, *Access to Ambulatory Care and the U.S. Economy* (Lexington, Mass.: Lexington Books, 1979).

140. About half the states with mandatory rate-setting programs (specifically Connecticut, Maryland, Massachusetts, and Washington) use independent commissions to set rates. For analyses of the effectiveness of state rate-setting programs, see Bruce Steinwald and Frank A. Sloan, "Regulatory Approaches to Hospital Cost Containment."

141. These changes include freezes in fees paid to physicians, fee increases below the rate of inflation (expecially Medicare's Economic Index), erosion of Medicaid eligibility by failing to adjust income standards for inflations, reductions in covered services and limits, and reform of the reasonable cost method of reimbursing hospitals. All of these changes have the effect of reducing private physicians' and hospitals' willingness to treat Medicaid and Medicare patients.

142. U.S. Department of Commerce, Bureau of the Census, City Government Finances in 1976-77 (Washington, D.C.: U.S. Government Printing Office, 1978), p. 7 ff.

143. In 1978, 12.7 percent of central city families, 5.3 percent of noncentral city, metropolitan families, and 10.8 percent of nonmetropolitan families had incomes below the poverty level. U.S. Department of Commerce, Bureau of the Census, *Money Income and Poverty Status of Families and Persons in the United States: 1978* (Advance Data), series P-60, no. 120, November 1979.

144. "Statement of the American Hospital Association (AHA) to the House Committee on Ways and Means, Subcommittee on Health, on the Hospital Financing Crisis Confronting Many Public and Private Nonprofit Hospitals," February 21, 1980. Because all hospitals did not respond to the AHA survey, the percentage estimate of hospitals in deficit is subject to error.

145. U.S. Department of Commerce, Bureau of the Census, *City Government Finances in 1976-77* (Washington, D.C.: U.S. Government Printing Office, 1978); idem, *County Government Finances in 1976-77* (Washington, D.C.: U.S. Government Printing Office, 1978); and idem, *Finances of Special Districts* (Washington, D.C.: U.S. Government Printing Office, 1978).

146. American Hospital Association, *Hospital Statistics*, 1978, p. 8.

147. Ibid., p. 180.

148. Unpublished data from the American Hospital Association reported in J. Hadley, "Background Information on the Reimbursement of Hospitals' Teaching Expenses," Urban Institute Working Paper 1302-01 (Washington, D.C.: The Urban Institute, December 1978), p. 24.

149. U.S. Department of Commerce, Bureau of the Census, *City Government Finances in 1976-77; County Government Finances in 1976-77*; and *Finances of Special Districts.*

150. Ibid.

151. Excluding New York City's medical vendor payments reduces per capita spending in the high-poverty areas to $92.

152. LuAnn Aday, Ronald Andersen, and Gretchen Fleming, *Health Care in the U.S.: Equitable for Whom?* (Beverly Hills, Calif.: Sage Publications, 1980).

153. Ronald Andersen, Joanna Lion, and Odin Anderson, *Two Decades of Health Services* (Cambridge, Mass.: Ballinger, 1976).

154. U.S. Department of Commerce, Bureau of the Census, *Social and Economic Characteristics of the Metropolitan and Nonmetropolitan Population: 1977 and 1970*, Special Studies P-23, no. 75, 1979, pp. 5, 16.

226

155. Ibid.

156. U.S. Department of Health, Education, and Welfare, Public Health Service, National Center for Health Statistics, *Limitation of Acitvity Due to Chronic Conditions*, series 10, no. 111, DHEW Publication No. (HRA) 77-1537 (Rockville, Md.: Health Resources Administration, June 1977).

157. Estimates are adjusted for age and sex. See Aday et al., *Health Care in the U.S.*, p. 190.

158. John Holahan et al., "Paying for Physicians' Services under Medicare and Medicaid," *Milbank Memorial Fund Quarterly/Health and Society* 57 (1979):192-203.

159. American Medical Association, *Profile of Medical Practice*, 1978, pp. 217, 221, 227.

160. Mary Fruen, Jack Hadley, and Samuel Korper, "Effects of Financial Incentives on Physicians' Specialty and Location Choices," *Health Policy and Education* 1 (1980):150-2.

161. American Medical Association, *Profile of Medical Practice*, 1978, p. 255; tables 23 and 25 in this report.

162. Victor Cohn, "Economic Squeeze: Terminal Illness for Inner-City Hospitals," *The Washington Post*, October 4, 1979, p. A3.

227